In Praise of Kings

In Praise of Kings is a study of Gujarat in the long-neglected fifteenth century. The interregnum between the Delhi sultanate and the Mughal empire has conventionally been regarded as a period of decline. By contrast, this book shows the cultural and political dynamism of an important South Asian region at this critical moment in its history.

This book highlights how, after the fall of the Delhi sultanate, the political landscape of fifteenth-century Gujarat was dominated by Rajput warrior chieftains and the Muzaffarid sultans. The interaction between these competing political players have been traditionally viewed as a clash between two religious groups. Querying this perspective, the book demonstrates how both the Rajputs and the sultans fashioned a common warrior ethos that was constructed with diverse literary and cultural elements.

Notably, the study draws on rarely used literary works in Sanskrit and Gujarati to reconstruct the royal courts of fifteenth-century Gujarat and recasts the fifteenth century as a period of creative transformations. It also questions the deeply entrenched perception that Gujarat was predominantly a land of traders and merchants. Through a close analysis of original primary sources, it shows how Gujarat's warrior past was also integral to this region's history and identity.

This book will be of interest to students and scholars of medieval and early modern South Asian history and literary culture, as well as to those concerned with wider questions of the formation of regional traditions and identities.

Aparna Kapadia teaches History at Williams College, USA. She writes about the history of Gujarat and western India, and the cultural and intellectual histories of early modern and modern South Asia. She is also the co-editor of *The Idea of Gujarat: History, Ethnography and Text* published in 2010.

In Praise of Kings

Rajputs, Sultans and Poets in Fifteenth-century Gujarat

Aparna Kapadia

CAMBRIDGE
UNIVERSITY PRESS

CAMBRIDGE
UNIVERSITY PRESS

University Printing House, Cambridge CB2 8BS, United Kingdom

One Liberty Plaza, 20th Floor, New York, NY 10006, USA

477 Williamstown Road, Port Melbourne, vic 3207, Australia

314 to 321, 3rd Floor, Plot No.3, Splendor Forum, Jasola District Centre, New Delhi 110025, India

79 Anson Road, #06–04/06, Singapore 079906

Cambridge University Press is part of the University of Cambridge.

It furthers the University's mission by disseminating knowledge in the pursuit of education, learning and research at the highest international levels of excellence.

www.cambridge.org
Information on this title: www.cambridge.org/9781107153318

First published 2018

Printed in India at Thomson Press (India) Ltd.

A catalogue record for this publication is available from the British Library

ISBN 978-1-107-15331-8 Hardback

Contents

List of Maps

Acknowledgements

This book has been in the making for nearly a decade. When I began the project as my doctoral dissertation at the School of Oriental and African Studies (SOAS), I intended to write a history of Gujarat, a region whose pre-colonial past had received surprisingly little attention despite crucial significance in the political and economic development of India. Over the years, however, the context for the research coincided with other significant developments. In recent times, the politics of India's medieval past has become more fiercely contested than ever before. Underpinning this contestation is a political imagination of the subcontinent's pre-colonial history as one shaped by conflict between religious communities. Nowhere is this more evident than in Gujarat and western India. In this imagination, little space remains for an understanding of interactions between social groups as driven by multiple and overlapping motivations and affiliations set within specific historical contexts. Through a focus on a period of transitions in a richly diverse region, I hope to have broadened the space of discussion and highlighted the complex fabric of India's pre-colonial past.

I have accumulated several debts in writing this book. My dissertation advisor, Daud Ali, helped to shape the project through the example of his own scholarship and his insightful and constructive comments on the text. I am grateful for Daud's continued support and interest in my work. My interest in regional and cultural history began at the Centre for Historical Studies in Jawaharlal Nehru University, New Delhi. Kunal Chakrabarty sparked my initial curiosity about regional narrative traditions. During the early years of my graduate study, I was also privileged to learn from scholars like Neeladri Bhattacharya, B. D. Chattopadhyaya, Vijaya Ramaswamy, Himanshu Prabha Ray and Kum Kum Roy. Fleur D'Souza and Siddhartha Menon's engaging history classes at St Xavier's College and Rishi Valley School respectively alerted me to the exciting possibilities of a career in the discipline.

In transforming the dissertation into a book, I have also benefitted from comments and discussions with several scholars. I am particularly grateful to

Francesca Orsini for her timely and perceptive suggestions at a crucial stage. Rosalind O'Hanlon's mentorship during my postdoctoral years at the Oriental Institute, Oxford University, helped to sharpen ideas in this monograph. Christopher Minkowski offered several suggestions for the translation of the Sanskrit works. Thanks are also due to Faisal Devji, Rachel Dwyer, Douglas Haynes and Sunil Sharma for always being generous with their scholarship, time and intellectual support. Interactions with and comments from scholars working on pre-colonial histories of South Asia – Allison Busch, Whitney Cox, Sumit Guha, Sunil Kumar, Luther Obrock, Ramya Sreenivasan, Cynthia Talbot, and Audrey Truschke, in particular – have helped to refine many of the ideas presented in this book.

Tanuja Kothiyal and Samira Sheikh read several drafts of the manuscript and offered insightful suggestions and comments. No words can adequately express my gratitude to them for their unconditional support, expertise and friendship. Marisha Kirtane and Samir Patil always responded to my unreasonable demands on their time. They provided the astute non-academic perspectives that helped to improve clarity and coherence. This book has benefitted from several conversations with Kaushik Bhaumik. I am also indebted to Prashant Kidambi who mentored this project from its inception.

I am grateful to the editorial team at Cambridge University Press for their patience. Katie Van Heest's developmental inputs and Deborah Jones's editorial support have immeasurably improved the outcome. Three anonymous referees for Cambridge University Press suggested ways to contextualize the ideas and arguments of this monograph. Their suggestions have sharpened the final product.

Williams College has provided a congenial intellectual environment to complete this book. My colleagues at the College, and especially the Department of History, welcomed me warmly in their midst. Their support and encouragement of my research and teaching as well as their unstinted friendship eased the challenges that accompanied the writing of this book. Thanks are also owed to friends and former colleagues at Ambedkar University, Delhi, where I took my first steps into the world of university teaching.

The initial dissertation project was supported by a fellowship from the Felix Trust. An Additional Fieldwork Grant from SOAS and an Isobel Thornley Fellowship from the Institute of Historical Research funded the later stages of dissertation research. The award of an Andrew Mellon Postdoctoral Fellowship at the University of Oxford allowed me the time to work on the early drafts of the manuscript. I also appreciate the support from the Hellman Fellows Fund and the Oakely Center at Williams College, which facilitated the final stages of research and writing. Williams College's generous sabbatical leave policy provided the uninterrupted time needed to see this book to completion.

I am grateful to several libraries and archives in India, the United Kingdom, and the United States for granting me access to their resources. Thanks are due in India to the Library of the Asiatic Society and the Forbes Gujarati Sabha in Mumbai, the B. J. Institute in Ahmedabad, the Hansa Mehta Library at the M. S. University and Oriental Institute in Baroda, and the Bhandarkar Oriental Research Institute in Pune. In the UK, I have benefitted from the repositories of the British Library (Asia and Africa Collections) and the SOAS library; and in the USA from the Library of Congress in Washington DC and the Widener Library at Harvard. I would also like to offer my heartfelt thanks to the Williams College Library, particularly to the inter-library loan service through which I was able to access a number of valuable research materials. I am grateful to Cory Campbell at the Williams College Office of Information Technology for preparing the maps.

Versions of chapters 3, 4 and 5 have been previously published. Chapter 3 appeared in *After Timur Left: Culture and Circulation in Fifteenth Century North India* edited by Francesca Orsini and Samira Sheikh (Oxford University Press, 2014); extracts from Chapter 4 were published in *The Medieval History Journal* (vol. 16, issue 1, 2013), and sections of Chapter 5 in *The Idea of Gujarat: History, Ethnography and Text* edited by Edward Simpson and myself (Orient Blackswan, 2010). I am grateful to the editors and publishers for granting me permission to use this material.

I have been very fortunate to have been part of a vibrant community of scholars of South Asia in three countries. Aparna Balachandran, Preeti Chopra, Carolyn Heitmeyer, Farhana Ibrahim, Abhishek Kaicker, Aditi Saraf, Aditya Sarkar and Uditi Sen have all been wonderful interlocutors and compatriots in this journey, making every moment a worthwhile enterprise. Many other friends have also sustained me through their emotional and intellectual support. I particularly wish to thank Meera Asher, Milena Behrendt, Christophe Carvahlo, Amal Eqeiq, Jacqueline Hidalgo, Ann Leibowitz, John Lloyd, Christophe Kone, Vedica Kant, Pia Kohler, Mahesh Menon, Sudhir Sitapati, Mishka Sinha, Archana Rao, Darshak Shah and Abha Thorat-Shah. Virchand Dharamsey was always willing to share his extraordinary scholarship and knowledge of the many histories of Gujarat. Geeta Kapur and Vivan Sundaram; Arun Adarkar and Fiona Shrikhande; and Aruna and Priya D'Souza have been the most supportive and generous extended family.

My parents, and my sister Payal Kapadia, as well as Ranabir Das, have been an endless source of encouragement and inspiration. To them I remain ever-grateful. Nandita Prasad Sahai, dear friend, mentor, fellow traveler, left this world a little too soon. It is to Nandita's memory that I dedicate this book.

A Note on Transliteration and Usage

In the interest of readability, I have kept the use of diacritical marks to the minimum. I have used these only for book titles and in direct quotes. In such instances, the words are transcribed according to the American Language Association-Library of Congress (ALA-LC) charts.

- Common words from Indian languages have not been italicised.
- All English translations are mine, unless indicated otherwise.
- Dates are rendered in the Common Era throughout the book.

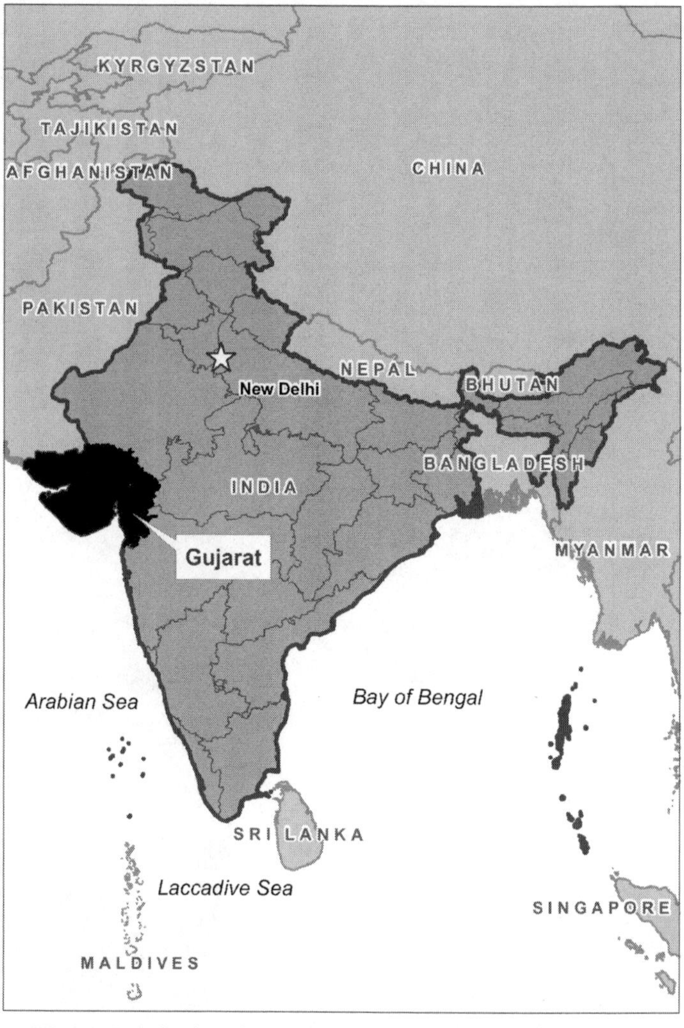

Map 1: Relative location of the modern state of Gujarat in India.

Source: GADM database of Global Administrative Areas

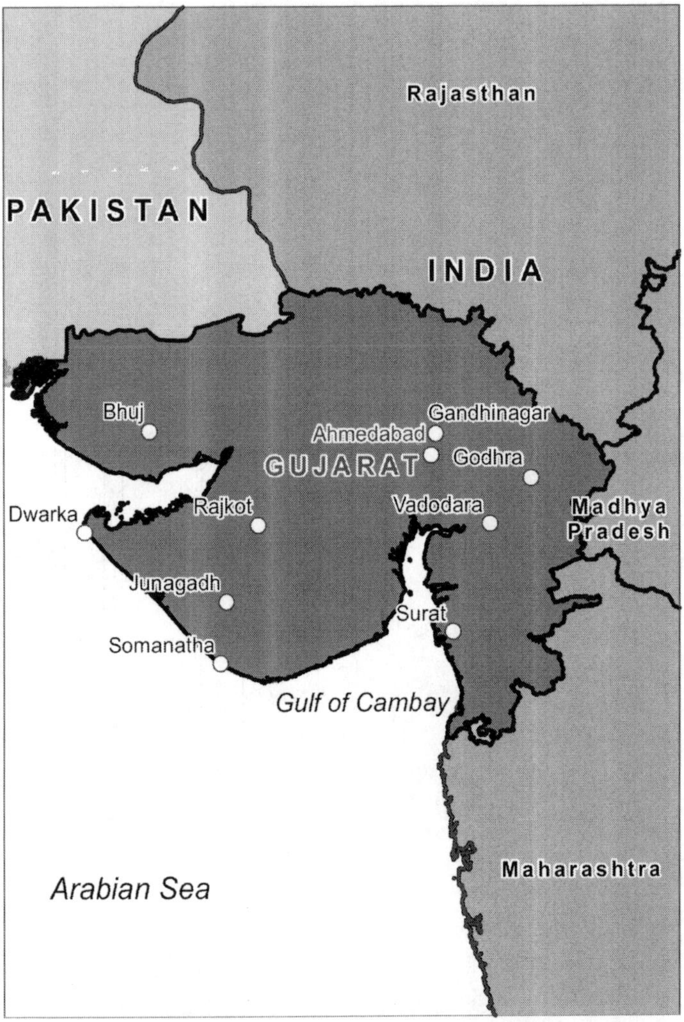

Map 2: The modern state of Gujarat, India, with key cities and towns.

Source: GADM database of Global Administrative Areas.

Introduction

Gangadhara, a multilingual poet of the fifteenth century, having achieved renown in south India, decided to seek further glory in the faraway kingdoms of Gujarat.[1] From the court of King Pratapadevaraya of Vijayanagara (r. 1426–1447), he set forth on a long and arduous journey of hundreds of miles.[2] At the time, Gujarat roughly comprised much of the territory that is part of the state today, including the peninsulas of Saurashtra, also known as Kathiawad, and Kachchh.[3] Gangadhara first went on a pilgrimage to the holy city of Dwarka. Next, he proceeded to the court of Sultan Muhammad Shah II (r. 1442–1451), at Ahmadabad. This was a flourishing city, a new capital of the Gujarat sultanate that had only recently been built by the Sultan's father, Ahmad Shah (r. 1411–1442). At the Ahmedabad court, to the great delight of Sultan Muhammad, Gangadhara vanquished the local poets with his excellent lyrical skills. Gangadhara then went on to two other courts in the region –

[1] The story of Gangadhara's travels is based on a Sanskrit play which Gangadhara composed for Raja Gangadas, the Chauhan ruler of Champaner, a kingdom located in eastern Gujarat. See Gangadhara, *Gangadāsa-Pratāpa-Vilāsa-Nāṭakam*, II, 17–18. In the play, the poet tells us that he is proficient in six languages but does not specify which ones. For more on Gangadhara's compositions, see Chapter 3.

[2] Pratapadevaraya was also referred to as Devaraya II. He was well known as a great patron and was himself a poet writing in Kannada.

[3] The modern state of Gujarat came into existence on 1 May 1960, as a part of a long movement to divide the former Bombay State into the linguistic states of Gujarat and Maharashtra. However, the region, with its varying ecologies, had taken shape from the thirteenth century onwards, and already roughly corresponded to its present boundaries. By the time it was incorporated into the Delhi sultanate in the early fourteenth century, the term 'Gujarat' had been adopted as a convenient appellation for the different constitutive units. For a brief history of the region's modern cartographic history, see Kapadia and Simpson, 'Gujarat in Maps'.

Champaner, to the east of the capital, and Junagadh, to its far west – composing panegyrics for the Rajput chieftains of these fort kingdoms.

In the mid-fifteenth century Gujarat was becoming well known as a place where poets and scholars were sure to find supportive audiences.[4] Sanskrit continued to be popular: Gangadhara's skills in this Indic High language were favoured not only by modest Rajput kings but also desired in the court of a Muslim sultan. At the same time, a multilingual milieu was also emerging. As political action shifted away from the subcontinent's traditional centre, Delhi, Gujarat, an ecologically and socially diverse region, saw a variety of groups vying for political power. Poets, writers, and scribes were crucial to the ways in which these new rulers of local and regional entities imagined their polities and asserted their rights to rule in this changing political context. Gangadhara's ability to make good in the different courts that constituted Gujarat evidence the region's political, cultural, and literary vibrancy. Yet the century during which Gangadhara made his journey is viewed in the conventional historiography of pre-modern South Asia as one of political and cultural decline. In most surveys of Indian history, the fifteenth century is given little attention, and is often designated the 'period in waiting' or the 'twilight' before the rise of the Mughals in the sixteenth century.[5]

This paradox is the starting point of the questions that animate this book: what kind of political ethos can we discern from works like Gangadhara's compositions in praise of Gujarat's kings? Who were these kings whose courts supported both local and trans-regional poets in the fifteenth century? And what does their presence say about the politics and culture of Gujarat during

[4] A number of Sanskrit poets from various parts of India appear to have visited Gujarat throughout the course of history. Bilhana, the Kashmiri poet, visited Patan sometime in the eleventh century and was patronised by the Chaulukya king Karna's minister Sampatakara or Shantu. Here he wrote a play entitled *Karaṇasundarī*. In the thirteenth century, Harihara, a Brahmin poet from Bengal, interrupted his journey to the holy site of Somanatha, at the behest of Vastupala, the governor of Sthambhatirtha or Khambhat (Cambay). Harihara is said to have composed a play based on the Jain governor's life before continuing his journey. For more information on the works of these, and other, Sanskrit poets in Gujarat, see Panchal, 'A Glimpse into the Sanskrit and Other Forms of Drama in Medieval Gujarat', 293–310.

[5] K. S. Lal's book is the only comprehensive political history of this period. Lal's work focuses on the decline and subsequent recovery of Delhi as a regional kingdom in this period. See Lal, *Twilight of the Sultanate*. A small number of general surveys of Indian history provide a corrective to the dominant view on the fifteenth century. These include: Keay, *India: A History* and Asher and Talbot, *India Before Europe*.

this time? Why would a successful poet from a region with a well-established tradition of patronage, like Vijayanagara, undertake a difficult journey to find new patrons in Gujarat in particular?

I use literary narratives produced in the courts of Gujarat to answer these questions and explore the ways in which regional and local rulers were represented, and represented themselves, in a century of transitions between *c.* 1398 and 1511. These narratives include biographical praise-poems in Sanskrit as well as in Dimgal, a poetic language tradition associated with the oral genealogist-historians of western India.[6] The result is a portrait of fifteenth-century Gujarat as a rich, multi-layered, and multi-lingual political landscape. At the start of this period, Gujarat was an unsettled region, a frontier in which a number of different mobile political players of obscure origins, ranging from warlords to chieftains, who later came to be referred to as Rajputs, and sultans with imperial ambitions, were making competing territorial and economic claims. By the mid fifteenth-century, the sultans would overpower the competition to establish a regional imperium. Whatever the size of their actual domains, these men sought to define themselves in a landscape of shifting authorities and ambiguous sovereignties; patronising poets and commissioning panegyrics was one way they asserted their newfound status. Turning our gaze to such regional specificities, and regional texts, highlights the changes in the subcontinent, driven by smaller political and territorial entities, and proves the fifteenth century to have been a time of influential change that has hitherto not been fully investigated and accounted for.

Two developments have conventionally been viewed as markers of political and cultural change in the history of pre-modern north India: first, Delhi's sack at the hands of the famous Turko-Mongol warrior, Timur, in 1398 and the Delhi sultanate's consequent decline, and second, the rise of the Mughal empire, which is credited with the inauguration of unprecedented political and cultural innovations. The intervening period between 1398 and 1555,[7]

[6] Dimgal, a linguistic tradition, sometimes called a language, was in use in Gujarat and Rajasthan from at least the fifteenth century onwards. This tradition is associated with 'bards' or poets of the Charan caste. Whether Dimgal is a poetic style or a separate language remains a controversial matter. The main issue around which the debate is centred is whether Dimgal should be distinguished from Pimgal, a prose language used in Rajasthan and Gujarat. For a detailed survey of the tradition/language, see Bhati, *Prācīn Ḍiṇgaḷ Gīt Sāhitya*.

[7] This is the period between Timur's invasion and Humayun's return to India from Iran, from when the Mughal empire would be firmly based in the subcontinent.

sometimes referred to as 'the long fifteenth century', is often overlooked as many of the sources available from this time are not the sorts commonly considered 'hard evidence'. Major imperial accounts, building projects, and other material remains are scarce. However, even when such evidence is available, as in the case of the regional sultanate of Gujarat (1407–1580), literary narratives that were produced in abundance during this period give insight conventional sources cannot. The writings explored in this monograph – primarily biographical praise poems – reveal the ideologies, aspirations, and self-expressions of those who may have commissioned them. Expanding the conventional archive to include these effusions illuminates what is obscured in the historiography of fifteenth-century Gujarat as a 'twilight' time of political fragmentation and cultural regression.[8] Upending prevailing conceptions, this book uncovers the fifteenth century as an era of tremendous dynamism. Taking a fresh look at this century's cultural diversity, and the creative political processes that it engendered, can throw light on the history of pre-Mughal South Asia in important new ways.[9]

Society and Polity in a Regional Setting

Gujarat had been a province of Delhi since *c.* 1304. In 1407, amidst the chaos that followed Delhi's destruction at Timur's hands, the last governor sent to Gujarat by the Delhi sultan, Zafar Khan son of 'Wajih al-Mulk', declared himself independent of his former masters. Zafar Khan took the title of Muzaffar Shah, and with this declaration inaugurated a regional imperium that would last for over a hundred and fifty years. Gujarat had the advantage of a long association with the Indian Ocean trade networks. This favourable position was further enhanced by the sultans' control over important coastal and

[8] Francesca Orsini and Samira Sheikh have emphasised the value of the literary archive to better understand this period as it is often the lack of conventional sources that had led scholars to ignore this important century. See Orsini and Sheikh, *After Timur Left*.

[9] My book adds momentum to a small but significant and growing body of scholarship challenging the notion of this period as a time of regression. See Orsini and Sheikh, *After Timur Left*. The essays included in this volume provide a rich picture of how a milieu of multiple languages and literary forms was emerging in this century. Also see Jha, 'Beyond the Local and the Universal,' 1–40; 'Literary Conduits for "Consent"', 322–50. Samira Sheikh's work on Gujarat not only provides an important revisionist history of the region in this period but is also a significant intervention in creating an understanding of society and polity in a regional setting during this important century. See Sheikh, *Forging a Region*, 2010.

overland trade routes that connected Gujarat to the rest of the subcontinent.[10] According to the eighteenth-century historian Ali Mohammad Khan, it was this resulting prosperity that led the fifteenth-century ruler of Delhi, Sultan Sikandar Shah, to complain that the 'support of the throne of Delhi is wheat and barley but the foundation of the realm of Gujarat is coral and pearls'.[11] Years later, Gujarat's wealth also made it the prized province of the Mughal empire: two of its major rulers, Shah Jahan and Aurangzeb, had both served as its governors before ascending Delhi's throne.

The region Muzaffar Shah (r. 1407–1411) and his descendants came to control was characterized by a vast ecological diversity and consequently, different economies of trade.[12] Different parts of the region were interconnected by the trade routes that extended overland to other parts of the Indian subcontinent as well as to the western Indian ocean. Gujarat's location and ecology rendered it a frontier that encouraged the movement and settlement of traders, pastoralists, peasants, military, and political adventurers. Its long coastline had been home to a variety of trading communities and their mercantile interests, while the central plains of the east were centres of manufacturing and agriculture. The Saurashtra and Kachchh peninsulas had supported pastoral and semi-pastoral life for centuries. Many of these pastoralists went on to adopt the upwardly mobile social identity of Rajputs as they established stronger territorial ties in these locales during the fifteenth century. Gujarat in the fifteenth century was also marked by considerable urban and agricultural expansion, which facilitated settlement.[13] As they established their rule, the sultans were able to 'settle' different parts of this diverse region and increase its interconnectedness through the

---

10 For a history of Gujarat's internal trade routes until the fourteenth century, see Jain, *Trade and Traders in Western India*. André Wink has also demonstrated how the balance of power in the Indian regional context was affected by shifts in Indian Ocean trade. See Wink, *Al-Hind*, vols. 1 and 3. For Gujarat's trading history after the Portuguese arrival in the region, particularly during the sixteenth century, see Pearson, *Merchants and Rulers of Gujarat*.

11 Bayley, *Local Muhommadan Dynasties of Gujarat*, 20.

12 For a recent overview of the term 'Gujarat' and a history of the term's relationship to the territories it constituted, see Sheikh, *Forging a Region*, 25–27.

13 This is particularly visible in the numerous grants for wells, tanks, and mosques made to faciliate the settlement of forested regions, including those extending from eastern Rann of Kachchh to Patan and those lying between Patan and Cambay. For details of building patterns as reflected in epigraphs, see table in Sheikh, *Forging a Region*, 77–80.

expansion of trading networks and further development of cities. A number of administrative and military measures also encouraged this process.

The sultans' attempts to make inroads into Gujarat were not unchallenged; likewise their success was not a foregone conclusion. Throughout their rule, the sultans faced considerable resistance from chieftains and rulers of local power centres, who had often acquired their patrimonies during Chaulukya rule. With Chaulukya decline in the twelfth century, many of these regional strongmen were able gain control over lands around the core administrative area. The fifteenth century saw an expansion of this state of affairs, with the competition between political aspirants growing as Delhi weakened. Thus, in Gujarat, on the eve of the regional sultanate's establishment, many of these chieftains – including the Rathods in Idar, the Chauhans in Champaner, the Chudasamas and the Gohils in Saurashtra – had built strong local political ties. Their forts, located on the outer boundaries of what had been the region's centre, Anhilvada–Patan, and later Ahmadabad, were of great strategic significance, as was their control of the resources in the surrounding areas.

The history of Gujarat in the fifteenth century was shaped by alternating periods of conflict, negotiation, and accommodation between these small but significant local power bases and the regional sultans, for whom the control of these resources was crucial to their centralising initiatives and to the establishment of their rule.[14] The narratives surveyed in this book are expressions of this landscape in which political configurations were in flux and multiple groups were vying to establish their political and social positions. *Raṇamallachanda*, a poem narrating the story of the Rathod chieftain Ranmal (Chapter 2) provides a striking example of this. Ranmal's fort at Idar, strategically located on the trade route connecting the sultanate capital at Anhilvada–Patan, was one of the first local power bases coveted by Zafar Khan. Yet, while Ranmal is depicted in the poem as a fierce warrior single-handedly resisting and triumphing over the Khan's massive armies, he is a chieftain devoid of lofty titles or a prestigious lineage, thus indicating his modest and hitherto unestablished status. Moreover, he is also depicted as conquering territories encompassing much of Gujarat – territories that would have been far beyond his reach. Other historical accounts do not corroborate the

[14] Recently, Richard Eaton and Philip Wagoner have studied the power struggles between what they term the 'primary centres' of power on the Deccan plateau, and the 'secondary centres' that lay on the plateau's frontier. The local chieftaincies of Gujarat can also be viewed in similar terms vis-a-vis the regional sultanate. See Eaton and Wagoner, *Power, Memory, Architecture*.

claims about Ranmal in these verses. Yet the poet allows the reader/audience to consider possibilities that lie beyond historical realities – a large empire, or comparisons with well-known, and often unconventional, historical and mythical heroes – creating a history and legacy for the protagonist in a time when new social identities of men like him were still evolving.

The struggle between the chieftains and sultans in the dominant historiography of Gujarat and in the popular imagination is often narrowly viewed in terms of clashes between two religious groups: the 'Hindu' Rajputs and the 'Muslim' sultans. In this line of thought, which has had a lasting impact, the introduction of Turkic rule is considered the end of civilisation and as a rupture in Gujarat's heroic history.[15] However, the political flux that shaped the establishment and consolidation of sultanate rule in the region cannot be comprehended through such simplistic religious binaries. The rise of the new chieftains and the breakaway sultans may be more productively understood as an outcome of the 'military labour' market that had been emerging in central

[15] The influential scholar-politician K. M. Munshi's writings are a primary example of this view in which the Chaulukya–Vaghela rulers are seen as the sole representatives of Gujarat's 'glorious' 'heroic' past. See Munshi, *The Glory that was Gūrjaradeśa*, vol. 1 and *Gujarāta and its Literature*. Several other accounts of the region's history have also underscored the role of the Chaulukyas as representing the 'glorious' past of Gujarat. *Gujarātno Madhyakālīna Rājput Itihās* (*The Medieval Rajput History of Gujarat*, first published during 1937–39), for instance, viewed the Chaulukya–Vaghela dynasties as the great warrior rulers of the medieval period. Their reign, according to the book's author, Durgashankar Shastri, was one in which the region attained the height of its prosperity, but in the centuries after 'Ala' al-Din Khalji's attack, he notes, Gujarat saw the destruction of its 'Hindu Empire' and along with that the destruction of its 'Hindu culture and prosperity.' See Shastri, *Gujarātno Madhyakālīna Rājpūt Itihās*, vol. 1, 504. Similarly, A. K. Majumdar's *Chaulukyas of Gujarat* also granted this dynasty the pride of place in the region's medieval history. For him, the Chaulukyas were the 'virile captains of war', who saved the country from the disorder that followed the end of the Gurajara-Pratihāras and the Rashtrakuṭa empires of northern India. See Majumdar, *Chaulukyas of Gujarat*, 1. Two other historical works, one by M. S. Commissariat and the other by S. C. Misra, are general accounts that are less prone to such biases even though they take a dynastic approach. See Commissariat, *A History of Gujarat*, vol. 1, vol. 2, and Misra, *The Rise of Muslim Power in Gujarat*. More recently, Sheikh's work on the society and polity has provided a much-needed corrective to the histories that foreground the role of the Chaulukyas and Vaghelas as Gujarat's legitimate rulers. Instead, Sheikh shows how the region was 'forged' through historical processes that had been at work since 1200 and how Gujarat's diverse elements were integrated through the 'religious marketplace' facilitated by the Muzaffarid sultans in the fifteenth century. See Sheikh, *Forging a Region*.

and north India since the 1200s.[16] This was a landscape of rich mobility wherein talented military adventurers could attain a considerable degree of success through their ability to recruit manpower and supply elephants and horses. The Delhi sultans were the largest employers of these services, creating space for entrepreneurial leaders, with a loose and contingent allegiance to central authority, to establish their own landed chieftaincies or even regional-level kingdoms.

In fact, Zafar Khan's own father and uncle had been beneficiaries of this very system, as they had won the favour of the Delhi sultan, Firoz Shah, by supplying his military. These men, a certain Saharan and his brother Sadhu, were, most likely peasants or pastoralists, non-Muslim Tank Rajputs from Thanesar in northwestern India (modern-day Haryana). They encountered the prince Firuz Khan (who would later become Firuz Shah Tughluq) when he was separated from his retinue during a hunting expedition. The two brothers, who were already somewhat prominent within their locality and could gather horsemen and footsoldiers by the thousands, decided to help the prince, whom they recognised as having royal links. They further ingratiated themselves with the prince by giving him their sister in marriage and joined his retinue, eventually becoming very prominent among his courtiers. Both brothers eventually converted to Islam and became followers of a prominent Sufi saint. Saharan received the title of Wajih al-Mulk. It was Wajih al-Mulk's son, Zafar Khan, who went on to become the last governor of the prosperous province of Gujarat before declaring himself an independent sultan. The progress of his career is indicative of how rapidly military adventurers could rise in this landscape.[17]

The eventual collapse of Delhi's power in the fourteenth century led to the further expansion of the military labour market and the formation of a number of new political alliances between the rising sultanates and those who commanded the resources they required to cement their rule. Consequently, new groups were also integrated into the political networks during the fifteenth century. Chief among these were Afghans and other migrants from the northwest, as well as diverse men of unknown origins who came to be encompassed by the label of Rajput. In return for military services, these men

[16] Kolff, *Naukar, Rajput and Sepoy.*

[17] This summary is based on Sikandar Manjhu's account. See Sikandar, *Mir'āt-i Sikandarī*, trans. 1–3. Cynthia Talbot's discussion on the Kyamkhani lineage of Rajasthan shows a more detailed elaboration of the process by which upward mobility of this kind could be achieved during this period. Talbot, 'Becoming Turk the Rajput Way,' 211–43.

were able to acquire lands that they could pass on to their descendants as well as gain varying degrees of political status.[18]

If the entrepreneurial military labour market was one of the defining forces shaping Gujarat's polity at the time, another factor was the struggle by the local centres of powers to assert their status. The ways in which the local chieftains sought to have their authority recognised, offers even more clear evidence that the framework of religious binaries is seriously misleading. As many of these warrior groups became more successful, both in terms of their territorial gains, and political prominence, they also aspired to royalty. One way in which they pursued this aspiration was by drawing on pre-existing norms of the exalted Kshatriya status that had been deployed by Indic polities for centuries. In their public epigraphs, many of these groups, including a number of chieftains from Gujarat, made claims on this prestigious identity by forging links with the ancient solar and lunar lineages (*surya* and *chandra vamsha*), claiming royal titles and links with Puranic deities, and in many cases also making grants of land to Brahmins and projecting themselves in stock terms as protectors of Brahmins and cows.[19]

The currency of the Kshatriya status was so strong even in the fifteenth century that the powerful Muzaffarid sultans, self-proclaimed Muslim rulers who had access to several other avenues of expressing their political superiority and royalty, also chose to make claims on this identity. According to the account of seventeenth-century historian Sikandar Manjhu, which traces the sultans' Rajput ancestry back by several generations, the Tanks belonged to the solar lineage, which linked them to the Puranic hero, Rama.[20] A full-blown expression of this is visible in the Sanskrit poem addressed to Mahmud Shah Begada (1459–1511), which also links him to the solar lineage, and portrays him as a paramount Indic king or *chakravarti,* blessed by Sarasvati, the goddess of learning, who chooses to establish herself in the sultan's court (Chapter 4). In the poem, Sultan Mahmud Begada is adorned with multiple titles usually reserved for great Indic kings, and described as equal in virtues and attributes

[18] Alongside military men, Hindu and Jain merchants were also invited by the various sultanates to settle in their territories and, as inscriptional accounts from the period show, they gained prominent positions. For the expansion of Jain patrons, see De Clercq, 'Apabhramsha as Literary Medium in Fifteenth-Century North India' in Orsini and Sheikh, *After Timur Left*, 339–64.

[19] Chattopadhyaya, 'Origin of Rajputs,' 57–88.

[20] Sikandar, *Mir'āt-i Sikandarī,* trans., 1.

to a plethora of Puranic deities. Thus, despite the options available to him, pre-existing ideologies of Indic kingship and royal status appear to have held significance to this regional Muslim monarch.

The evolution of the quest of Kshatriya status would eventually result in many of the local chieftains making claims on the 'Rajput' identity. The heroes from the Rathod, Chauhan, and Chudasama lineages that appear in the following pages, have all been recognised as such from the sixteenth century onwards. B. D. Chattopadhya's groundbreaking work on Rajasthan suggests that 'Rajput' was an assimilative category that allowed for transition from tribal to state polity from the sixth century onwards and in which prestigious descent played a crucial role.[21] On the other hand, Dirk Kolff suggests that, during the thirteenth to the fifteenth centuries, 'Rajput' was an open-ended category that provided social status to a wide range of itinerant warriors who continued to circulate in northern and northwestern India; it was only in the sixteenth century, Kolff writes, that the term Rajput came to be associated with aristocratic monarchical lineages.[22] In the narratives discussed, from the courts of Gujarat, both the older warrior ethos and the gradually emerging descent-based category of Rajputs can be found. Moreover, the universal royal ideal of Kshatriya kingship was integrated into the ways the identities of these groups developed. While a warrior like Ranmal Rathod (Chapter 2), is referred to as a Kshatriya, the panegyric addressed to him is a bricolage of different tropes that draw from local legends, contemporary history, as well as Puranic mythology. It is these, rather than his lineage and descent, that define him as a hero and chieftain. In contrast, in the biography of the Chudasama king, Mandalik (Chapter 3), whose family had ruled the fort of Junagadh in Saurashtra for centuries, we can see a descent-based identity acquiring significance. Interestingly, among all the narratives studied here, descent from the prestigious solar lineage, as well as a genealogy tracing historical descent, hold the most significant place in the epic-poem addressed to the Muslim sultan, Mahmud Begada (Chapter 4). A close reading of narratives from the local and regional courts throws light on the fluid nature of the 'Rajput warrior' identity and reveals how those who claimed it harnessed a plethora of widely-recognised rhetorical elements to do so.

---

[21] Chattopadhyaya, 'Origin of Rajputs,' and 'Political Processes and the Structure of Polity in Early Medieval India' in *The Making of Early Medieval Indian*, 183–222.

[22] Kolff, *Naukar, Rajput and Sepoy*, 71–74.

A rich body of scholarship now exists on the elite clan-based Rajput kingship and warrior tradition that evolved from the sixteenth century onwards as elite Rajputs were incorporated in the Mughal imperial system. It was during this period that the category of 'Rajput' came to be crystallised around prestigious descent, something that was held in significance by the imperial Mughals as well.[23] Less is known, however, about the specific elements of the elite warrior ethos and descent-based identity that were emerging in the fourteenth and fifteenth centuries, when the idea of the 'Rajput' was still open-ended and could include a number of different elements and innovations. The collection of narratives brought together in this book reflects crucial aspects of the ways in which the warrior ethos and identities were creatively developing, but had not entirely become set in stone, in the fifteen-century milieu.

Society and polity as represented in the narratives from Gujarat's courts offer a view of a vibrant and evolving warrior ethos. The warrior chieftains of these works, composed by Brahmin poets and preserved in written form, belonged to elite traditions and circulated within the setting of elite courts. The trajectories the warriors took in each case differed, but often rather than simplistic religious differences, it was the common pool of ideological resources that shaped the ways in which they chose to fashion their political claims through the works of their poet panegyrists.

Literary Innovations for Elaborating a Warrior Identity

As Gangadhara's experience with the regional and local courts of Gujarat shows, here and in many other parts of India, patrons big and small were seeking the services of poets and composers who could articulate their newly acquired positions, or at least their aspirations. The fifteenth-century Telugu poet Srinatha travelled across the Andhra region and was called upon not only by the Vijayanagara king Harihara II, but also by the ambitious elites of the region, who wished secure their social positions by emulating current courtly trends.[24] Similarly, in several small hinterland towns that popped up all over

---

[23] See Ziegler, 'Marwari Chronicles' and 'Some Notes on Rājput Loyalties During the Mughal Period', in *The Mughal State*, 68–210; Kolff, *Naukar, Rajput and Sepoy*; Mita, 'Polity and Kingship of Early Medieval Rajasthan: An Analysis of the Nadol Cāhmāna Inscriptions,' in *Kingship in Indian History*, 89–117.

[24] Rao and Shulman, *Classical Telugu Poetry*, 118. For an elaboration of the poet's role in fashioning the identity of the Andhra elites and the region itself, see Rao and Shulman, *Śrīnatha*.

central India, warlords and chieftains – men who may not even have had strong forts let alone an actual court – commissioned poetic works in the north Indian vernacular, Hindavi, modifying classical genres to suit their own specific contextual contingencies.[25] Likewise, in Gujarat, a great deal of literature in the fourteenth and fifteenth centuries comes from these relatively small centres of power: Ranmal's Idar fort (Chapter 2) was most likely of a modest size at the time when Sridhara Vyasa composed his panegyric celebrating the chieftain. Gangadas and Mandalik (Chapter 3), on the other hand, were holders of larger fortifications at Champaner and Junagadh, respectively, which the regional sultans found more challenging to conquer.[26]

The texts surveyed here can broadly be categorised as eulogistic biographies of the lives and deeds of individual chieftains and kings. While the roots of royal biographies can be traced to the Vedic period, biographies of historically known kings and individuals became popular across the subcontinent from the early medieval period onwards.[27] These are not always birth-to-death narratives; rather they often include events that may have been regarded by the patron or poet as worthy of transmission to a contemporary audience and preservation for posterity. The narratives may also go beyond historical realities, sometimes including supernatural interventions, as was the convention in these genres. Nonetheless, they all demonstrate a keen awareness of the patrons' specific historic and political context.

The poet-composers of these narratives played a central role in the creation of the self-image of new warrior groups, some of whom, as the protagonists of the compositions in this book, also managed to acquire varying degrees of elite status. Ranmal's ancestors belonged to the cadet line of the Rathod clan, and had gained territorial control of Idar during the Chaulukya reign in Ahilvada–Patan around the eleventh century. The Chudasamas, on the other hand, had become the most prominent rulers of Saurashtra over several

---

[25] Sreenivasan, 'Warrior-Tales'. Imre Bangha has also discussed how Valmiki's classical Rāmāyaṇa epic was modified in the vernacular in fifteenth-century Gwalior. See Bangha, 'Early Hindi Epic Poetry in Gwalior,' in Sheikh and Orsini, *After Timur Left*, 365–402.

[26] Mahmud Shah Begada would eventually overpower both of these fortifications and lay the foundations of sultanate cities in Champaner and Junagadh.

[27] For histories of the biographical tradition in pre-modern South Asia see Pathak, *Ancient Historians of India*, 1–29. Also, Ali, 'Temporality, Narration and the Problem of History', *Indian Economic and Social History Review*, 237–59; and, Thapar, *The Past Before Us*, 471–506.

centuries.[28] These chieftains, originally pastoralists with links to Islam, came to claim elaborate royal titles and ties to the Puranic deity Krishna's *yadava* lineage; such efforts are partucularly visible in the eulogistic biographical poem, *Maṇḍalīkanṛpacarita*, addressed to their last major ruler Mandalik (Chapter 3).

The Chaulukya and their successors, the Vaghelas, who preceded the rulers of Delhi in Gujarat, had been great patrons of Sanskrit as well as the other trans-regional languages, Apabhramsha and Prakrit. Hundreds of public inscriptions and important eulogies evidence how the Chaulukya-Vaghelas presided over an Indic polity that drew from the prevailing conventions of the cosmopolitan ideal of kingship. Furthermore, the Chaulukyas and Vaghelas also supported the Jain faith, members of which often had close ties to the state. The eleventh-century Jain scholar-monk, Acharya Hemachandra, who is considered one the most important Jain intellectuals, was based at the court of two of the most prominent kings of the Chaulukya dynasty. A number of compositions, including the Sanskrit-Apabhramsha-Prakrit grammar, *Siddharhemacandra,* played an important role in shaping Chaulukya ideas of rule both within the region and outside of it. At the same time, within the numerous Muslim trading communities that had settled in Gujarat's thriving urban centres, Arabic and, to some extent Persian, were introduced into the region's literary landscape. This multilingual tradition, which had already been established during Chaulukya–Vaghela rule beginning in the tenth century, reached an unprecedented scale during the fifteenth-century regional transformations.

The Muzaffarid sultans actively patronised literature and learning in Arabic and Persian, perhaps on a larger scale than in other contemporary courts. Scholars and men of religion from across the Islamic world were invited to settle in the region, which emerged as a vibrant location for intellectual communities to flourish. [29] This also provided impetus for the first expressions of an Indo-Persian vernacular, Gujari, a form of Hindavi or Hindi.[30] As Sufis and scholars

---

28 For a history of the Chudasamas' rise in status and their eventual fall as the rulers of the Saurashtra peninsula, see Sheikh, 'Alliance, Genealogy and Political Power,' *Medieval History Journal*, 29–61.

29 For a history of the creation of Muslim intellectual communities in Gujarat and the role of the sultans in facilitating them, see Balachandran, 'Texts, Tombs and Memory'.

30 On Gujari see Dar, 'Gujarat's Contribution to Gujari and Urdu,'18–36; Nayak, 'Gujarī Bhāshā,' *Svadhayaya*, 268–85; Pathak, 'Gujari: The God-Given Great Gift to the World,' in Siddiqi, *The Growth of Indo-Persian Literature in Gujarat*, 98–104. Also, Sheikh, *Forging a Region,* 204–14.

from north India settled in the cities of Gujarat, they often composed works in this regional tongue. Yet Sanskrit and bilingual inscriptions using both Sanskrit and Persian, and sometimes Gujarati, also a regional language, continued to be commissioned both by local communities as well as court officials; there was a considerable increase in the number of such inscriptions during the fifteenth century. Furthermore, the tradition of Jain literary production not only endured under the Delhi sultanate, but flourished as Jain scholars continued to compose works in Sanskrit and Apabhramsha.

Vernacularisation was taking new forms outside the courtly milieu as well. In the early fifteenth century the poet Bhalan adapted the classical Sanskrit work *Kādambarī* by transforming both the tale and the genre into the regional language and idiom.[31] But this was also the period in which Narasimha Maheta, the poet who is regarded as Gujarat's first poet or *adi-kavi*, composed his vast oeuvre of Vaishanava devotional poems in Gujarati. Narasimha's poetry transformed the Gujarati language as his compositions were not Sanskrit poems in 'Gujarati but Gujarati poems in Gujarati'.[32] Moreover, Narasimha carved out new possibilities of patronage for the poet in the devotional congregational realm rather than through state support, revolutionising the regional literary traditions.[33] This elevated Gujarati to a language of poetry both akin to Sanskrit but also distinct from it. Alongside these major changes in the development and status of the Gujarati language, immense varieties of local and specialised community dialects also blossomed at this time; the regional languages of Saurashtra and Kachchh, and Khojki, the medium of devotional expression used by the Ismaili Khojas, are some example of these. Both at the popular and courtly levels then, the inhabitants of Gujarat had a variety of languages and idioms to choose from.

It is against this backdrop that the choices the chieftains and sultans and their poets made, to fashion their ideas of self, kingship, and the region, may be viewed. Instead of the evolving regional vocabularies, the chieftains of Gujarat chose to express their political aspirations in Sanskrit. What is more, while the sultans were patrons of a variety of languages, and did in fact commission large-scale historical writings in Persian and Arabic, in the mid-fifteenth century, they too claimed the benefits of the universal Kshatriya values of kingship that

[31] Yashaschandra, 'From Hemacandra to Hind Svarāj,' 581.
[32] Yashaschandra, 'From Hemacandra to Hind Svarāj,' 584.
[33] Yashaschandra, 'From Hemacandra to Hind Svarāj,' 586.

the Sanskrit eulogistic and epic traditions had to offer. Similarly illuminating is the widespread use of Dimgal, which was a language tradition that was not specific to Gujarat but was understood amongst warrior elites across western India. Unlike Sanskrit, however, Dimgal was associated with specialist oral performers, namely Bhats and Charans. These genealogist-poets held close ties with the Rajput ruling groups all over western India and Gujarat. Thus, while the narratives studied in this book display a close relationship to the context in which they are produced, the medium of communication their composers deployed were decidedly trans-regional.

I view these texts as having active, 'dialogic and discursive' relationships to their particular contexts.[34] Consequently, I situate these narratives firmly within the historical contexts to which they belong.[35] In their use of the transregional languages and familiar idioms, these narratives draw their legitimacy from the conventions of respected genres. Yet they also exhibit innovation, shaped by and, in turn, shaping the patrons' political and social aspirations. The 'particular' and the 'place' are crucial to the ways in which the protagonists are fashioned in and presented by the composers of these narratives: the local and universal are constantly intertwined to create the protagonists' world. In the play about the Chauhan king, Gangadas of Champaner, and in Mandalik's biography, both set in local courts, this interplay is visible throughout the narratives (Chapter 3). In the regional sultan's biography, however, the universal takes precedence over details of historical accuracy (Chapter 4).

Bringing these texts together and reading them closely illuminates the aspirations and self-articulations of elite warrior groups in fifteenth-century Gujarat, as they negotiated the political processes that were in motion at the regional and local levels. On one hand, through Sanskrit, these groups were able to forge links to the prestigious and universally recognised Kshatriya warrior status; on the other hand they could also draw on the more open-ended warrior ethos through languages akin to the oral traditions. The political prestige associated with the classical language of power appears to have

[34] Inden, 'Introduction: From Philological to Dialogical Texts,' 13.

[35] A number of scholars have contributed to the analysis of narratives that may have not been considered 'historical' or containing a sense of the past until about three decades ago. A growing body of scholarship now exists on pre-modern historical accounts and ways in which they may be read within their contexts and specific genres. The most recent among these studies include Zutshi, *Kashmir's Contested Pasts*. Also, see Thapar, *The Past Before Us*.

remained foundational in establishing the patrons' self-image as successful kings. On the other hand, pre-existing genres and linguistic conventions could be substantially modified to suit the needs of the patrons: the Sanskrit play and the biography of the Chudasama chieftain as well as the sultan's Sanskrit biography are examples of how new groups could be incorporated into classical genres that were usually associated with Indic kings from great lineages of the past. Far from composing conventionalised narratives about cardboard heroes, the poets of these works drew upon a rich pool of ideological and linguistic resources to represent their patrons in a time and space in which sovereignties and identities were not fully established. I argue that, in producing these kinds of narratives, the poets were making deliberate attempts to write both their patrons' personal histories, and more importantly, inscribe them into the wider histories unfolding at the time.

While the fifteenth century was not the source of great canon-making literature, it was a period in which a vast body of literary works, in a plethora of languages and genres, was created in order to articulate a variety of community-based and religious identities.[36] Placing such narratives within a longer history of local and regional state formation provides both a counter-argument and a corrective to the dominant historiography of South Asia. The fifteenth century has been a black hole of sorts in the historiography of the subcontinent in general, but this lacuna has had an especially deep impact on the historical studies of Gujarat. The dominant view – both in scholarship and in the popular imagination – considers Turkic rule as a rupture in Gujarat's heroic Rajput past. By paying close attention to the vibrant literary culture of the Rajput and sultanate courts, we can also recognise the political and cultural continuities – not ruptures – that were at work.

Re-discovering the Fifteenth-century Warriors

In the mid-nineteenth century, an officer of the East India Company of Scottish descent, Alexander Kinloch Forbes (1821–1865), was stationed in Ahmadabad and Mahi Kantha in Gujarat as the Assistant Collector. Like many of his colleagues at the time, Forbes was interested in unearthing the history of the place he was sent to administer. Forbes's attention was caught by the works of Jain scholars who had written the histories of the Chaulukya

[36] Orsini and Sheikh, Introduction to *After Timur Left*.

and Vaghela kingdoms. However, he was especially captivated by the people he refers to as 'bards', the different communities of Bhats and Charans, who specialised in the oral narration of the pasts and genealogies of the various Rajput kingdoms that dotted the region. It was in their records and traditions that Forbes found the stories of the chieftains and warriors who had been part of the fifteenth-century political configurations. On the basis of these sources, along with translations of a few Jain and Persian works, Forbes went on to compose what has become a classical account of Gujarat's past, *Rās Mālā: Hindoo Annals of Western India* (1856), in which he constructed the history of Gujarat as the history of the Rajput chieftains. Forbes's *Rās Mālā*, which foregrounded the Rajput polities, their origins, and their interactions with the sultans, still stands out as distinct from later histories of the region (Chapter 5). These works, particularly the accounts of the colonial nationalist elite in the late nineteenth and early twentieth centuries, gave precedence to the Indic Chaulukya–Vaghela polities, viewing the sultanate-Rajput interactions as indicators of the fifteenth-century decline.

The communities of Bhats and Charans, the preservers of the genealogies and histories of the Rajput chieftains, were integral to their polities, not only as historians but also as diplomats and guarantors. These men often accompanied their patrons during battles, inspiring the warriors to fight and composing poetry in their honour. They were also considered descendants of the Mother Goddess and therefore enjoyed a sacred status in the communities they served. Because of this status, the Bhats and Charans became a crucial link in the preservation of not only lineages but also of the heroic ethos. In the centuries that followed the fifteenth, while the courtly milieu of the entrepreneurial polities was transformed under the Mughal rule, it was their battle narratives, sustained by oral tradition, that continued to flourish and circulate.

It was these narratives of the Bhats and Charans that Forbes documented. While the fifteenth-century narratives that I have analysed, such as *Raṇmallachanda, Gaṅgadāsapratāpavilāsanāṭaka, Māṇḍalīkamahākāvya*, and *Rājavinoda*, were not among Forbes's discoveries, his work on oral compositions plays a crucial role in the understanding of the period. Oral traditions further confirm the complex interplay of ideas and power between the mobile polities of the region in which the sultans and Rajputs played significant roles. Although his history is not free of colonial bias, the oral traditions recorded by Forbes present a fluid, rather than entirely confrontational, picture of the politics of the region, differing sharply from much of the scholarship that would appear in the years to follow.

Plan of the Book

With the exception of the first, the chapters in this monograph are centred on one or two individual narratives. Chapter 1 provides the setting; a historical map that sets the stage for the ways in which the region and its politics evolved in the fifteenth century. It traces three important developments that shaped the fifteenth century society and polity: first, the establishment of the Indic polity of the Chaulukya–Vaghelas; second, the rise and decline of the Muslim empire of the Delhi sultanate, and third, the emergence of the local Rajput chieftains, who were once pastoralist warriors, and who began to settle down and establish their patrimonies in the region before the foundation of the great fifteenth-century polity of the Muzaffarid sultans. While discussing each of these political formations, I also map the linguistic and literary choices that were made during this period to articulate ideas of kingship and authority as well as express community identities.

The changes in the early fifteenth century are reflected in the literary culture of the Rajput chieftains, the topic of Chapter 2. This chapter centres on *Raṇmallachanda,* a battle narrative in which Ranmal, the Rathod chieftain of Idar, fights against the new governor sent by the Delhi sultan. Ranmal, in this narrative, is supported neither by an elaborate court nor a long genealogy linking him to an illustrious royal lineage. Instead, Ranmal is portrayed as a solitary hero concerned with the defence of his patrimonies and honour. This work is in Dimgal, prefaced by Sanskrit, and interspersed with words from the Persian register. The story has the fluid quality of an oral narrative and, interestingly, is composed by a Brahmin poet, Sridhara Vyasa. It is also laden with stock descriptions of a Kshatriya warrior's duty to protect Brahmins, women, and cows against the atrocities of the Muslims. This multilingual layering of genres, traditions, and tropes, reflects the crystallising self-representation of chieftains, such as Ranmal, who appear, simultaneously, to be seeking a place in the larger varna hierarchy, as well as maintaining ties with the more fluid warrior traditions in this period. The two languages serve different functions: the Sanskrit section portrays Ranmal, a local chieftain with limited territorial control, as a great Indic king, whereas the Dimgal portion depicts Ranmal as a warrior, and his triumphs on the battlefield, replete with copious descriptions of blood and gore.

As the fifteenth century progressed, the more successful of the Rajput chieftains in Gujarat also patronised Sanskrit poetry alongside oral traditions, which continued to shape their notions of identity and authority.

In the narratives discussed in Chapter 3, *Gaṅgadāsapratāpavilāsanāṭaka* and *Māṇḍalikanṛpacarita,* which are addressed to chieftains who controlled strategically located hill kingdoms, we find resonances of the cosmopolitan order that existed during the erstwhile Chaulukya world. Unlike Idar, the Chauhan kingdom of Champaner and the Chudasama kingdom of Junagadh are depicted as having elaborate courts, courtiers, and genealogies that proclaimed links with prestigious Puranic heroes. Above all, their rulers saw themselves as repositories of all the virtues demanded of true Kshatriya kings. Nevertheless, their political aspirations remained modest and limited to the areas they already controlled. Despite the violent battles with the enemy sultanate or *yavana* rulers depicted in the narratives, these men sought control and fame in their own local territories rather than the entire region. The use of the cosmopolitan Sanskrit and the aestheticised *kavya* genre was meant to establish the patrons' rule firmly within the region, rather than transport their fame across the subcontinent.

Chapter 4 examines a significant Sanskrit text entitled *Rājavinoda*, 'pleasure of the king', by a poet named Udayaraja. Drawing on the classical *kavya* tradition of Sanskrit poetry and using the markers of an Indic paramount king or *chakravarti,* whose kingdom is the centre of Indian subcontinent, this text allowed Mahmud Begada, a Muslim sultan, to draw on the eclectic ideological resources available to him. In contrast to the Sanskrit works composed for the local Rajput chieftains (Chapter 3), or the multilingual text in honour of Ranmal (Chapter 2), which highlight the context of the protagonists' rule, the panegyric addressed to Sultan Mahmud conveys deeply universal values of kingship that could be applied to any great king.

The Rajput chieftains of Gujarat, their literary world, and the articulations of kingship and authority that emerged during the fifteenth century, had long-term implications in the making of Gujarat as region. While the sultans were overpowered by the Mughals at the end of the sixteenth century, and the Mughals in turn by the Marathas and the British, the Rajput kingdoms endured and went on to constitute the over two hundred princely states that comprised Gujarat on the eve of independence. The significance of this historical legacy was first articulated in a text entitled *Rās Mālā: Hindoo Annals of Western India* by a colonial administrator named Alexander Forbes in the mid-nineteenth century. Forbes drew primarily upon the oral accounts and written sources related to these Rajput groups that were abundantly available through the local elites to write a 'modern' history of the region. The end result was something of a hybrid of his colonial imperialist ideals, 'modern' history, and older articulations of kingship and authority that were based in the Rajputs' own itinerant martial pasts. The fifth chapter is a reading of *Rās Mālā.* There we see that, contrary to the popular perception of Gujarat as a land of merchants and traders, it was the history of the Rajputs and their interactions with the sultans that went into the making of one of the first attempts to articulate the idea of Gujarat as a modern region.

1

Setting the Stage

Contextualising Fifteenth-century Gujarat

In the fifteenth century, the Sultanate of Gujarat emerged as the most powerful of the kingdoms that succeeded the Delhi sultanate. The regional sultans of Gujarat, sometimes referred to as the Muzzafarid or the Ahmadshahi dynasty, were erstwhile nobles of the Delhi sultanate who declared their independence in 1407 from the already dwindling authority at Delhi, and their rule in Gujarat lasted until the 1580s – over a hundred and fifty years – when the Mughal emperor Akbar (r. 1556–1605) defeated the last ruling sultan on the plains of Saurashtra. The Muzaffarids integrated the diverse frontier region and its different geographical and social elements. And in doing so they created a distinctive vocabulary and idiom of 'Gujarati' regional rule.[1]

In *c.* 1407, Zafar Khan, the former noble of Delhi and governor of Gujarat, reluctantly declared himself the independent sultan of the province. While Delhi had been sacked at the hands of Timur in 1398, the prestige the former capital and its rulers commanded remained intact.[2] Therefore, many of the regional governors of provinces such as Jaunpur, Malwa, and Gujarat did not so much revolt against their former masters as seek less confrontational means of consolidating their power.[3] Zafar Khan, Gujarat's governor, took the title of Muzaffar Shah, laying the foundations of what was to become one of the longest-lasting regional sultanates to emerge during the fifteenth century. At

---

[1] For a detailed analysis of the ways in which the regional Muzaffarid sultans achieved the integration of the region, see Sheikh, *Forging a Region*.

[2] Gujarat had been incorporated as a province of the Delhi sultanate in the early fourteenth century and was administered by a governor sent from the capital until 1407.

[3] Digby, 'After Timur Left: North India in the Fifteenth Century,' in Orsini and Sheikh *After Timur Left*, 47–59.

the time that Zafar Khan declared himself sultan, throwing off the shackles of the moribund Delhi sultanate under Mahmud Tughlaq II (r. 1324–1351), the region had long been an imperial province, referred to both as 'Gujarat' or by the name of its capital, Anhilvada (or Naharwala in the Persian chronicles). The regional sultans, Muzaffar Shah and his successors, particularly Sultan Mahmud Begada (r. 1459–1511), strove to integrate different geographical, political, and societal elements of the region. By 1480, Mahmud Begada, who styled himself 'Gujarati', had established military control over most of the territories of the modern region, as well as, at times, parts of Malwa, southern Rajasthan, and the southern coastal lands stretching almost all the way to present-day Mumbai.[4] It was most of this territory that, with Akbar's conquest, went on to form the Mughal province or *subah* of Gujarat.

Three major developments preceded this regional imperium and set the stage for the political and cultural transformations that Gujarat would undergo in the fifteenth century. The first of these was the Chaulukya–Vaghela empire (*c.* 942–1304), an Indic polity that lasted over three hundred years until the establishment of the Delhi sultanate's rule over Gujarat in 1304. It was during this time span that some of the processes of regional integration began, which were brought to fruition in the fifteenth century. This was also the period during which the core territories from which Gujarat would be ruled for subsequent centuries were stabilised. Further, the Chaulukyas, and the Vaghelas who succeeded them, managed to reap the benefits of Gujarat's long-standing links with the Indian Ocean trade networks as well as with the Arab and Persian merchants active on the coastal areas of the region; this growth in commercial activity bears witness to the emerging cosmopolitan society at the time.

Despite being of humble origins, the Chaulukyas, and later the Vaghelas, established a vast polity that claimed universal Indic ideals; this is particularly evident in the literature and architecture they patronised. They expressed their royal ideologies in the cosmopolitan languages of Sanskrit, Prakrit, and Apabhramsha. Simultaneously, they laid claim to Puranic norms of kingship, supporting a sizable number of Shaiva temples. But the Chaulukyas, and particularly the Vaghelas, also favoured the Jains, a trading community that came to be closely associated with the state due to its mercantile skills and achievements. By the twelfth century, the Chaulukyas had adopted a royal order and vocabulary that drew upon the age-old universal Indic traditions of kingship; however, they also fostered a polity in a territory populated by

[4] Sheikh, *Forging a Region,* 27.

newly ascendant warrior chieftains, Brahmin and Jain scribes and scholars, and a wide range of immigrant and local trading groups that benefitted from Gujarat's oceanic and internal trade routes.

The second major development contributing to the transformation of Gujarat was the conquest of the Chaulukya–Vaghela territories by the rulers of the Delhi sultanate in the closing years of the thirteenth century. Gujarat, particularly the Somanatha temple located on its western frontier, had witnessed incursions from the north and northwest during the previous centuries as well. These attacks had been had been characterised by plundering raids rather than any attempts by the attackers to establish stronger political ties with the region. It was only with the Delhi Sultan 'Ala' al-Din Khalji's conquest that Gujarat became more enduringly politically and economically linked to the transregional empire of Delhi, and thus to the wider Persianate world.[5] The Delhi sultanate, with its new political, cultural, and military norms, was the final blow to this old order that was already in decline. Yet, once in the province, the governors sent by the Delhi authorities had to accommodate local realities and were quick to establish links with the local power structures; it was these links that would eventually facilitate the formation of the independent sultanate of Gujarat in the fifteenth century. Even at the height of its power, and despite its expansionist ambitions, the Delhi sultanate's control over the provinces remained tenuous as local chieftains and imperial representatives stationed on the ground grew in strength. Persian was adopted as the language of courtly splendour from this time onwards by a number of Turkic powers; the sultans of Delhi were no different. However, numerous Sanskrit and bilingual inscriptions were also commissioned in this period and included the new dispensation in their vocabularies. Similarly, the Jains and other mercantile communities continued to grow in prominence during the Delhi sultanate rule over the region.

With the decline of the Chaulukyas and Vaghelas, space was created for a third crucial political process that would shape the region in the subsequent years. From the twelfth century onwards, Gujarat had seen the migration of men of obscure lineages into the region from the north and northwest. These men – warriors, pastoralists, merchants – began to settle in the region. With the end of Chaulukya–Vaghela rule, these men grew stronger in their patrimonies, building forts and laying claim to the region's resources. These local chieftains

[5] 'Ala' al-Din Khalji first attacked the Anhilvada kingdom in 1298, but it was only after his second incursion in 1304 that the region was established as a province of the Delhi empire; it remained so until 1407.

had not been destroyed by the new imperial wave of the Delhi sultanate but in fact been reconstituted and would ultimately become the most important political elements the new dispensation was forced to negotiate with. These men, later known as Rajputs, also established courts in which new vocabularies of kingship would be developed in the aftermath of the Chaulukya cosmopolis.

New power structures were forged and contested during the period between the establishment of the Chaulukya dynasty in *c.* 940 and the end of Delhi sultanate rule in Gujarat in *c.* 1407. Literature, and to a certain extent material culture, also underwent great change, largely due to the courtly patronage patterns of Chaulukyas and the Vaghelas. While several conventional accounts view the end of the Chaulukya–Vaghela reign at the hands of the Delhi sultanate, with its wholly different political, cultural, and military conventions, as representing the end of the 'glory' of Gujarat, the discontinuities from the Delhi sultanate proved short-lived, giving way rather quickly to the Gujarat sultanate, which represented further transformation in the patronage landscape that was to shape the fifteenth century.

The Chaulukya–Vaghela Polity, *c.* 940–1304

Around the year 942, Mularaja, a scion of the Chaulukya family, is said to have killed his maternal uncle, Chavada or Chapotkata Samantasimha of Anhilpataka, on the central plains of Gujarat, and established a dynasty in his own name that would rule over Gurjaradesha, the name the region was known by at the time, for over two centuries; after that, another branch of the family, the Vaghelas, established themselves as the Chaulukya's successors. The Chavadas, from whom Mularaja usurped the throne, were the local feudatories of the northern Indian dynasties of Gurajara–Pratiharas. Later sources inform us that they were most likely previously forest dwellers who had managed to acquire land and establish territorial control over parts of northern and eastern Gujarat.[6] With Mularaja's takeover of the Chavada capital at Anhilpataka, or what would subsequently be known as Anhilvada–Patan, began the three-hundred-year rule of a regional Indic polity of the Chaulukya-Vaghela dynasties that participated in what Sheldon Pollock has called the Sanskrit cosmopolis, and adopted a vocabulary of universal kingship that dominated in India and Southeast Asia

[6] Merutungacharya, *Prabandhacintāmani*, 18–20. The *Ratnamāla*, composed by the twelfth-century Brahmin poet, Krishnaji, also mentions a similar story about the establishment of Chapotkata or Chavada rule. See Krishnaji, *The Ratan Málá*.

throughout the first millennium of the common era.[7] The establishment of the Chaulukya rule over the city of Anhilpataka also marks the beginning of a period in which Gujarat experienced a number of transformations in terms of expansion of settlements and the rise of new political and social groups. This formed the basis of a nascent regional cohesion upon which the Gujarati or Muzaffarid sultans were able to lay the foundations of their independent kingdom in the fifteenth century.

The Chaulukyas have widely been associated with the end of the pan-Indian imperial dynasties, the Gurjara–Pratiharas of Kanyakubja, which held sway over most of north India until the end of the tenth century. Following the decline of this power and its rival kingdom, the Rashtrakutas in the Deccan, several smaller dynasties such as the Paramaras, Chandellas, Kalachuri, Chaulukyas, and Gahadavalas came to control different parts of northern India. This proliferation of dynasties, as B. D. Chattopadhyaya has asserted, was related to the continuing process of state formation at the regional and local levels, which, in turn, was connected to the growth of trade and urban centres from the early medieval period onwards.[8] The rise of Chaulukya rule in Anhilvada–Patan and its subsequent territorial expansion can be related to this process.

Beginning with Mularaja's (r. 942–996) accession, the Chaulukyas embarked on an energetic expansionist programme; over the next century, they would extend their rule into territories across Gujarat and parts of southern Rajasthan and Malwa. Their vast epigraphic records suggest that this included the subjugation of clans and forest-dwelling groups like Bhils on the peripheries of what was to become the core of their kingdom, Anhilvada–Patan. The Chaulukyas' quest for territorial control reached something of a peak under Jayasimha Siddharaja (r. 1094–1143), who is accepted, by contemporary writers and later historians alike, as the dynasty's greatest ruler. Siddharaja defeated Khengar or Navghana of Girnar in Saurashtra and conducted successful campaigns against Malwa as well as its surrounding forest regions. The Chahamanas of Nadula and Shakambhari accepted Chaulukya overlordship during this period.[9] Siddharaja's successful campaigns increased the size of his territory and the Chaulukya kingdom achieved its maximum expanse –

---

7 For elaboration on the Sankrit cosmopolis see Pollock, *The Language of the Gods* and 'The Sanskrit Cosmopolis, 300–1300,' 209–217.

8 Chattopadhyaya, 'Urban Centres in Early Medieval India,' 155–86, and 'Political Processes and the Structure of Polity,' 183–222.

9 For an account of Chahamanas of Nadula as feudatories of the Chaulukyas, see Mita, 'Polity and Kingship of Early Medieval Rajasthan,' 89–117.

encompassing Saurashtra, southern Rajputana, and parts of Malwa – during his reign.[10] With Kumarapala (r. 1143–1174), who followed Siddharaja as the dynasty's next most prominent king, Chaulukya domains extended to the Vindhya ranges, at least as far south as the river Tapti, and as far north as the southern reaches of Rajasthan. Saurashtra and Kachchh to the west were also a part of Kumarapala's domain.

A few decades after Kumarapala's rule, Chaulukya power in Gujarat saw the beginnings of the internal strife and external chaos that would eventually lead to the relinquishment of the Anhilvada territories to the Vaghelas, who had formerly been their courtiers. This was also the period when Delhi launched an attack on the region: in 1197, the Ghurid ruler, Mu'izz al-Din Sam's general, Qutb al-Din Aybeg, looted Anhilvada, although this did not result in the acquisition of territory for the Delhi sultan.[11] The Vaghelas retained power in the region by claiming descent from the Chaulukyas but were able to maintain only nominal control over parts of Saurashtra and north Gujarat. With the conquest of Gujarat by 'Ala' al-Din Khalji's army in 1297–98, the Vaghelas lost control over central Gujarat, although branches of the family continued to exist in north Gujarat and central India.[12]

Settlement expanded and trade continued to thrive through the many political changes that occurred beginning in the eleventh century. As they augmented their territories, the Chaulukyas also built towns and settlements along the important trade routes, taking advantage of their lucrative revenues and encouraging mercantile activities. Soon after its takeover by Mularaja, Anhilvada grew into a prosperous urban centre. Similarly, Siddharaja Jayasimha extended Siddhapur and also built the large Shaiva temple complex of Rudramahalaya. Several other towns located in the hinterlands of major

[10] Majumdar, *Chaulukyas of Gujarat*, 82–83. Inscriptions attributed to Siddharaja, or bearing his name, have been found in several parts of the region, including Udaipur, Sambar, and Ujjain. The Dohad inscription of 1140 also speaks of Siddharaja Jayasimha as the ruler of *Gurjara-mandala* and notes that he imprisoned the kings of Saurashtra and Malwa. See Dhruva, 'The Dohad Inscription,' 158–62.

[11] The Chaulukya empire had already witnessed two other attacks from the north and northwest. The first of these was in 1126 against Bhima (r. 1022–1064) under whose reign, Mahmud Ghazna attacked the Somanatha temple, and the second was in the reign of Mularaja II (r. 1176–1179), who resisted attacks by Ghurid sultan Mu'izz al-Din Muhammad bin Sam, also known in Indic sources as Hammira (Amira) and the lord of the Turushkas.

[12] The Baghela ruling family of Rewa also traditionally claimed its descent from the Vaghelas of Gujarat.

trade routes also flourished during this period. Bhinmal, or Srimala, which lay on the route to Sind from western India, grew into an important town, and Dabhoi, Kapadvanj, Godhra, and Dohad emerged as successful centres of trade on the eastern route between the Malwa hinterland and Khambhat or Cambay.[13] Port towns like Cambay and Somanatha also prospered, reaching a scale far greater than that of the mainland's urban centres.

The Chaulukya–Vaghela rulers' temple-building spurred the growth of metropolitan areas. Kings including Mularaja and Siddharaja built large temples and encouraged Brahmins to settle in the towns of Gujarat, making generous gifts of villages to them for their support. In addition to asserting their political dominance over the region and their rivals, the temples also facilitated the development of the urban economy and society. The inscriptions on public and administrative epigraphs from the period bear witness to this fact, often indicating the place of origin of the Brahmins who settled in Gujarat. Mularaja's Balera copper plates, dated as early as *c.* 995, for instance, record the grant of a village to Dirghacharya, a Brahmin who had migrated from Kanyakubja in north India.[14] Similarly, an endowment from Chaulukya king Karna's reign records the grant of a village in south Gujarat to a Brahmin whose family was originally from Madhyadesha.[15] Numerous such examples exist of donations and grants to Brahmins, including those who had been settled in the region for generations and come to occupy specific parts of it, such as the Modha Brahmins of Modhera or the Nagars, who saw Vadnagar (Visnagara or Vishalnagara) as their traditional home.

From their modest beginnings as descendants of forest chieftains in the tenth century, the Chaulukyas, by the end of the twelfth century, had extended their sway over much of Gujarat, and their empire included territories in southern Rajasthan and western Malwa. Most significantly, with the establishment of Chaulukya power, a strip of territory extending from north to south, roughly from the area north of Patan to Cambay on the coast, became the core territory from which Gujarat would be ruled in subsequent centuries.[16]

Along with the expansion of their empire the Chaulukyas embarked on an ideological programme, participating in the universal ideals of kingship that were the norm during this period. The large-scale temples they built and the

---

13 Sheikh, *Forging a Region,* 32.

14 Konow, 'Balera Plates of Mularāja,' 76–79.

15 Acharya, *Historical Inscriptions from Gujarat* 2, 18–24.

16 Sheikh, *Forging a Region,* 67.

Chaulukya court itself, emerged as sites for the extensive patronage of literary activities, including the composition of epic poems, dramas, and significantly, a vast number of inscriptions granting lands, primarily to Brahmins, but often also accompanied by long genealogies and eulogies to the ruling kings and their ancestors.

The vast array of public inscriptions documenting donations and land grants from the Chaulukya–Vaghela period bears witness to the image of kingship these rulers sought to project. The records of the practical administrative matters of these grants were always preceded by genealogies and praise poems or *prashastis* dedicated to the patrons. In composing these, poets at the Chaulukya court drew from the pool of inscriptional practices of *kavya* that were available at the time to establish their patrons' power and fame. Typical examples of this can be seen in the work of poet Shripala, who served at the courts of Jayasimha Siddharaja and Kumarapala, two of the dynasty's most prominent rulers. As Pollock has pointed out, Shripala, in his Vadanagara and Bilpank *prashastis*, appears much more concerned with announcing his patron dynasty's power upon the earth than with the accuracy of the genealogy of the kings or the facticity of their military achievements.[17] Instead, his aim is 'to give voice to what is enduring and charismatic about kingly power' and to demonstrate the different constituents of fame such as philanthropy, building projects, and battles, all of which were practices that were familiar across the landscape of the Sanskrit *prashasti*.[18] The titles of the patrons, which were drawn from Puranic hierarchies of Indic kings, and the rulers' close association with Puranic deities also reinforced the function of eulogies to grant their patrons universal fame. The ideals of kingship these eulogies conveyed were not, therefore, meant to be specific, but general, universally recognised, traits of great kings. Sanskrit inscriptions of considerable length continued to be patronised throughout the thirteenth century, when the Vaghelas succeeded their former overlords. [19]

Through their literary patronage, the Chaulukya rulers of Anhilvada aspired to the spread their kingly glory far beyond their kingdom of Gujarat. In addition to the wide number and variety of inscriptions commissioned by the Chaulukya

[17] Pollock, *Language of Gods*, 145. For biographical details of the poet, see Sandesara, 'Śrīpāla: The Blind Poet-laureate,' 252–59.

[18] Pollock, *Language of the Gods*, 145.

[19] Gadre, 'The Nānaka Praśastis,' 74–79. Another important example of a *prashasti* from this period comes from the reign of a later Vaghela king, Saraṅgadeva. See Bühler, 'The Cintra Praśasti of Sarangadeva,' 271–87.

and Vaghela kings, a vast array of other literary works produced by poets and writers associated with their courts evidences the existence of a vibrant scholarly circle that blossomed under their rule.[20] This diverse body of literature included works in Sanskrit as well as Apabhramsha and Prakrit, the two other cosmopolitan languages in use at the time. The literati, that were an important part of the Chaulukya and Vaghela kingly aspirations, were also instrumental in the creation of an image of the kings not only as powerful Kshatriya rulers but also as generous patrons of literature and poetry *vis-á-vis* their rivals, particularly the rulers of the neighbouring kingdom of Malwa. The Jain scholar-monk Hemachandra's work on Sanskrit-Prakrit-Apabhramsha grammar, the *Siddhahemacandra*, was composed at the behest of Jayasimha Siddharaja and displays a keen awareness of the relationship between language and power. In this period, works like *Siddhahemacandra* were meant to confer royal glory upon the king, and scholarly renown upon the grammarian, and grant spiritual benefit to them both.[21] Hemachandra's grammar was meant for the larger world, not solely the immediate context in which it was produced.[22] The Jain preceptor held an important position at the court of Jayasimha Siddharaja and Kumarapala; several Jain sources even suggest that Hemachandra converted the two kings to the Jain faith. The *Siddhahemacandra* was composed with the implicit purpose of eclipsing the Sanskrit grammar by the legendary king Bhoja (1011–1055), who was widely known for his literary skills and patronage.[23] Copies of the grammar were apparently sent to other kingdoms of the subcontinent, particularly Kashmir, which was viewed as the centre of learning and the abode of the goddess Sarasvati.[24]

For the Chaulukya rulers, literary patronage went hand in hand with the construction of a wide range of temples. The temple complexes built by the Chaulukyas not only became centres of economic activity but also symbolised their dominance over the region. The ultimate object of *dharma* for the Vaishnava or Shaiva king was the construction or patronage of a temple. It was with this that he 'hoped to top off the cosmo-moral order constituted by his

[20] For a brief survey of literary works patronised by Chaulukyas, see Majumdar, *Chaulukyas of Gujarat*, 403–20. For details of the scholars and literary productions at under the Jain ministers Vastupala and Tejahpala see Sandesara, *Literary Circle of Mahāmātya Vastupāla*.

[21] Pollock, *Language of the Gods*, 182.

[22] Pollock, *Language of the Gods*, 182.

[23] Pollock, *Language of the Gods*, 181.

[24] Sandesara, *Literary Circle of Mahāmātya Vastupāla*, 11.

imperial kingdom.'[25] As several of their inscriptions indicate, the Chaulukyas viewed the kingdom itself as being blessed by Shiva, and kings like Kumarapala were adorned with titles such as 'one who has obtained the boon of the lord of Uma, that is, Shiva' (*umapativaralabdha*). The numerous attacks on the Somanatha temple during the Chaulukya period show that these buildings were not only storehouses of wealth but were viewed as symbols of the rulers' power – even by those outside the kingdom.[26]

The end of the Vaghela rule saw the rise of the Jain merchant–minister brothers, Vastupala and Tejahpala, whose vast marble temple buildings dedicated to their faith evidence another form of political representation that had emerged in the region prior to the arrival of Islamic rule. The two brothers, as has been noted, controlled the entire administrative and military operations of the Anhilvada kingdom and became protagonists in a number of Sanskrit texts and epigraphic praise poems composed in the same elaborate styles used in compositions written for kings.[27] The support of these rulers for building

[25] Inden, 'Hierarchies of Kings in Early Medieval India,' 133.

[26] For the political significance of the Somanatha temple and the complex history of Muslim raids on it, see Davis, *The Lives of Indian Images*, 'Images Overthrown', 88–112 and 'Reconstructions of Somanāthā', 186–221, and Thapar, *Somanatha*. Soon after his accession, Mularaja built a temple dedicated to Shiva as Mulaswami (Mula's Lord) and later another temple dedicated to Somanatha at Mandali-nagara, apparently at the god's own bidding. Such was the king's dedication that he is also said to have travelled to Somanatha daily to worship the divinity. This is unlikely, as the round trip between Anhilvada and Somanatha is over 700 miles. Tradition has it that Somanatha, pleased by his dedication, promised to bring the ocean to Anhilvada. When the diety arrived, as promised, a number of pools in the town turned brackish proving that the ocean had actually accompanied him. To celebrate the Somanatha's arrival, Mularaja built the Tripurushaprasada temple at Anhilvada. This temple was further adorned with a 'jewelled peak' after Mahmud Ghazna's attack on the kingdom. Apart from the Rudramahalaya temple at Siddhapur, Jayasimha Siddharaja also built Sahasralimga lake at Patan. In addition to this, at the behest of his mother, Mayanalladevi, he remitted the taxes being levied on the Anhilvada-Saurashtra border to the pilgrims going to Somanatha. Similarly, later kings, including Kumarapala, who was known to be a follower of the Jain faith, also maintained their patronage and devotion to Shiva, and more specifically to his incarnation as Somanatha. Campbell, *Gazetteer*, 160–161, 172.

[27] See for instance *Hammiramadamardana*, a play by Jayasimha Suri written sometime between *c.* 1220 and 1230, and the *Vastupāla-Tejahpāla praśasti* by the same author. For the text of the play and the *prashasti* see Dalal, *Hammiramadamardana of Jayasimha Suri*. Also see Bühler, *The Jagadūcharita of Sarvānanda*.

projects also encouraged the development of a regional architectural style.[28] This regional style, often referred to by art historians as the 'Maru-Gurjara' style, reached its most elaborate form from the eleventh century onwards and was extensively patronised by the Chaulukya kings.[29]

Aside from the Puranic kingly ideals, the Chaulukyas also shared a close and complex relationship with Jainism, as a number of scholars and poets who served at their courts were adherents of this faith. While the epigraphic records share in the Puranic discourse of kingship, many other texts composed by the Jains reveal a somewhat different view of Chaulukya rulers; as kings who were morally superior to their rivals because of their association with the sect. Apart from their practical involvement with everyday political affairs, the Jains also engaged in the broader discourse on the nature of kingship.[30] In their many historical and literary narratives from this period (and also in the subsequent centuries) they portrayed the way in which the rulers should act towards the Jain community and in that sense advanced a distinct theory of kingship.[31] Vaghela king Ajayapala's Jain minister Yashahapala, for instance, composed a play called the *Moharājaparājaya*, or 'conquest of king moha or illusion', describing Kumarapala's conversion to the Jain faith and the triumph

---

28 The architectural style in the western Indian region encompassing Gujarat, Rajasthan, and Sindh began to develop distinctive features from the eighth century onwards. Alka Patel has recently noted that while Chaulukya ascendancy had little to do with the initiation of this process of architectural consolidation, it is possible that the extensive royal, noble, and householder patronage was instrumental in bringing about its culmination. Patel, *Building Communities in Gujarāt*, 5–6.

29 On the architectural styles of Chaulukya temples and details of the building activities of individual rulers, see Dhaky, 'The Chronology of Solanki Temples of Gujarat,' 1–81.

30 Cort, 'Who is King?' 86.

31 Cort, 'Who is King?' 86. For a detailed discussion on the different genres of Jain history, see Cort, 'Genres of Jain History,' 469–506. Toshikazu Arai's study of the *Prabandhacintāmaṇi* shows how its fourteenth-century Jain author, Merutunga, claims the moral superiority of the religion over Brahminical kingship. Merutunga's narrative begins with stories of exemplary kings of north India, but it is primarily concerned with the kings of Gurjaradesha or Gujarat (the Chaulukyas) and Malavamandala or Malwa (the Paramaras). The kings of these counties are portrayed as archenemies and their attributes are contrasted with one another. As Arai has demonstrated, despite being Shaivas, the Gurjara kings are viewed by the author as representing the superior Jain ideals of kingship through their austerity and fortitude, whereas the kings of Malwa, though generous patrons of the arts, are represented as Brahminical rulers who were wont to succumb to worldly pleasures. See Arai, 'Jaina Kingship in the Prabandhacintāmaṇi,' 92–132.

of the good moral values represented by the Chaulukya kings.[32] Moreover, as noted, the Jain ministers, Vastupala and Tejahpala, also acquired a degree of prominence that made them the subjects of literary compositions and eulogistic inscriptions in the likeness of kings. The story of another Jain merchant, Jagadadeva or Jagdu, from the Vaghela period, also in Sanskrit, indicates how prosperous merchants could also aspire to political power. Jagdu, the merchant from Bhadreshwar in Kachchh, not only supplied the Vaghela king, Vishaldeva, with grains from his stores during a famine, but also built a fortification wall around the city for its protection, constructed a Shaiva temple, and sponsored the repairs of a mosque, despite being a Jain himself.[33]

Aside from adopting Puranic and Jainistic ideals of kingship, the Chaulukyas also achieved a degree of societal integration by patronising other religious communities. While in this period Vaishnavism remained secondary to Shaivism and the Jain faith, several Vaishnava temples were endowed by prominent members of society.[34] With the settlement of various itinerant pastoralist warrior groups in the region, a number of local cults and their shrines also flourished. Furthermore, the urban centres of Gujarat had attracted various Muslim trading communities for centuries through the Indian Ocean maritime networks. Port cities like Veraval and Cambay had been to home to vibrant communities of Arab and Ismaili traders who had commissioned religious and domestic structures encouraging the rise of a local style of Islamic architecture. Inscriptions and epitaphs found at Cambay, Patan, Veraval, Junagadh, and Somanatha speak of a number of endowments made by Muslims and also record the deaths of notables including men of religion, prominent merchants, and women during the Chaulukya rule.[35] Similarly, the existence of bilingual inscriptions in Arabic or Persian and Sanskrit from this period are indicative of the acceptance of Muslim patronage to places of worship under Chaulukya–Vaghela rule even towards its tail end.[36]

---

[32] Sandesara, *Literary Circle,* 15 and Majumdar, *Chaulukyas of Gujarat*, 411–12.

[33] Bühler, *The Jagadūcharita of Sarvānanda.*

[34] Dhruva, 'The Dohad Inscription,' 158–62.

[35] Desai, 'Arabic Inscriptions of the Rajput Period from Gujarat,' 1–24. Desai also studies thirty epigraphs from Cambay and finds that a number of the people mentioned in them were from different parts of Iran. Also, see Desai, 'Some Fourteenth Century Epitaphs', 2–58.

[36] A Persian-Sanskrit inscription from 1304, for instance, records an endowment made to the Jami mosque in Cambay during the reign of Karan Vaghela. The Sanskrit portion of the inscription acknowledges the endowment and asks the local chieftains to do the same. Details of this inscription can be found in Desai. 'A Persian-Sanskrit Inscription,' 13–20.

By the end of the thirteenth century, the Vaghelas did not control the same territorial expanse as their predecessors, the Chaulukyas. Despite the dismantling of the Chaulukya–Vaghela rule, however, the richly diverse society that developed during their exceptionally long dispensation had a lasting impact on the way the region would evolve in the centuries that followed.

Delhi Sultans in Gujarat, *c.* 1304–1407

In the early decades of the fourteenth century, the Vaghelas were violently overthrown by the Delhi sultanate armies. 'Ala' al-Din Khalji (*c.* 1296–1316), the most expansionist of the Delhi rulers, launched an attack on Vaghela King Karandeva's capital in 1304, bringing a decisive end to the long reign of the Chaulukya–Vaghela Indic polity. While Gujarat, particularly the prosperous Somanatha temple, in the Saurashtra peninsula, had seen several incursions from the north and northwest over the past two centuries, including a recent attack by Khalji in *c.* 1298,[37] it was his second attack, roughly around 1304, that was to have a lasting effect on the region. Various historical accounts tell us of Karandeva being forced to flee first to Deogir in the Deccan and thence further south to Warangal, where he sought asylum with Raja Rudradeva. Although Gujarat, due to its trade links across the Indian Ocean, was one of the earliest regions in the subcontinent to come in contact with Islam, Khalji's conquest extended Delhi's rule and established a Muslim governor or *muqta'* there.[38] The numerous public inscriptions that followed this event and proliferated in the subsequent decades are indicative of the beginnings and rapid acknowledgement of a new political dispensation.[39]

[37] In 1299 'Ala' al-Din Khalji sent his brother Ulugh Khan and his *wazir* Nusrat Khan to attack Gujarat. The incursion was most likely aimed at the sacking of Somathantha in emulation of Mahmud of Ghazni's attacks in the previous century. It seems that Karandeva Vaghela's attempts to stop their entry in to Gujarat were thwarted and Somathatha and Anhilvada were sacked. Nusrat Khan went on to plunder the prosperous port city of Cambay. According to some Jain and Rajput accounts, he also overran parts of the Kathiawad peninsula. After this attack, which was the first of two campaigns ordered by Khalji into the region, the Delhi army returned to the capital with enormous booty. Vaghela power was re-established until a second attack in *c.* 1304. See Jackson, *Delhi Sultanate*, 195–96. See also, Padmanabha, *Kaṇhadāde Prabandha*, 14–15. For Jain account, see Bühler, 'A Jaina Account of the End of the Vaghlelas of Gujarat,' 194–95.

[38] Jackson, *Delhi Sultanate.*

[39] Desai, 'Khaljī and Tughluq Inscriptions from Gujarat,' 1–40.

The Khalji incursion into Gujarat linked the region's fortunes closely to those of Delhi and eventually led to the formation of the independent sultanate of Gujarat in the fifteenth century. The Delhi sultans benefitted from the immense vitality of the regions' trade routes and mercantile links that had been fostered by the previous rulers. Already successful urban centres like Anhilvada-Patan and Cambay continued to benefit the Delhi sultans. With Delhi's conquest of these towns, Gujarat's revenue far exceeded that of other provinces; its governorship was therefore much coveted by the courtiers of Delhi, some of whom were willing to pay significant bribes to be appointed to Anhilvada or Cambay.[40] The significance of trade for the region was understood by the earliest governors sent to Gujarat. Alp Khan, the governor appointed to the province soon after the 1304 attack, is known to have adopted a generous and conciliatory attitude towards the various trading communities in the region, including the Arabs, the Ismailis, and the Jains. Inscriptions from Petlad and Cambay testify to his benevolence towards Muslim merchants, but Alp Khan is also remembered in a number of Jain accounts.[41] Noteworthy are two accounts about the Jain merchant Samara Sah, who is memorialised for the restoration of Jain temples at Shatrunjaya. Both the accounts, the *Samrā-rāsu* and the *Nābhinandanajinoddhāraprabandha,* speak of Alp Khan's cordial relations with the merchant and his granting of an official order or *firman* to restore the Jain temples, as the great merchant had sought to do.[42]

The extension of territory that had begun with 'Ala' al-Din was gradually replaced by direct rule under the Tughluqs who succeeded them, but the absorption of territories brought its own administrative and militaristic problems.[43] The Tughluqs faced constant rebellions at the hands of nobles stationed in Gujarat. Sultan Muhammad bin Tughluq (r. 1325-51) in fact spent the final three years of his rule chasing the rebel governor Taghi in Kathiawad, or Saurashtra, and the Thar regions, where he succumbed to illness and died in 1350. The sultan's presence in north Gujarat and the Saurashtra peninsula appears to have resulted in his gaining a degree of submission from the local chieftains, who were rewarded with the customary robes of honour and other

[40] Misra, *The Rise of Muslim Power,* 130.

[41] Misra, *The Rise of Muslim Power,* 67.

[42] The text of *Samrā-rāsu* is published in Dalal, *Prācīna-Gūrjara-Kāvyasamgraha,* 27–38. For *Nābhinandanajinoddhāraprabandha*, see Harakhcand.

[43] Jackson, *Delhi Sultanate,* 255.

gifts.[44] A bardic account collected in the nineteenth century also speaks of Muhammad's conquest of the coast and the defeat of the Gohil chieftain Mokhraji at Piram. The fact that the Gohil rulers of Bhavnagar trace their ancestry to Mokhraji is indicative of political pliancy and suggests that, though the chieftain was subjugated and his fortress at Piram destroyed, Gohil authority in the locality did not come to an end.

By the start of Firuz Tuqhluq's (r. 1351–88) rule in Delhi in 1362, Gujarat's governors, like the governors in other provinces of the empire, were becoming more powerful and displaying a degree of independence decades before Delhi's demise in the fifteenth century. One of these was Mufarrih Sultani, who held the title of Farhat al-Mulk Rasti Khan, and governed Gujarat from 1377 to 1391. Later writers such as Firishta view Rasti Khan's actions as leniency towards and complicity with the 'Hindu' or the infidel chieftains.[45] Eventually, the governor, Zafar Khan, managed to gain control of the local power bases, overthrow Delhi's rule in the province, and establish himself as an independent sultan.

While Gujarat was ruled as a province of the Delhi empire, it was also integrated into what has been termed the 'Persian cosmopolis', which had its own values of political power and cultural ideals.[46] The Delhi sultans promoted the use of the Persian language and Persianate cultural norms were established in the parts of the subcontinent they ruled. Gujarat featured in the works of the great poet Amir Khusrau (1253–1325), whose Persian *masnavi*, *Duval Rāni va Khiẓr Khān*, was commissioned by the Khalji prince Khizr Khan. This is a historical romantic tale of the love between Khizr Khan and Duval Rani, the daughter of the Gujarat king Raja Karandeva Vaghela. The princess, it is believed, was captured along with her mother during Khalji's conquest of Gujarat. Khusrau's *Khaza'in al Futuh,* composed around 1311–1312 to praise Khalji's victories throughout India, and Ziya' al-Din Barani's *Ta'rīkh-i Firūz Shāhī* form important sources for the history of Delhi's connections to province of Gujarat during the sultanate period.[47] While the new sultans of Delhi were of Turkish origin, they were steeped in Persian culture. The Indo-Persian culture, that drew on the Ghurid and Ghaznavid tradition of patronage of scholars and

[44] Misra, *Rise of Muslim Power,* 116–23.

[45] Firishta, *History of the Rise of Mahomedan Power*, Vol. 4, 2.

[46] Eaton and Wagoner, *Power, Memory, Architecture*, 21–27.

[47] For an English translation of *Duval Rāni va Khiẓr Khān,* see Losensky and Sharma, *In the Bazaar of Love*, 117–30.

poets, was founded as early as the eleventh century in Ghaznavid Punjab and its surrounding area.[48] As the Delhi sultanate grew more stable and confident in its rule during the thirteenth and fourteenth centuries, this culture matured. At this time, Persianised Turkish dynasties were supreme in other parts of the Islamic world as well. The successive dynasties of the Delhi sultans, being in constant contact with Iran and Central Asia, patronised the development of a local Persian culture.[49] This inaugurated a long period of Persian historical writing that was to continue into the nineteenth century. The efflorescence and spread of the various Sufi orders during this period also played an important role in facilitating the development and circulation of Indo-Persian culture in Delhi and throughout the subcontinent.[50]

Delhi's imperial rulers did embark on a focused patronage of Persian and Persianate culture in the region, but a number of older traditions also continued to exist during this period. The end of the Chaulukya–Vaghela rule meant that patronage to large-scale temples, and consequently Brahmin and Jain scholars who composed works in Sanskrit, Prakrit, and Apabhramsha, was no longer available. This phenomenon has conventionally been viewed in terms of a simple binary clash between Hindu and Muslim rulers in which the latter replaced the older traditions entirely with Islamic ones. A closer examination of the overall patronage landscape in Gujarat during the brief hundred years as a Delhi Sultanate province, however, provides a more complex picture.

Public inscriptions – which, as we have seen, were an important form of writing that communicated state ideology as well-formed visible records for administrative and legal purposes – acknowledged the presence of Khalji and Tughluq sultans and governors located in Patan, Cambay, Dholka, and other sites across the region.[51] While Persian was used for writing inscriptions during the Chaulukya–Vaghela reign only in rare instances, from this period onwards, Gujarat witnessed a greater production of inscriptions in the language. This was as expected, but Sanskrit inscriptions recording grants of land or donations by a variety of social groups were found all over the region even after the sultanate gained power. Some of the inscriptions from

[48] Alam et al. *The Making of Indo-Persian Culture*, 24. The Delhi sultans patronised political theorists like Ziya' al-Din Barani (d. 1357) as well as poets like Amir Khusrau (d. 1325) and Hasan Sijzi Delhlavi (1254–1328).

[49] Alam et al. *The Making of Indo-Persian Culture*, 24.

[50] Digby, 'Before Timur Came,' 298–356; Eaton, *The Rise of Islam on the Bengal Frontier*.

[51] For some early inscriptions of the Delhi sultans, see Desai, 'Khaljī and Tughluq Inscriptions from Gujarat,' 1–40.

this period were bilingual – in Persian and Sanskrit – a tradition that further proliferated in Gujarat during the Muzaffarid rule in the fifteenth century on a variety of public buildings.[52]

The patronage of Islamic structures in Gujarat displays a similarly complex history. The sultans of Delhi were Muslims, and the Khalji annexation did lead to the construction of new religious sites commissioned by officials appointed to Gujarat. Many older temple structures which were now 'dilapidated and deliberately dismantled' were repurposed to provide foundations for new sites.[53] For example, the Jami mosques at Bharuch and Cambay, built during Tughluq reign, are known to have been erected in place of Hindu temples reusing the temples' very stones. However, Gujarat was also home to diverse Muslim communities that had settled in the region several hundred years prior. The mosque, as an architectural feature and place of worship, was thus not unfamiliar to its inhabitants at the time of the Khalji conquest. In fact, before and after the Khalji annexation, many important buildings in urban centres were built by wealthy merchants. There appears therefore to have been, as Alka Patel suggests, 'a delicate play and balance of power between the state and its representatives on the one hand, and on the other the economic sustenance of the region as vested in these astute merchants.'[54] The architecture of Gujarat from the twelfth to the sixteenth centuries shows that during the fourteenth century, when Gujarat was a province of Delhi, there was a sudden explosion in architectural scale indicating that 'prosperous merchant-magnates vied for Khalji- and Tughlaq-deputed governors for political recognition in the eyes of the Delhi overlords.'[55] Thus, the support for Islamic structures was not entirely driven by a unified agenda of religious and political propaganda by the new government, but rather appears to have been driven more by the local economic and social contingencies. With the settlement of greater Muslim populations in the region, Sufis and holy men, as well as scholars, were drawn to the cities of Gujarat, a tradition of migration that would continue on a larger scale in the following century.[56]

---

[52] For a detailed analysis of bilingual inscriptions from fifteenth-century Gujarat, see Sheikh, 'Languages of Public Piety,' 189–209.

[53] Patel, 'From Province to Sultanate,' 72.

[54] Patel, 'From Province to Sultanate,' 72.

[55] Patel, 'From Province to Sultanate,' 72–73.

[56] Jyoti Gulati Balachandran has shown that during the Muzaffarid Sultanate of Gujarat a regional community of learned men, including religious scholars, teachers, and spiritual masters, emerged on the central plains of eastern Gujarat. The migration and settlement

Another aspect of the conquest of Gujarat by the rulers of Delhi in 1304 was the end of the Chaulukyas' and the Vaghelas' patronage of Jain cultural traditions. However, Shvetambara Jains, who had been growing in prominence in the region from the tenth century onwards, continued their literary productions in abundance even after the defeat of the Vaghelas. Jain narratives like the aforementioned *Samrā-rāsu* and *Nābhinandanajinoddhār-aprabandha* speak of the generosity with which the new sultanate governors treated Jains. As traders and bankers, Jains interacted closely with the state. The continuation of Jain literary production is noteworthy, as it disproves the popularly held notion that Jainism (as well as other non-Muslim sects) saw a decline under the Muslim sultans of Delhi, particularly after their conquest of Gujarat. The changing political circumstances affected the concern that Jain intellectuals expressed through their literary output.[57] As the life of Jain monk and scholar Jinaprabhasuri (*c.* 1261–1333), the leader of a branch of the *Kharatara Gaccha*, and his most famous work, the *Vividhatīrthakalpa*, or 'description of various holy places', show, the Jains adapted to the new dispensation in an attempt to make the community accessible to the courtly world of the sultanate. Rather than becoming inward-looking, as the dominant scholarship has suggested, works like *Vividhatīrthakalpa* suggest that the Jains took a pragmatic approach in order to preserve their community's privileges in the light of new challenges. The Jain merchant groups continued to hold prominent positions under the regional sultanate and subsequently in the Mughal court.[58]

Local Polities

New political and cultural elements were introduced into Gujarat with the end of the Chaulukya–Vaghela rule and the establishment of Gujarat as a province of the Delhi empire in the fourteenth century. Delhi's authority in the region was maintained through governors from outside the province, representatives of the state who grew stronger as the distant central control weakened. The

of these men into the region gave rise to the production of Persian and Arabic texts as well as the construction of tomb shrines commissioned by the sultans. See Balachandran, 'Texts, Tombs and Memory.'

[57] Vose, 'The Making of a Medieval Jain Monk,' 26.

[58] Audrey Truschke has recently shown how Sanskrit and Persian traditions interacted in the Mughal court where Brahmin and Jain scholars participated in a vibrant, multilingual, and multicultural intellectual environment. See Truschke, *Culture of Encounters*.

governors stationed in Gujarat were quick to grasp the value of its thriving trade, as well as the significance of its local nodes of power, as we have seen in the case of the ambitious governor Farhat al-mulk. As the direct influence of Delhi began to diminish towards the end of the fourteenth century, it was these two major resources, trade and the local chieftains, that governors would harness in order to strengthen their control over the region. While new elements were introduced into the realm of culture as well, pre-existing traditions continued to flourish and were reconfigured in the light of the changing realities.

These local chieftains that the Delhi sultanate governors had to contend with were part of the complex sub-regional elaboration that had emerged in the wake of Chaulukya decline. Kachchh and Saurashtra had been home to pastoralists and semi-pastoralist groups for centuries, and during the Chaulukya rule a number of such militarised clans of obscure origins moved into different parts of Gujarat. By the twelfth century, many of these groups had obtained land from the Chaulukya rulers and established strongholds in the areas they had acquired in return for military service. These men, who came to control strategically significant nodes of power and resources, existed in the interstices of a large empire. They did not always leave behind elaborate historical records, but their presence can be discerned from numerous inscriptions, memorial stones, and oral narratives, along with the small body of literary works to which they extended patronage despite their limited territorial and economic resources.

The settlement of these men coincided with ongoing processes of state formation at the regional and local levels. But socially, it also coincided with the process of 'Rajputisation' whereby they aspired to rearticulate their social status and find a place of prestige for themselves within the wider varna social hierarchies. These chieftains also made grants to Brahmins, as is recorded in numerous Sanskrit inscriptions, and commissioned genealogies linking themselves to more exalted pasts. The chieftains and their lineages formed the political substratum of the region from the thirteenth century onwards. As they became more powerful in their local patrimonies, often located on important trade routes, they laid claim to the region's resources. In the wake of their political ascendency, the Delhi sultans, and more significantly, the regional sultans, were forced to negotiate and counter these groups in order to create a stable rule. These groups, many of whom came to be known as Rajputs, had a lasting impact on the region over the centuries that followed, even after the fall of the regional Muzzaffarid sultanate, and came to form the fundamental political fabric of the region until the end of the colonial rule.

These lineages in Gujarat did not use the term 'Rajput' to describe themselves until the sixteenth century, but instead used the word *garasiya* or 'landowner'. This word could refer to landowners of various levels, including small *zamindars* and chieftains of hill fortresses, or chieftains who belonged to prestigious lineages. However, it was during this period, between the twelfth and the fifteenth centuries, that these groups were establishing networks and alliances that would eventually facilitate their claims to Rajput status at a later date.[59] Some of these chieftains, such as the Gohils in Saurasthra, Rathods of Idar or the Chauhans of Champaner, claimed relations with older, prestigious clans of Rajasthan; others, such as the Chudasamas of Junagadh or Jhalas and Jethvas, had migrated from Sindh and the northwest, and still others, like the Bhils and Kolis, already lived in the hills and forests spread across the region.

The dismantling of the Vaghela kingdom at the hands of the Delhi armies in *c.* 1298 created a political vacuum whereby further movement into the eastern and central territories up to the coast became possible. Despite the fact that the Delhi sultan captured Asaval, Anhilvada–Patan, Somanatha, Vanthali, and Cambay, migrations continued, with settlements being established around these core areas. Even before the Vaghelas were overthrown, their power in the region had begun to wane and the pastoralist warrior groups, many of whom had been their former vassals, were able to occupy territories around the heartland. The Rathods established themselves at Idar, a short distance away from Anhilvada, after Arjundeva Vaghela's reign (1267–80). The Chudasama and Jhalas chieftaincies of Saurashtra were also nearly equal in strength and stature to the Vaghelas. In the early fourteenth century, central and eastern Gujarat became prime territory for migrant bands in search of patronage, alliance, or marriage.[60] The Jhalas, the Gohils, and the Rathods all rushed to grab territories in this region.[61] The fortifications at the eastern hill of Champaner, strategically located between Malwa and Gujarat, also arose during this time.

The Delhi sultans had to continuously negotiate with these forces as well as other migrant groups, including Afghans. The governors from Delhi had to control and keep an upper hand over local elements, and often made alliances with them in order to do so. The Muzaffarid sultans who followed in the wake of Delhi's decline in the region had to constantly work to control these players. It was only during the reign of Sultan Mahmud Begada (r. 1459–1511), the fifth

[59] Shiekh, *Forging a Region,* 67–70.

[60] Kolff, *Naukar, Rajput and Sepoy*, 71–85.

[61] Sheikh, *Forging a Region*, 69.

ruler of the dynasty to come to the throne that administrative and militaristic measures ensured that these groups would be incorporated into the regional empire. The patrilinies established between the twelfth and the fifteenth centuries were resilient entities – they outlasted the regional rulers, as well as the Mughals and the Marathas that followed, and went on to be constituted as Native or Princely States by the British. On the eve of independence, Gujarat was home to over two hundred such states, many of whom traced their descent to the groups that had acquired political ascendency during this period.

Conclusion

In sum, the political processes that began with the Chaulukyas had an impact on the longer history of Gujarat, setting the stage for the full-fledged regional configurations that would emerge in the fifteenth century. The expansionist programme the Chaulukyas embarked on resulted in an extension of agricultural and urban settlements in new areas in the north and northeastern parts of the region surrounding their capital Anhilvada–Patan. This area became the base from which the later rulers, the Delhi sultans, the regional Muzaffarid sultans, and the Mughals would control the region. In their ideological inclinations, the Chaulukyas and their successors, the Vaghelas, participated in the Sanskrit cosmopolis that had emerged all over the subcontinent, claiming links to Puranic deities in their vast temple building projects and inscriptional records. Poets and scribes further fostered patrons' kingly identities through the vast array of literary works that the Chaulukyas and Vaghelas patronised during their rule. In addition to supporting the Brahminical Shaiva faith, the Chaulukya kings, such as Kumarapala, and more so the Vaghela rulers, were also closely associated with Jainism, which extremely popular in the region as manufacture and trade rapidly flourished. The growing trade also led to the settlement and success of a number of local and transregional Muslim trading communities. The end result was the formation of a diverse social fabric that would develop even more complex layers in the subsequent centuries.

While the Delhi sultanate introduced a new ideology and language of kingship into the region, many of the elements of the older Sanskritic order were not destroyed. Support to large-scale temples ceased, but some aspects of the courtly society that the Chaulukyas and Vaghelas had developed persisted. Sanskrit inscriptional practices made headway through patronage from the emerging local power holders, including the Rajput chieftains and merchants all over the region. Similarly, the Jains continued to prosper as traders, scholars, and men of religion and remained closely associated with the state. In the aftermath of the Chaulukya–Vaghela rule, the Delhi governors also had to contend with the local political elements, primarily the Rajput chieftains. It was in the courts of these chieftains that new and significant forms of courtly patronage would take shape in the fifteenth century, albeit on a smaller scale.

The end of the Indic polity of the Chaulukya–Vaghelas and the decline of the Indo-Persian empire of Delhi resulted in the convergence of local processes and the subcontinental ones in Gujarat. A wide range of small and large local power bases was established as the Delhi governors grew more powerful. In 1407, when Zafar Khan, the last governor sent to Gujarat by the Delhi sultan, declared himself the independent ruler of the region, the Delhi empire had already been reduced to a small area around the city for a few years. The stage was set for a new configurations of power and patronage in Gujarat.

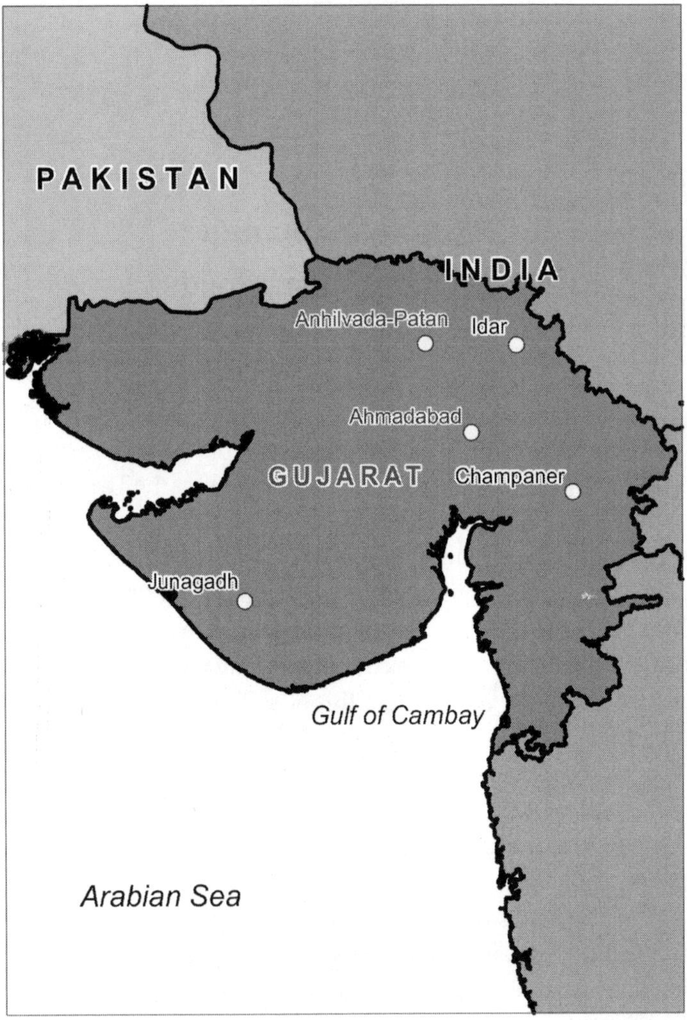

Map 3: Locations of historic places mentioned in the book within the modern state of Gujarat.

- Ahmadabad (modern: Ahmedabad): Gujarat sultanate capital, founded by Ahmad Shah c. 1411.
- Idar: Hill fort controlled by Rathods
- Junagadh: Chudasama kingdom; conquered by Sultan Mahmud Begada in 1483.
- Champaner: Chauhan kingdom; conquered by Sultan Mahmud Begada in 1494.
- Anhilvada-Patan: Also known as Naharwala. Chaulukya-Vaghela capital; later headquarters of Delhi sultanate and Gujarat sultanate until c. 1411.

Source: Esri; GADM database of Global Administrative Areas.

2

Raṇmallachanda
A Warrior Imagined

In 1394, Zafar Khan, the new governor appointed by the Delhi sultan to the province of Gujarat, launched an attack on the hill fort of Idar. Idar was located on the periphery of the province, northeast of Anhilvada–Patan or Naharwala, the headquarters of the Tughluq sultans of Delhi in Gujarat. Ranmal, the ruler of the fort and its surrounding area, had challenged the new governor's claims to authority, and refused to pay the customary tribute owed to the representative from Delhi. Only a few years before this attack, in 1391, Sultan Nasir al-Din Muhammad Shah III of Delhi (r. 1390–1393) had appointed Zafar Khan, the son of Wajih al-mulk, a respected nobleman of the court, to quell a rebellion that was brewing in the capital at Anhilvada–Patan. Farhat al-mulk Rasti Khan (*c.* 1376–1392) was the governor of the province at that time, and had been appointed by Muhammad's predecessor, Sultan Firuz Tughluq. Rasti Khan governed the province successfully, and his hold over it increased due to the control he had over the local chieftains. Some sultanate sources go so far as to suggest that he gained the loyalty and support of these men, who held small but successful power bases all over the region.

After the death of his overlord, Firuz Shah, Rasti Khan gradually began to assert his independence over the province with support from the local chieftains. Seventeenth-century historian of Gujarat, Sikandar Manjhu, notes that Rasti Khan became rebellious; he also describes how the Delhi sultanate nobles stationed in the province complained of the tyranny of his administration.[1]

[1] Sikandar, *Mir'āt-i Sikandarī*, trans., 5. Sikandar Muhammad (also Sikandar Manjhu Gujarati) was the son of an official who served the Mughal emperor, Humayun, as a librarian. His father accompanied the emperor in his campaign against Gujarat in the latter half of the sixteenth century and continued to live there after his master's

Following Manjhu, Muhammad Qasim Firishta goes further in saying that the governor had joined forces with the 'infidel' chieftains and even promoted idol worship.[2] While this may have been a later attempt to tarnish his reputation, both these sources imply that the governor was displaying signs of dissent and was emboldened by local support outside of the imperial administration. His rise in the region thus posed a threat to the authority of Delhi as well as to the local Muslim nobles. Consequently, the next reigning sultan, Nasir al-Din Mahmud Shah (r. 1394–1413), decided to send another powerful man from the centre, Zafar Khan, to put an end to Rasti Khan's insubordination and revive Delhi's fortunes in Gujarat.

After failed negotiations, in which Zafar Khan offered to mediate with the sultan on Rasti Khan's behalf, a battle ensued between the two men's forces near Patan. Zafar Khan overpowered Rasti Khan and his allies, and founded a town named Jitpur (city of victory) at the site of his triumph.[3] He took over as the governor of Gujarat, with its capital in Anhilvada–Patan. Yet Zafar Khan's task was far from complete. In order to maintain hold over the region, he had to bring the areas surrounding the capital under his control. His governorship was challenged, right from the start, by local chieftains such as Ranmal of Idar and Rai Bhara of Junagadh, who refused to accept his authority or pay tribute.[4] Ranmal and others like him were the very chieftains Rasti Khan had allied with in order to govern the province successfully. It was only after these men had been subjugated, and their claims over the land they controlled renegotiated, that Zafar Khan and his successors consolidated their rule as independent sultans of Gujarat.

As a new imperial political dispensation was being established in the early decades of the fifteenth century, tendencies for resistance evolved among local warrior chieftains who held sway over hinterland regions such as Idar. These ideas of resistance were articulated and celebrated in narratives that

departure. Very little is known about the life of Sikandar, whose account of the history of the region, written very soon after the fall of the Muzaffarshahi sultans in 1572, remains an invaluable source. See Desai, 'Mir'at-i-Sikandarī as a Source,' 235–78.

2 Firishta, *History of the Rise of Mahomedan Power*, Vol.4, 1.

3 Sikandar, *Mir'āt-i Sikandarī,* trans., 5–6.

4 Sikandar notes that soon after Zafar Khan had subjugated Idar, the chieftain of the Junagadh or Jahrand in Saurashtra, Rai Bhara, rose in rebellion. Zafar Khan overpowered him and marched against the Somanatha temple that was also located on the peninsula. See Sikandar, *Mir'āt-i Sikandarī,* trans., 5–6. Also, Sikandar, *Mir'āt-i Sikandarī*, Hindi trans., 11.

were often composed for, and at the behest of, these local rulers. The case study here concerns the encounters between the last governor of the Delhi sultanate, Zafar Khan, and the above-mentioned chieftain, Ranmal of Idar. The action revolves around a literary work titled *Raṇmallachanda*, a poem in praise of Ranmal's martial deeds.[5] It is the story of Idar's Rathod chieftain, who controlled the region during the late fourteenth and early fifteenth centuries, and his encounter with the Delhi governor, Zafar Khan, who would later declare himself Muzaffar Shah, the sultan of Gujarat. Composed primarily in the tradition of Dimgal *virakavya*, or heroic poetry, by a Brahmin poet named Sridhara Vyasa, the text is in Old Gujarati but prefaced by verses in Sanskrit and interspersed with Persianised words.[6] It is one of the earliest available narratives to speak of how established local power structures were disrupted and displaced in the wake of Delhi's dwindling fortunes and following the rise of a new imperial authority in the region. The Rathod chieftain's encounter with Zafar Khan encapsulates the processes through which the chieftains negotiated their own positions *vis-à-vis* the new power. Through *Raṇmallachanda*, it is possible to discern how these transformations were perceived, articulated, and reformulated by the chieftains themselves as they negotiated the changing political landscape and sought to establish themselves within the world of warrior elites that was emerging all over western India. This multilingual text also offers insight into the ways in which the varieties of literary resources available at the time could be harnessed to enhance the prestige of an otherwise modest chieftain.

The poet depicts the Delhi governor's encroachment on Ranmal's territory and portrays his protagonist as a courageous warrior hero who thwarts every attempt by the sultanate forces to capture his kingdom. To do so the poet prefaces his poem with Sanskrit verses that draw on elements from the classical cosmopolitan literary tradition to conjure an image of a typical Kshatriya king. These include comparisons to Puranic deities as well as praise of Ranmal's cultural achievements and generosity. However, these elements are closely interwoven with the vernacular and oral literary traditions that speak of a warrior identity of the kind that Dirk Kolff has discussed.[7] This

---

[5] Sridhara Vyasa, *Raṇmallachanda,* 145–71. Henceforth *Raṇmallachanda*. The numerals that follow indicate the verse numbers of the poem. Also, see Gahlot, *Rā Raṇmalla Chanda.*

[6] The language used in the poem is sometimes also referred to as Old Gujarati or Old Western Rajasthani. For details on the grammar and connections with Gujarati and Marwari, see Tessitori, 'Notes on the Grammar of Old Western Rajasthani,' 1–106.

[7] Kolff, *Naukar, Rajput and Sepoy.*

identity was an open-ended one and allowed for the inclusion of fighting men of varying origins. In Sridhara Vyasa's composition, we see an eclectic assembly of elements from different cultural and linguistic traditions of the times and the existence of an intricate dialogue between them. In what follows, I argue that this multiplicity is reflective of the emergent ideas of kingship, authority, and heroism in the local kingdoms of Gujarat in the early fifteenth century.

In the late fourteenth and early fifteenth centuries, the already-distant power of Delhi was crumbling in Gujarat. Rasti Khan, it will be recalled, had been undermining Delhi's authority, whether by tyrannising the population or by exhibiting leniency towards local chieftains – the 'infidels' – an infraction the Mughal-era historian Firishta accuses him of. These changes coincided with a period in which groups of obscure origins were establishing themselves politically and socially in the region; many of these, like the Rathods, had migrated from the north and northwest under the Chaulukyas during the tenth and eleventh centuries. In a narrative such as the *Raṇmallachanda*, we see the early local manifestations of what was to emerge as a pan-Indian warrior identity in the form of the category of 'Rajput'. This amalgam of an identity was the result of a gradual diffusion of the ideas that developed at the regional and local levels as chieftains and mercenary warriors negotiated their own social and political positions in relation to the new regional sultanates.

A Dialogue between Literary Traditions

Raṇmallachanda is the tale of the eponymous Rathod chieftain Ranmal and his encounter with Zafar Khan, the governor of Anhilvada–Patan, between 1391 and 1403. Sridhara Vyasa's account of the encounters between the two adversaries begins with ten invocatory verses in Sanskrit. These act as something of a preface in which the poet introduces the subject of his work:

> Having bowed down to Shankara, the lord of the *gaṇas*, I begin this fascinating *chanda*,
>
> I will narrate the exploits of Ranmal, the mighty rival of the *yavana* king [the Delhi sultan].[8]

[8] *Raṇmallachanda*, 1.

After the initial invocation in Sanskrit, the tale begins, forcefully and in the Dimgal style, with the information that the commander of an army of seventeen thousand soldiers has sent a message to the sultan. This dispatch informs him that Ranmal, the unparalleled *hindu*, has captured all the grain that had been collected as revenue by the sultanate forces.[9] Further, we are told:

> Inordinately fond of battle, Ranmal does not accept the orders and authority of the Sultan,
>
> Just as the brave Hammira, the Rathod (*kamadhajja*) twirls his moustache [in defiance].[10]

The Sultan responds by ordering his vast army to launch an attack on the defiant chieftain. Most of the tale that follows is about the nature of the battle that ensues – dramatic scenes in which war drums and trumpets resound as the armies move forward. The poet also describes the equipment used and the destruction brought upon the respective armies. The sultanate commander, however, makes one more attempt to frighten the rebellious Ranmal into surrender. Still, Ranmal refuses to comply. The narrative then goes on to describe the armies and elaborate battle scenes. After the gory deaths of hosts of *yavanas*, a word referring to the men from the sultanate forces, the battle finally ends in Ranmal's victory. Interestingly, not too many men from Ranmal's army appear to have been injured.

In *Raṇmallachanda*, its Brahmin poet displays his knowledge of classical Sanskrit with the opening verse but composes the bulk of his work in the oral tradition of Dimgal *virakavya*, the heroic poetry that was gaining popularity and prestige in western India among warrior clans. This was a style developed and popularised by the communities of Bhats and Charans who served as genealogists, poets, and preservers of history for these clans throughout the medieval period and right up to the nineteenth century.[11] However, not much is known about the poet Sridhara Vyasa himself. He is associated with two other works concerned with Puranic themes, but does not say much about himself

[9] *Raṇmallachanda*, 11.

[10] *Raṇmallachanda*, 12. This motif occurs repeatedly in the narrative. Ranmal as well as his adversaries twirl their moustaches on several occasions to assert their defiance and arrogance. See *Ranmallachanda*, 19, 20, 54, 60, and 64.

[11] Some Gujarati literary scholars link the *chanda* genre, a metrical style, to *gurjara-apabhramsa* literature, which they view as the precursor to the *charani dimgal*. See Shastri, 'Rās ane Phāgu Sāhitya,' 216–17.

within these narratives.[12] The only known manuscript of the *Raṇmallachanda* is preserved in the form of a *pothi* along with two other texts, one of which is Padmanabha's *Kānhadade Prabandha*, 'biography of Kanhadade', a well-known narrative about a similar warrior chieftain, Chauhan Kanhadade, from another modest hill fort in southern Rajasthan.[13] The pairing of the narratives may suggest that Ranmal's story was read along with other tales of the heroic warrior traditions of the Rajputs. However, the alliterative and onomatopoeic language of the oral Dimgal tradition it is composed in also indicates that it was most likely also meant for oral recitation.

The Sanskrit preface to Sridhar Vyasa's composition is short: ten verses compared to the seventy-verse Dimgal portion. Yet, its presence is not arbitrary. As we shall see later in this chapter, these verses link the chieftain of the modest fort of Idar to the universal Indic ideas of kingship, including claims over the protection of the entire earth, great charitable acts, and the cultural and scholarly pursuits that brought such kings fame. In the post-Chaulukya era, large-scale support of Sanskrit as the language of political power was reduced. However, as noted in the previous chapter, Sanskrit continued to be used in the inscriptions sponsored by aspiring local warlords, merchants, and some elite women to record grants or donations. Similarly, the mercantile communities of Jains maintained their support of Sanskrit and Apabhramsha works.

This was also the period in which early forms of Gujarati were being used in literary works outside of the courtly milieu. Sanskrit was one of the many possible options Sridhara Vyasa could have deployed; he also could have omitted it entirely as the Charani battle narrative tradition would have held equal, or even more, import in the projection of Ranmal's martial persona and growing status. It is possible then that the poet's use of Sanskrit added distinctive prestige and would contribute to the protagonist and eventually his clan's elite aspirations. The poet's innovation lies not only in the juxtaposition of the two languages itself, but also in the ways in which he is able to modify the Sanskrit eulogy to include the protagonist's specific contextual contingencies: Ranmal is the destroyer of the great paramount kings (just as he is of the *yavanas*), but he is not supported by a prestigious lineage, nor does he perform material or financial acts of charity, but rather builds the tombs of his enemies. Ranmal, as the holder of a modest fort, may have lacked an elaborate court or

---

[12] These are entitled *Īśwarīchaṁda* and *Bhāgavat Daśamaskaṁda*. See Jani in Paniker, *Medieval Indian Literature*, 48, and Joshi et al., *Gujaratī Sāhityano Itihās*, 216.

[13] Sridhara Vyasa, *Raṇmallachanda*, MS no. 1541 of 1891-95. Bhadarkar Oriental Research Institute, Pune.

resources for large-scale munificence but he did, according to his panegyrist, have all the trappings of a brave warrior.

In the rest of the *Raṇmallachanda*, Sridhara Vyasa presents a narrative more akin to the oral traditions associated with the heroic ethos specific to western India and makes frequent use of alliterations, which lend his text performative character. These forms lend themselves to recitation with considerable dramatic force. Thus, a typical verse in the text reads:

> *damadamkār damāma damakkīya, ḍhamḍham ḍhamḍham ḍhol ḍhamakīya,*
> *taravar taravar vesa pahaṭṭiya, tara tara turak paḍii talahaṭṭīya.*[14]

It is nearly impossible to replicate these alliterations in an English translation, and the onomatopoeic representations of drums and battle sounds, which contribute so strongly to the drama, cannot be reproduced in English. The translation can only go as far as:

> The drums beat loudly, the *ḍhols* resound noisily (*ḍhamḍham ḍhamḍham*), Rapidly (*taravara taravara*) changing their garbs, the turak [Turks] fall in position at the base of the hill.

The alliterative style thus reveals an aural character reflecting the greater tradition of Rajput oral narrative in which poets composed works before battles. With their staccato alliterations, such verses, it is said, reproduced the sounds and moods of war, preparing and energising audiences of Rajput warriors for battle, and inspiring unwavering death wishes in their hearts.[15]

At certain points in the narrative the poet also alters familiar words to make them resonate with the mood of the scene. When read aloud, the *Raṇmallachanda* conjures an image of the dusty and noisy battlefield of Idar hill. The language is also freely interspersed with vernacularised forms of Persian and Arabic words. These include, among others, words such as *banda*, *barjara* (bazaar), *firman*, *foja* (fauj, army), *halal*, *haram*, *khan*, *mal*, *mir*, *mallik*, *suratrahana* (also *suratran*, or sultan) and a variety of ethnonyms. The detailed descriptions of the confrontation, including names of specific generals, the variety of ethnic groups in the Muslim army, as well as other activities, such as the collective act of praying or *namaj* just before going into battle, also mark

---

[14] *Raṇmallachanda*, 47. For a comprehensive discussion on Dimgal prosody, see Kamphorst, 'Rajasthani Battle Language,' 33–39.

[15] Kamphorst, 'Rajasthani Battle Language,' 47.

it as an early example of the literary tradition of compositions in Old Gujarati that deal with similar themes. For instance, the aforementioned *Kānhaḍade Prabandha* by the Nagar Brahmin poet Padmanabha, composed somewhat later than the *Raṇmallachanda, c.* 1455, is the story of a Chauhan chieftain's encounter with 'Ala' al-Din Khalji in Jalor while the latter was on his way to conquer Gujarat. Much longer than the *Raṇmallachanda*, the *Kānhaḍade Prabandha* displays a similar affinity for Persianised words and intricate detail, including lists of weapons of war, types of horses, names of specific people, and even descriptions of the food that they ate.[16]

The story of Ranmal was popular in the oral traditions in Gujarat, as well. Similarly, Ranmal appears repeatedly in other historical sources from the period. One possible implication of the lack of written circulation is the popularity of the tale in the oral traditions. In the early decades of the fifteenth century, men like Ranmal were still struggling to maintain their sovereignty over the lands that they had occupied and lacked the resources for courtly accoutrements such as the patronage of buildings or civic structures. The relative scarcity of textual materials and buildings attributed to these emerging chieftains can be partially explained by these economic and social constraints. Yet the numerous memorial stones and oral narratives that even now dot the landscape of Gujarat, Kathiawad, and Kutch bear witness to the enduring significance of the presence of warriors like Ranmal in the region.[17]

The decline of the traditional Chaulukya–Vaghela kingdom (along with those of the Paramaras of Malwa or the Yadavas of Devagiri in other parts of the subcontinent) and the rise of the Delhi sultanate in the north from the twelfth century onwards interrupted long-established forms of social and political authority, which were further modified as successor sultanates attempted to consolidate their hold over provinces including Bengal, Jaunpur, Malwa, and Gujarat. Real political changes led to changes in the vocabulary through which kingship and authority were articulated by the local elites in their literary traditions, particularly during the fifteenth and sixteenth centuries. In these works, often written in Sanskrit or regional languages, battles between a local chieftain and a Muslim sultan became the central theme. The sultans in that scenario were often portrayed in exaggeratedly evil terms. The Muslim

---

[16] See Padmanabha, *Kānhaḍade Prabandha.*

[17] For a detailed description and discussion of memorial stones as an important element of Gujarat's warrior ethos see Swayam, 'Sites of Ritual Construction of Identities,' 303–39.

rulers, whose literary effusions in Persian also displayed a prejudice against the 'infidels', felt a similar need to assert authority.[18] Yet, as recent studies have revealed, such works were not created in conscious opposition to one another but in fact display close cultural affinities in the idioms, imagery, and tropes they used; they reflected a shared literary and cultural tradition of exchange and negotiation based on their contemporary political contexts.[19]

For the local warrior chieftains, the primary moulders of kingly ideology in the medieval and the early modern periods were not always the Brahmins but the various communities of Charans, traditionally the historians and storytellers of the region. The status and position of the Charans was derived from the fusion of both secular and religious qualities and duties: they were considered to be *deviputras*, or the sons of the goddess. The Charans' ritual significance lay in the fact that they were mediators between the goddess and the kings, so they played important roles in maintaining the social status and

---

[18] The existence of such literary narratives led Aziz Ahmad to suggest that these were in fact located in two different linguistic, religious, and historical cultures. He referred to them as the 'Muslim epics of conquest' and 'Hindu epics of resistance'. The two kinds of literary narratives, for Ahmad, were thus completely distinctive, having developed in ignorance of each other, and differing in their readership as the Muslim epics were composed in Persian while their Hindu counterparts used either Sanskrit or the vernaculars. According to Ahmad, while they did not develop in 'conscious opposition' to one another, 'one of them was rooted in the challenge of asserting the glory of Muslim presence and the other in the repudiating it'. See Ahmad, 'Epic and Counter-epic in Medieval India,' 470–76.

[19] Michael Bednar's study of the narratives, which Aziz Ahmad divided into the two distinctive cultural categories, is one example of this recent scholarship. Bednar engages in close readings of these narratives and studies their tropes to show how these apparently distinctive literary traditions in fact interacted closely with one another. While the Persian tradition, represented here by Amir Khusrau, made extensive use of Indic imagery, the Sanskrit and vernacular traditions represented the Muslims as carriers of an emerging Rajput identity. Bednar's study reveals that in crossing these literary boundaries these narratives display a 'single social, cultural, and historical attitude that existed in a literary and cultural symbiosis.' See Bednar, 'Conquest and Resistance in Context.' Though not arguing directly with Ahmad, other recent studies on literary narratives from the medieval period have also suggested that the 'epics of conquest' and 'epics of resistance' were not watertight but reflected a shared literary and cultural tradition of exchange and negotiation based on their contemporary political contexts. Ramya Sreenivasan's recent work on the narratives of the Rajput queen Padmini, for instance, suggests a rich exchange between the Persian and Indic tradition but also reveals a close interaction between other languages and genres all over the subcontinent. See Sreenivasan, *Many Lives of a Rajput Queen.*

legitimacy of their overlords. Charans accompanied these warriors in battles, sang of their glory in war, and, as late as the nineteenth century, served as guarantors and diplomats for their lieges on account of their sacred association with various forms of the mother goddess. In many cases, they were held in higher regard than the Brahmins, even though they were ranked lower in the traditional varna hierarchy.

Brahmin poets were occasionally patronised by the more successful kings at their newly emerging courts to write of their glories in Sanskrit. However, it was the warlike ideologies of the Charans, their particular dialects, and the fluid textures of their narratives, meant for oral recitation, that came to shape the nature of kingship in the region. Similarly, the continuing existence of memorial stones that can still be found, sometimes in clusters of sixty or seventy all over Gujarat evidence a tradition of memorialising battles and violent deaths at the popular level. Such assemblages were closely associated with the Charans, who encouraged their patrons to die in battle but also resorted to self-harm and suicide themselves in order to maintain their own social and ritual positions.

In its use of Sanskrit, the oral Dimgal tradition of the Charans or bards, and Persian register, Sridhara Vyasa's narrative of Ranmal also reflects the poet's awareness of the multiple literary traditions that were prevalent in the region and the ways in which they could be harnessed in order to produce a heroic account of Ranmal's resistance to Zafar Khan (later sultan Muzaffar Shah). By using multiple languages and details of localised information, *Raṇmallachanda* features a continuous dialogue between the literary and cultural resources that were available in the specific regional context of fifteenth-century Gujarat. The simultaneous use of multiple resources in itself reflects the fluid nature of a political scenario in which chieftains like Ranmal struggled to assert authority and establish kingly identity.

Situating the Warrior Chieftain

Of Zafar Khan's locally powerful chieftain-adversaries, Ranmal Rathod of Idar was one of the earliest. The mountainous region of Idar is located in the Sabarkantha district of present-day Gujarat and connects the chains of the Vindhya and Aravalli ranges on the Gujarat's northeastern frontier. Its ruler, *ra* or raja Ranmal appears on many occasions in the chief Persian sources on the region, namely, the *Mir'āt-i Sikandarī* and the *Mir'āt-i Aḥmadī*; he is also documented by the Mughal-era historian Firishta, who wrote of the various

Muslim dynasties in India. Persian chronicles, like the *mir'āts* and Firishta's accounts, portray a considerably different picture of the Rathod chieftain than the one presented by his Brahmin panegyrist. The Persian histories are often coloured by an inclination to highlight the victory of Islam over the lands of the 'infidels', but, studied in conjunction with other sources from the region, they are invaluable in revealing the imperial imagination's perception of local chieftains.

The seventeenth-century Gujarati historian, Sikandar Manjhu, mentions at least three encounters between Zafar Khan and the Rathod chieftain in his *Mir'āt-i Sikandarī.* The *Raṇmallachand* also speaks of previous meetings between the two. Whatever the actual number of encounters may have been, it does seem that the hill fort of Idar, strategically positioned at the intersection of routes leading from Gujarat to both southern Rajasthan and Malwa, was one of the first forts to be targeted by the early sultans of the Muzaffarid dynasty. As the controller of this crucial location, Ranmal appears to have held an important position in the politics of region.

In *Mir'āt-i Sikandarī,* the raja or chieftain of Idar is depicted not only as the very first of the chieftains to have rebelled against the new governor, but also as one who often took advantage of the political dissensions at Anhilvada–Patan to secure his own position. Sikandar mentions that shortly after Zafar Khan had conquered Patan, he was given the news that the raja of Idar had rebelled.[20] An army was thus commissioned to besiege the fort, plunder its riches, and harass its inhabitants. Finally, Ranmal accepted defeat and made submission. After this, we are told, Zafar Khan was engaged in restraining the rulers of Asirgardh and Burhanpur, who were transgressing the limits of their territories and making incursions into some of the provinces that had submitted to Gujarat.[21] During this period, he also marched against Rai Bhara, the chieftain of Jharand (or Junagadh), and, according to Sikandar, destroyed the famous Somanatha temple.[22]

Again, in 1397–98, Zafar Khan besieged the fort of Idar to subdue the 'infidels' there.[23] But, continues Sikandar, on hearing of Timur's conquests in the north, Zafar Khan made peace with the raja and returned to Patan. It was when his grandson Ahmad Shah came to the throne (*c.* 1411) that the rulers of Patan finally again encountered the Idar chieftain. Ahmad's title was disputed by his cousin Firuz Khan, who proclaimed himself king at Bharuch. Ahmad

[20] Sikandar, *Mir'āt-i Sikandarī,* trans., 6.
[21] Sikandar, *Mir'āt-i Sikandarī,* Hindi trans., 10
[22] Sikandar, *Mir'āt-i Sikandarī,* Hindi trans., 11.
[23] Sikandar, *Mir'āt-i Sikandarī,* trans., 7.

Shah temporarily suppressed his cousin's rebellion, but shortly thereafter, in 1412, Firuz Khan and his supporters joined Ranmal and took shelter at Idar fort. The confederacy was soon besieged by Ahmad Shah. Upon realising that the Sultan had gained the upper hand, the Rathod chieftain not only submitted Firuz Khan's horses and elephants to him but also plundered his former ally's camp. Amid the chaos, Ranmal was let off after paying a suitable tribute to Ahmad Shah. [24]

Ranmal did finally send his son to offer submission, something we learn because he also appears a few times in Firishta's account of Zafar Khan's early years in the region. In this account, too, much of which is based on Sikandar's narrative, Ranmal seems to alternate between making trouble and offering his submission to the great power. Forgiveness for the lack of payment, according to Firishta, was granted on the transmission of a large sum of money and jewels. Like Sikandar, Firishta also mentions that around the year 1398, Zafar Khan suspended his attack on Idar due to the arrival of Timur's army but resumed it later in the year. However, he adds that this was also a period in which Delhi was in a state of confusion and many rivals were contending for the crown.[25] Zafar Khan and his son Tatar Khan chose not to participate in this competition at this time, instead concentrating on stabilising their hold over Patan. Therefore, in 1401, Zafar Khan once again attacked Idar to levy tribute, but Ranmal fled to Vishalnagar, leaving the fort to be occupied by the governor's forces. Ranmal's alliance with Ahmad Shah's cousin Firuz, who had promised the Rathod chieftain independence in exchange for his help in providing men and horses for his campaign, is documented in a rather elaborate account. Despite being able to hold out against Ahmad's forces by taking refuge in the hills, Ranmal eventually abandoned his allies and submitted to the Sultan. In fact, notes Firishta, Ranmal seized Firuz Khan's horses, elephants, and other effects, and sent them to the Sultan in order gain favour for himself. [26]

Taken together, the Persian histories of the region provide a glimpse into just how a chieftain such as Ranmal would have been able to participate actively in

[24] Sikandar, *Mir'āt-i Sikandarī*, Hindi trans., 12–13. Later in the same account, we again find the Idar chieftain's son, Punja, forming a confederacy with other chieftains, namely, Trimbakdas of Champaner and the raja of Nandod (in Rajpipla, Rewa Kantha district) along with other rebels from Ahmad's court, in an abortive attempt to invite Hoshang Shah of Malwa to usurp the throne of Ahmedabad. Also see Firishta, *History of the Rise of Mahomedan Power*, Vol.4, 6–21.

[25] Firishta, *History of the Rise of Mahomedan Power*, Vol.4, 4–5.

[26] Firishta, *History of the Rise of Mahomedan Power*, Vol.4, 9.

the politics of the region. His strategic location and military resources allowed him to form alliances with the Sultan's adversaries in order to occasionally assert his independence. Yet, when the alliance proved less advantageous, he was also able to seek the imperial power's forgiveness and maintain peace at the cost of a temporary submission. The portrayals of the sultans' encounters with Idar betray the tensions and ambiguities that shaped the political landscape at a time in which different power brokers sought to retain or gain control over much of the region. The Muzaffarids, descendants of Zafar Khan, would soon emerge as the most powerful of these players, and establish themselves as independent rulers.

In the nineteenth century, the colonial officer Alexander Forbes recorded the legend about the way in which Ranmal's line of Rathods made incursions into Idar. This account documents the formation of the town under Rao Sonugji, one of Ranmal's ancestors who belonged to a cadet line of the Rathods. According to this narrative, Sonugji had wrested Idar from its tyrannical ruler, a 'Pūreehār Rajpoot'. The latter's Brahmin minister betrayed his master and invited Sonugji to establish his line of Rathods there. This was at the end of the Chaulukya rule in Anhilvada, under the king Bhimadeva II, sometime in the late thirteenth century.[27] Ranmal expanded the territories of his father, Burhutji, and made vassals of men from the Solanki and Chauhan families (presumably because their influence was now in decline).[28]

Forbes also recounts Ranmal's encounter with Muzaffar Shah, but this is based on Firishta and *Mir'āt-i Aḥmadī's* accounts of the same, which in turn draw from Sikandar's narrative, and need not be repeated here. A version of Forbes's oral account was recounted by the Rajasthani poet Shyamaldas in his monumental nineteenth century history of Rajputs, *Vīr Vinod*.[29] Not much is known about Sonugji's immediate descendants until Ranmal, who is remembered for his encounters with Zafar Khan. In 1924, Ranmal did find a place among the greats of the Rathod clan in a Gujarati language history commissioned by the State of Idar. The author of this 'History of Idar State' simply replicated Forbes's version of the Ranmal story in his account of the royal family's ancestors.[30]

Writers other than his panegyrist, Sridhara Vyasa, give a sense of how men like Ranmal may have harnessed their abilities to obey and disobey the imperial

[27] Forbes, *Rās Mālā*, 233–37.

[28] Forbes, *Rās Mālā*, 300.

[29] Shyamaladas, *Vir Vinod*, 994–95.

[30] Joshi, *Īḍar Rājyano Itihās*, 96–103.

authority in order to hold on to their own sovereign rights. The common strand that runs through these accounts, and Sridhara Vyasa's narrative, appears to be Ranmal's desperate resistance to the integration of his territories into the new imperial authority. During their reigns, the early sultans of Gujarat, Muzaffar Shah, followed by his grandson Ahmad Shah, were constantly engaged in bringing chieftains such as Ranmal under their control. These local power brokers occupied strategic locations on trade routes and controlled a variety of material and human resources, access to which would ultimately allow the sultans to become the overlords of the region.

The Muzaffarid sultans, like other regional rulers, left behind numerous texts, inscriptions, coins, and monuments as testimonials to their rule. Those 'who occupied the continuum between the village headman and successful warlord'[31] may not have left behind a large official archive, but – like Ranmal, or the chieftains of Champaner and Junagadh discussed in the next chapter – did aspire to a position among the north Indian political elite. In such small principalities these groups may not have had the resources to build large structures, but they did choose to assert their status through the patronage of poets and performers.[32] In Sridhara Vyasa's multilingual narrative, which also displays a striking performative quality, we can see this assertion of status through the poet's articulation of resistance and defiance, and the evocation of elements of the warrior ethos that was in circulation in western India during the fifteenth century.

With the emergence of the new regional sultanates, the fifteenth century witnessed the continuation of an ongoing socio-political process that appears to have been at work in the subcontinent, to varying degrees, beginning in the seventh century. This was the process through which caste formation converged with the political processes of state formation as diverse groups came to seek Kshatriya status and, therefore, a place in the larger varna hierarchy.[33] In the swathe of land comprising Sindh, Rajasthan, Gujarat, and central India, this process took the form of 'Rajputisation'. Here, certain social groups came to acquire certain common martial characteristics that can loosely be termed as the 'Rajput tradition' or an 'ideal code of conduct'. Whether it was the mercenary warrior that Kolff has discussed at one end of the continuum, or the

[31] Sreenivasan, 'Warrior-Tales,' 241–72.

[32] Sreenivasan discusses literary patronage by similar groups in towns like Dalmau, Sarangpur, and Chanderi in central India. Sreenivasan, 'Warrior-Tales,' 243.

[33] Chattopadhyaya, 'Origin of Rajputs,' 57–88.

more elite prince, this code of conduct had as its cornerstones martial values such as valour and chivalry, loyalty to one's clan and to one's master, keeping one's word, and preference for death over dishonour.

Idealised Kshatriya kingly norms, drawn often from the older Puranic tradition of the kind visible in the Chaulukya inscriptions, also became integrated into this newly emerging martial tradition. In Gujarat, at the turn of the fourteenth century, regional and imperial hierarchies were in flux, as was the martial ethos that would shape 'Rajput-hood' in a somewhat later period. In the story of Ranmal, Sridhara Vyasa draws on a number of conventional and unconventional tropes resulting in a narrative that is something of a bricolage of values and a social identity that may have, in this period, been undergoing several shifts. Four aspects of representation in the *Raṇmallachanda* in particular demonstrate the mix of elements that went into the making of this local chieftain in early-fifteenth century Gujarat. These representations include the display of a strong aggressive resistance to the imperial forces, descriptors of the battle that are distinctly warlike, Ranmal's persona as the hero of the battle, and his foils – the forces that he fights in order to establish fame and his superiority over the imperial power.

Resisting Authority and Imagining Domains

In its portrayal of the struggle against the sultanate forces, *Raṇmallachanda* reflects an awareness of the region's political history and the new authority structure arising. Among the tensions, negotiations, and accommodations attending that changeover was an emerging martial ethos among the chieftains. From the Chaulukya period onward, the agrarian frontier of the entire region of Gujarat, Saurashtra, and Kachchh had been expanding. Access to open, cultivable lands and stable pastures allowed itinerant communities to settle down, which also promoted state formation and the development of complex economic relations. With agriculture becoming more common in the region, land became a coveted resource. Similarly, in Baglan, southwest of Gujarat, the expansion of agriculture and pastoral lands also made land an important asset, even though a number of peripatetic communities remained.[34] In order for the economies of consumption, production, and interdependence to flourish, the agrarian regimes turned to trade via the Indian Ocean. Access to

[34] Guha, *Environment and Ethnicity*, 62–63.

the area's important ports, such as Bharuch, Cambay, and Surat, required the maintenance of mountain and forest passes through places like Idar. If these forested hills were an obstacle from one point of view, they were valuable as capital from another: they could be strongholds, bases, and posts, and in their recesses grew the timber needed for mansions and ships.[35]

Idar, it will be recalled, was also located on the borders of the kingdoms of southern Rajasthan and Malwa, and lay close to the frontiers of Patan, the headquarters of the Delhi sultans in Gujarat and, later, the capital of the independent sultanate prior to the founding of Ahmadabad. Its position at the intersection of a number of important trade routes likely created opportunities for profit-making through toll collection. In the last years of the fourteenth and early part of the fifteenth centuries, control over these resources in the hilly area of Idar would have been important for the ambitious Delhi governor wanting to maintain a hold over Gujarat. Like other chieftains who oversaw similar landscapes, Ranmal would have gained prosperity and authority through control of the hill fort. The fort, due to its location, would also have been the currency with which he could bargain with men making claims on the nascent kingdoms of Gujarat and Malwa.

Sridhara Vyasa's narrative articulates this aspect of the conflict that frames the chieftain's resistance right from the beginning: Ranmal has captured the grain and wealth from the Sultan's coffers through a massive raid. Repeated references to Ranmal's defiance of the imperial authority form the principal motifs in the text. The raid on the sultanate treasury is described as having caused much mayhem in the sultanate domains. The poet notes:

> In the night, Khambhat [Cambay] trembles, at dawn confusion prevails in Dholka,
> In the morning helpless cries resound in Patan, on hearing of your raid, O Ranmal.[36]

For the poet, the wealth captured by the Rathod chieftain belongs rightfully to him.

> For the sultan's commander *mīr* Rājāṇī of Modhasa, the wealth has been laid inauspicious,

[35] Guha, *Environment and Ethnicity*, 62.

[36] *Raṇmallachanda*, 14.

> You, O Ranmal, are the only Kshatriya to have legitimised [literally 'made *halāl*'] this treasure [that had been] submitted before the Khan.[37]

Ranmal, as we know, does not accept the sultan's authority, nor does he obey the *firman*, or imperial order. In response, the governor of Patan decides to launch a mighty attack on Idar, instructing his commanders to gather elephants and horses and ransack the fort and its surrounding territories. They set off with elaborate militarily paraphernalia, including banners and noisy trumpets, to besiege the rebel's territory. Upon nearing the fort, however, the commander decides to give the chieftain a second chance. He instructs his messenger to climb the fortress of Idar immediately and address Ranmal thus:

> Respect the Sultan's order, immediately handover the wealth of the treasury,
>
> Else, give up your lands *(garās)* and servants *(dās),* and accept the Khan's service with folded hands.[38]

It is this surrender of the *garas*[39] or patrimonies that became the key aspect of the struggle between the new sultans and the chieftains.

In his battle with the officials of the Delhi sultanate, Ranmal remains steadfast in his decision to fight for his rights over his territories. He would rather confront the enemy than offer them submission. Resting his strong arms on his sword, Ranmal obstinately addresses the sultanate messenger with these challenging words:

> On the day that my head bends so low as to touch the feet of the *mleccha* [the Sultan or sultanate forces], the sun will certainly not rise.[40]
>
> As long as the sun continues to shine in the sky, the shoulders of the Rathod (*kamadhajja*) will not stoop down before the enemy,
>
> The flames of the fierce submarine fire may get pacified, yet I will not yield even a furrow of land to the *mleccha*.[41]

He asks the messenger to remind the Khan that in the past he has won against many other sultanate commanders and nothing would prevent him this time, too, from destroying the seventeen-thousand-strong army sent by him. Emboldened by his past achievements, Ranmal reiterates his defiance:

---

37 *Raṇmallachanda*, 15.

38 *Raṇmallachanda*, 28.

39 This word is derived from the Sanskrit, *grās* or mouthful.

40 *Raṇmallachanda*, 29.

41 *Raṇmallachanda*, 30.

> Do not provoke me to a fight, O Malik, I am the annihilator of the *mlecchas* in war,
>
> When I rise to battle, even the Sultan means nothing to me.[42]

In the battle that follows, while the *yavanas* destroy the administration of hill fort and create havoc, the chieftain slaughters several of their soldiers.[43] Many lose their heads while others simply run away, leaving their belongings behind.[44] The mighty *yavana* warriors, who had once rushed to fight the chieftain, now grow pale at his sight.[45] The victory is finally Ranmal's as the Sultan's forces accept defeat, literally 'stuffing grass into their mouths'.[46]

By Sridhara Vyasa's account, then, Ranmal retains his independence and chooses not to accept the Khan's service. However, the poet adds nuance to this defiance of authority through Ranmal's rejection of the governor's claims on the resources and through the imperial imagination he attributes to the chieftain. This inventive narrative is far removed from the historical reality of Ranmal as the controller of modest, albeit significant, hill kingdom. After he has destroyed the sultanate forces, referred to as *yavanas* or *mlecchas*, Ranmal appears to be contemplating the options that lie before him. In the very last verse of the composition, he says:

> Should I raid the fortress of Dhar and set it free after extracting tribute?
>
> With a sword in hand should I destroy the enemy soldiers surrounding the citadel?
>
> Should I strike Bharuch with the strength of my spear and crush it with terror?
>
> Should I capture the umbrella [sign of royalty, *chatra*] of the *asura* [Sultan] and establish it over my own head?
>
> Should I enter Patan at dawn and annihilate the *dhagaḍas* [sultanate soldiers] there?
>
> Ranmal, the *rā* of Idar says, should I create a single umbrella [*ek catra*, one kingdom under his own ruler] under the sun? [47]

For Sridhara Vyasa, his protagonist has the potential to capture the powerful fortress of Dhar in Malwa, the prosperous port town of Bharuch, and Patan, the

---

[42] *Raṇmallachanda*, 34.
[43] *Raṇmallachanda*, 44.
[44] *Raṇmallachanda*, 45.
[45] *Raṇmallachanda*, 66.
[46] *Raṇmallachanda*, 69.
[47] *Raṇmallachanda*, 70.

centre of Delhi's authority in Gujarat. The poet's Ranmal also claims he can take over the authority (represented by the umbrella or *chatra*) of the Sultan and destroy his power by killing his men. In fact, this imagined Ranmal goes so far as to imply that he can create a united kingdom with himself as its head. Sridhara Vyasa does not say more about any of these tantalising prospects. We have no other accounts of Ranmal attempting to take over the lands of the Delhi sultanate. Thus, despite his lofty claims, Ranmal remains the hero of a local tradition and in fact a local chieftain who refrains from seeking more extensive political control. Yet, the poem's imagined domain leaves readers with a sense of possibility about a significant political player who was active and vocal in changing times.

The Imagery of Battle

One of the most striking features of *Raṇmallachanda's* construction of Ranmal as a warrior hero is the evocative imagery of the battle that he fights against the imperial army. Through the extensive use of alliterative and onomatopoeic figures of speech, the poet recreates the sights and sounds of the confrontation between the two adversarial forces. Sensory details punctuate the narrative, immersing the audience in the sounds, scenery, and heroism of the battlefield:

> Long banners flutter endlessly in the sky,
>
> Kettledrums sound fearfully, the war trumpets make a fearsome sound,
>
> The people rapidly run helter-skelter in all ten directions.
>
> Thus proceeds the *śaka* [sultanate] army against the one that shouts Shiva Shiva.[48]

Similarly,

> The swift *tokhāra, tāra, tattāra* horses are harnessed,
>
> With their saddles, they appear as birds spreading their wings in the wind.[49]

Apart from mention of the types of horses, the poet enumerates the types of weaponry and protective armour.[50] War elephants also repeatedly rumble through the account. Such descriptive passages appear throughout the narrative,

[48] *Raṇmallachanda*, 21.

[49] *Raṇmallachanda,* 25.

[50] *Raṇmallachanda*, 69.

but the battle scenes become especially gory as Ranmal prepares to fight the sultan, referred to in the text as *aspati*, Lord of Horses (Sanskrit *asvapati*). Now, the *yoginis* (goddesses associated with the Tantric worship of Shiva, the destroyer and Shakti his female counterpart) rejoice in anticipation of the soldiers dying in battle – so that they may drink the blood of the fallen:

> Lakhs of *yoginis* circle the skies distributing the holy offering (*prasād*), they produce loud shouts of victory,
>
> They goad him [Ranmal] on [by saying], rise O brave one,
>
> Rise with your weapons and destroy the evil *mlecchas*.[51]

Such gruesome descriptions form a crucial part of Dimgal heroic poetry, and can be seen as a kind of war propaganda created to inspire warriors by the Charan poets. In the *chands*, as Janet Kamphorst has pointed out, 'the warrior-role is emblematic for martial virtues'.[52] From such images of blood-thirsty goddesses and vultures we may infer the warrior's grim intentions and even his willingness to sacrifice himself in battle. While in Ranmal's narrative the hero does not meet his demise, in others, such as the extremely popular tale of Pabuji that Kamphorst studies, such imagery also has spiritual connotations if the protagonist dies in battle.[53] The blood and bodies of the warrior heroes who who meet their deaths in this way are regarded as sacrifices to the goddess and her *yoginis* and seen as auspicious. In the case of Ranmal's clash with the sultanate forces, however, it is the destruction he causes to the enemies that becomes the holy offering or *prasad* to the divinities.

In the Sanskrit portion of the narrative, too, Ranmal is depicted as a great warrior. He has destroyed 'the pride of paramount kings' and 'when on the battlefield, enemies count for nothing'.[54] However, while he is compared to Rama as well as other historical warriors in this section, the spectacular battle scenes of the Dimgal portion do not find mention here. This spectacle of the battle along with the underlying cause for it are crucial to building Ranmal's heroic persona. The poet repeatedly notes that Ranmal has captured the sultan's wealth and that the imperial armies are making claims on his lands. Likewise, Ranmal's martial prowess is continuously emphasised through mention of his ability to take on the forceful armies alone. The resounding sounds and gory

---

[51] *Raṇmallachanda*, 42, 43.

[52] Kamphorst, 'Rajasthani Battle Language,' 23.

[53] Kamphorst, 'Rajasthani Battle Language,' 23.

[54] *Raṇmallachanda,* 2 and 8.

imagery underscore his martial dexterity. In the absence of an illustrious lineage or an army as strong and powerful as the sultan's, Ranmal, the sole defender of his fort, must display his own prowess as a great warrior.

Furthermore, while *Raṇmallachanda* shares the features of martial epics like that of Pabuji mentioned above, and others such as the *Epic of Alha*, the similarities between these epics are limited to the oral style and inclusion of graphic battle scenes. The elevation of local goddesses and heroes to the status of divinities, a trope found in these other narratives, is not one shared by *Raṇmallachanda*. The protagonists of these other martial epics have been recognised as being part of a non-elite martial culture that lacked an anti-imperialist perspective, unlike the classical warrior epics. In contrast to the non-elite protagonists of other works, Ranmal does not in fact lose his life in battle nor does he have a low-status companion. Furthermore, *Raṇmallachanda* was composed by a Brahmin who had the knowledge of Sanskrit. It was also preserved as a written work, implying an aristocratic setting for its production. Thus, Ranmal's story appears to be closer to the more classical warrior narratives that emerged in western Indian courts among Rajput elites, indicating the poet's projection of Ranmal and his Rathod lineage's upcoming status.[55]

The Warrior Chieftain's Heroic Persona

Another aspect of Ranmal's construction as a heroic figure is the manner in which Sridhara Vyasa articulates his protagonist's persona as a warrior; that is, not as a single ideal, but as an eclectic montage. As if drawing strength from the fierce fighters around him, Vyasa's Ranmal embodies aspects of warrior personae recognised in and around the region.

In the Sanskrit portion of *Raṇmallachanda*, Sridhara Vyasa draws on elements from older inscriptional and poetic traditions. This section portrays Ranmal as a multifaceted Kshatriya king, not different from the universal great kings of the past. The poet describes Ranmal, the warrior chieftain as one:

> Who destroys the pride of the paramount kings, [the one who] brings warring armies to heel,
>
> The holder of valiant glory, that Ranmal, the supporter of the earth prospers.[56]

---

[55] I draw here from Cynthia Talbot's suggestion that early modern classical Rajput narratives, such as *Pṛthvīrāja Rāso,* shared some features of regional or local martial epics but were meant for elite audiences. See Talbot, *The Last Hindu Emperor*, 141–43.

[56] *Raṇmallachanda*, 2.

As a powerful Kshatriya king, he is also a well-rounded personality and a 'builder', though with his own style.

> Some kings build sacrificial posts, others erect stepwells and wells.
>
> Ranmal is the only one [known as] the maker of the tombs [for his adversaries].[57]
>
> [He] enjoys the pleasures of dance and drama with those who have similar interests, enjoys pleasures of passion when in the company of women,
>
> With the heroic warriors, he revels in the joys of heroism, such is the one and only Ranmal.[58]

Thus, while other kings build temples and do charitable works, Ranmal's achievements lie in his military ability. By implication, he earns his spiritual merits by destroying his enemies and constructing their tombs. Yet the poet does not forget to emphasise that Ranmal is also interested in the finer things of a king's life. With regards to his talents as warrior, Vyasa portrays Ranmal as no less mighty than the great Puranic deity Rama. The poet writes:

> Powerful demons were driven towards the lord of death's (Yama) abode for abuducting Sītā,
>
> Presently, the mighty Rathod (*kamadhajja*) takes them there.[59]

The Sanskrit preface to the longer Dimgal poem is brief. It does not contain a genealogy nor does it claim lofty titles for the protagonist who is never referred to as anything greater than a raja, the kind of king lowest in the Indic hierarchy of kings. Yet, these verses do not appear to be a mere attempt by the Brahmin poet to display his skills in the cosmopolitan language. Instead, in referring to his protagonist as a king at all, 'the protector of the earth', and one who can in fact destroy other paramount kings, the poet makes claims on the universal values of kingship that could only be availed through Sanskrit, the language of the gods. Interestingly, Ranmal rejects the traditional charitable acts associated with great kings and instead charts his own path to fame through the building of tombs, indicating that he may be aware of his enemies' religious affilations. He has after all been cast as the 'enemy of the *yavanas*' right from the start of the poem, a theme that continues throughout

57 *Raṇmallachanda*, 6.
58 *Raṇmallachanda*, 9.
59 *Raṇmallachanda*, 3.

the narrative. Another curious twist to the conventional elements of kingship, however, comes in a verse that claims:

> If it were not for Ranmal, the great opponent of the *pātasāha* [emperor],
>
> The *gurjara* kings would have been sold in the market by the *dhagaḍas* [sultanate soldiers].[60]

The poet does not clarify who these kings are, but it is difficult not to wonder if this were a way in which the poet was also making claims on the protagonist's growing status in the region. The Sanskrit verses, like the verses in the rest of the *Raṇmallachanda*, bring together an innovative mix of tropes to build the chieftain's heroic personality.

As in the Sanskrit, the Dimgal portion of the poet's account continues the theme of the Ramayana: in slaying the enemy forces, Ranmal is in fact recreating the events in the great epic.[61] However, Sridhara Vyasa also compares his protagonist to Rama's rival, Ravana, who is traditionally viewed as an *asura*, or demon. He notes, 'Excited by war, resembling Ravana in his zeal for fight, he (Ranmal) calls out (to the fleeing enemy saying) stop, stop (*rahi rahi*).'[62] In this unusual representation, the narrative overturns the traditional *deva–asura*, or god–demon, dichotomy. It was indeed conventional to describe the Muslim enemies as demons or *asuras* in the Indic literary traditions of the time. The representation of the protagonist as Ravana, an *asura* in the epic tradition, however, appears to turn the traditional rivalry on its head. Here, the poet only seems to evoke the demon king in his aspect as a warrior hero. Just like his opponent, Rama, Ravana, too, is a great king and fighter and not the demonised Other; the comparison is ultimately instrumental in further enhancing Ranmal's glory.

Ranmal's comparison to the Puranic divinities is also accompanied by comparisons to the historical heroes well known in the region. According to the poet, after Hammira, the Chauhan chieftain of Ranthambhor, who destroyed the sultan's (here 'Ala' al-Din Khalji's) armies with alacrity, Ranmal is the only hero who can now repeat this great act.[63] The Dimgal portion of the narrative draws similarly from the pool of locally available historical resources. In the mould of Hammira, Ranmal singlehandedly manifested the valour of the 'thirty-six

---

[60] *Raṇmallachanda*, 7.

[61] *Raṇmallachanda*, 58.

[62] *Raṇmallachanda*, 59.

[63] *Raṇmallachanda*, 4.

clans (*chattīs kulaha*)' associated with Rajput status.[64] His fighting technique is also similar to that of Hammira, who, 'dashing headlong, decapitated the *dhagaḍas*, causing their heads to roll on the ground'.[65] Several other references to the achievements of this Chauhan ruler are found in the *Raṇmallachanda*, but Hammira's battle against 'Ala' al-Din Khalji is not the only local memory that the poet recalls to enhance Ranmal's position in his fight.

Sridhara Vyasa writes also of Satal of Sambhar, a chieftain of a minor branch of the Chauhans named *sonigara*, who was known to have once rescued the idol of Lord Somanatha by attacking the 'Ghazni demon' (*asuraha gajjaṇavaī*) from all ten directions.[66] He then returned the diety to his proper place. By the fourteenth century, terms derived from the place name *Ghazni* were used more generically to describe the ruler of Delhi.[67] In this case, the term most likely referred to 'Ala' al-Din, whose campaigns in western India had a lasting impact on the region's historical memory. According to the poet, Ranmal granted Satal (or perhaps his descendants) a kingdom because he always honoured those who fought against the Lord of Horses.[68] As a ruler who was able to make such a grant, Ranmal appears to be both a superior and a benevolent king. The act additionally allows him to share in the prestige that was associated in medieval western India with the Shaiva temple of Somanatha. It is also worth noting that both Hammira and Satal belonged to the Chauhan and not the Rathod clans, suggesting that it was not his own lineage he was drawing from but another well-known one.

Drawing on the past is a common feature across several texts produced in the local chieftaincies of Gujarat and Rajasthan that were dealing with intense territorial rivalries and frequent military conflicts at this time. From the mid-fifteenth century onwards, newer lineages consolidated power and

---

[64] *Raṇmallachanda*, 31. Bardic accounts generally consider thirty-six to be the total number of 'authentic' Rajput clans. However, the names enumerated in different accounts vary and the lists in many of these accounts often mention fewer than thirty-six names. See Sharma, *Rajasthan Through the Ages*, 233, 444.

[65] *Raṇmallachanda*, 58.

[66] *Raṇmallachanda*, 62. The memory of *sonigara* Saṭal also forms a significant part of the *Kānhḍade Prabandha*, where he is represented as an important aid to the protagonist in his battle against the Sultan 'Ala' al-Din's attempts at carrying away the idol of Somanatha. See Padmanabha, *Kānhḍade Prabandha*, II, 65–98. For a detailed study of Kanhadade narratives see Kapadia, 'What Makes the Head Turn,' and Sreenivasan, 'The 'Marriage' of 'Hindu' and '*Turak*',' 87–108.

[67] Chattopadhyaya, *Representing the Other*, 30.

[68] *Raṇmallachanda*, 63.

established legitimacy by claiming genealogical (and thereby political) descent from lineages whose powers had been destroyed by 'Ala' al-Din's campaigns.[69] The invocation of the memory of these campaigns by bards and court poets became a convenient instrument through which a patron's legitimacy could be reiterated in politically uncertain times. The case of the *Raṇmallachanda* constitutes an early instance of the local memory of Hammira and his struggle against the Khalji ruler being linked with Ranmal's victories, real or imagined, against the representatives of the sultans.

Interestingly, however, Sridhara Vyasa evokes yet another, and perhaps more recent and dramatic, event whose memory may have been prevalent at the time. He compares his protagonist to Timur, the Mongol chieftain, who had nearly destroyed Delhi about a hundred years prior. He notes:

> Though he overpowered the Lord of Delhi with the prowess of his arms, he did not become conceited,
>
> In that, Ranmal, the thorn in the side of the *śaka* [the Sultan],
>
> is equal only to the deathly Yama-like Timur.[70]

In bringing together all these different warrior idols and ideals, the poet builds his protagonist's martial personality. Ranmal draws his prestige from all these different heroes, as he shares some elements of each of their achievements or personas. The poet thus gestures towards universal kingly ideals, but, within the same cosmopolitan register, also portrays Ranmal as the protector of the *gurjara* or Gujarat kings, imagining a clearly regional role for him.

Despite evoking mythological and literary conventions of the time, Ranmal's panegyrist does not always follow the norm in representing the protagonist as a hero. The tonal and textural divergence between the brief introductory portion of the narrative in Sanskrit and the following Dimgal verses is considerable. Nowhere else in the narrative do we find Ranmal engaging in the cultural and sensual activities that are alluded to in the Sanskrit preface. He is compared to Rama but, as we have seen, he is also portrayed as a warrior in the likeness of Ravana and aided by little other than his own skills and strength in his fight to protect his small territory from the enemy. Similarly, he does not have an elaborate court or a retinue of courtiers. What we are witnessing in Sridhara Vyasa's representation of Ranmal as great warrior and his brave resistance

[69] Sreenivasan, 'Alauddin Khalji Remembered,' 275–96.

[70] *Raṇmallachanda*, 5.

to the Khan, then, is the convergence of several features of fifteenth-century political and social changes at the regional level.

The brutal and vivid descriptions of war and the onomatopoeic verses create the aural and visual sense of a fierce battle for the audience, who must imagine the adversity that the protagonist encounters in the course of preventing his lands and honour from being taken away from him. Rather than being defined by his achievements as a patron or administrator, Ranmal as a ruler is lauded for his prowess in battle. His lineage thus need not be from a pure bloodline of Kshatriya rulers but can draw its inheritance from Puranic and local heroes alike, including figures such as Ravana who are conventionally associated with evil forces. His duty as Kshatriya or *vira* (brave warrior) lies in singlehandedly protecting his territories by not succumbing to the enemy forces. Yet, in the end, as he contemplates his options, he holds back from actually executing a confrontation with the Delhi sultanate governor outside of his own patrimonies. What we learn in the Persian sources, albeit those of a somewhat later period, is that the tensions and negotiations between the hill kingdom and the new governor, who later styled himself the sultan, would continue into his descendants' reign. However, in his battle against the *yavanas*, Sridhara Vyasa's Kshatriya hero remains a solitary fighter, a warrior chieftain defending his status and sovereignty by dint of his individual prowess.

Depictions of the Enemy

The descriptions of the sultanate officials and their armies also figure in Sridhara Vyasa's construction of his martial hero's personality. Ranmal is fighting his battle against no small army. Compared to the numerous mentions of the 'seventeen-thousand-strong army' of the sultanate or the *yavanas*, Ranmal's army is also only mentioned once throughout the narrative. The fighters who make up this vast fighting force are commanded by men of authority who can issue royal decrees and expect submission based on the strength of their arms, horses, and elephants. The commander of the sultanate forces is in fact described as the 'best among brave warriors', who, on hearing of Ranmal's insubordination, immediately gave orders to beat the drums announcing a war.[71] These men and their armies are feared all over the lands surrounding Idar:

[71] *Raṇmallachanda*, 37.

The loud, horse-faced fighters are courageous,
They are harsh, pillaging fierce Persians (*pāraśikā*),
They plunder entire villages, capture women, children, and cows,
The men look on as the lowly soldiers carry them away.[72]

The characterisation of Ranmal's rivals as themselves brave and fierce indirectly inflates the protagonist's dominance, as he becomes their annihilator.

It is noteworthy that Sridhara Vyasa does not use a term with religious connotations such as *musalamana*, which would have been well-known at the time, to describe the sultanate soldiers. He chooses to represent those who constitute the sultanate army in a variety of different Sanskritised terms, like *mleccha*, *asura*, *śaka*, and *yavana* as well as more specifically ethnic terms such as *bagālīya* (Bengali) or *pārasīkas* (Persians). The sultan himself is referred to as *aspati*, derived from the Sanskrit *asvapati*, or the Lord of Horses.[73] In representing the Muslims with this vocabulary, the poet is indeed following the conventions of his times rather than emphasising the difference between religious groups.

Over the past two decades, scholars have revisited a number of early medieval and medieval narratives from diverse literary and cultural traditions to demonstrate that representations of Muslims were often much less binary and oppositional than they might appear upon superficial reading.[74] Within the Sanskrit and vernacular narrative traditions from western India specifically,

[72] Sridhara Vyasa, *Raṇmallachanda*, 41.

[73] Cynthia Talbot finds a similar representation of the ruler of Delhi in her study of Sanskrit inscriptions from medieval Andhra. She concludes that the use of this term in the literature of this period to identify the Turkic rulers was a portrayal of them as one of multiple, not binary, competing groups like the *Gajapatis* or 'Lords of the Elephant Corps' in Orissa, or *Narapati* or 'Lords of Men' in Andhra. See Talbot, 'Inscribing the Other,' 708. B.D. Chattopadhyaya, in a study of inscriptions and literary texts from the eighth to the fourteenth centuries in different parts of the subcontinent, also finds that Muslim rulers are often represented as one of many claimants in situations of intense and constant competition. Even in the socio-religious sphere, Chattopadhyaya finds that the Muslims are represented as one of many ideological components that existed within different local contexts and historical situations. Chattopadhyaya, *Representing the Other?*, 58.

[74] Some important examples of this scholarship include: Talbot, 'Inscribing the Other,' 692–722; Metcalf, 'Too Little Too Much,' 951–67; Chattopadhyaya, *Representing the Other?*; Thapar, 'The Tyranny of Labels,' 990–1014 and *Somanatha*.

terms such as *mleccha* were used to denote Muslims. Used extensively in the *Raṇmallachanda*, the word *mleccha* had been carried over from the Vedic times, when it was used to refer to those who could not speak Sanskrit correctly.[75] Later in the epic and Puranic tradition, this term, along with *yavana* and *shaka*, came to be used for those groups of people who entered the subcontinent from the northwest and central Asia and gained considerable amounts of political power. The terms also came to connote a lack of culture and civilisation and were used for indigenous tribes and foreigners by authors who composed literary works and texts for inscriptions. In general, these groups were recognised as those who challenged or did not adhere to Brahminical norms. In the early medieval and medieval periods, these designations were revived to refer to Muslims, as was the characterisation of barbarian or 'outsider'.[76] The Muslims could thus be equated with the foreigners and tribal people because of their common disregard for Brahmanism.[77]

While Sridhara Vyasa makes use of these conventional terms, his account presents another image of Ranmal's enemy that seems to contradict the 'inclusive' nature of the terms. He, in fact, appears to be conscious of a religious difference when he uses the term 'hindu'[78] for Ranmal and *'rahamāṇiya',* or followers of Rahaman[79], for some of the sultanate soldiers. An awareness of the intricacies of the enemy's religious and ritual practices is also apparent in the following description of the scene of prayer:

> The multicoloured fabrics are spread out, the sound of the call to prayer fills the atmosphere, the name of god Rahaman is remembered,
>
> The soldiers perform communal prayers (*nimāj*) while the sultanate cavalry stands guard.[80]

These soldiers are also engaging in the stock actions associated with the Muslims: capturing Brahmins, women, and children. However, the *yavanas* are not alone in capturing men of religion. The poet notes:

> Ranmal cuts off their [the *yavanas*] heads; with a club he smashes the *mlecchas*,

[75] Thapar, 'Tyranny of Labels,' 1002.
[76] Talbot, 'Inscribing the Other,' 698. Also see Chattopadhyaya, *Representing the Other?*, 30.
[77] Talbot, 'Inscribing the Other,' 699.
[78] *Raṇmallachanda*, 48.
[79] *Raṇmallachanda*, 18.
[80] *Raṇmallachanda*, 49.

> When he suddenly throws his spear in the battlefield, they flee leaving their swords,
>
> He captures the holy men and kills their monkey-like commanders.[81]

Although we are told that helpless Brahmins and children look to Ranmal's army for protection,[82] this act of capturing the holy men indicates that both sides were probably engaging in such deeds. It can be suggested, as others have, that just as the desecration of temples was a political act, the capture of holy men may also have had civic implications and was conceivably committed by any side in the contest for power.[83]

Conclusion

Raṇmallachanda is a literary work evidencing fifteenth-century cultural innovations that were taking place in the modest hinterland courts of Gujarat at a time when the political landscape was rapidly changing. Local elites such as Ranmal were becoming prominent political players in a world in which the centralised imperial reach was fading and regional aspirants such as Zafar Khan (later Muzaffar Shah) were making inroads. These new regional contenders needed the military and economic resources that men like Ranmal, with their holds over strategic fort kingdoms, commanded. Yet, while they were rising in status, these aspiring chieftains may not have had the resources to commission multiple imperial histories nor sponsor large-scale building or epigraphic projects: as we have seen in *Raṇmallachanda*, too, the only physical space that Ranmal occupies is the fort and the battlefield on which he can display his prowess as a warrior. But in the fifteenth and sixteenth centuries, 'courts' like Ranmal's did become sites where new ideas, engendered at the

---

[81] *Raṇmallachanda,* 45.

[82] *Raṇmallachanda,* 40.

[83] These representations are quite different from how the Muslims are depicted in *Kānhaḍade Prabandha,* the later narrative by the Nagar Brahmin poet Padmanabha. This narrative speaks of the battle between Kanhadade, the Chauhan chieftain of Jalor, and 'Ala' al-Din Khalji, and contains similar, if more elaborate descriptions of battle scenery, horses, and weapons than in the *Raṇmallachanda.* Unlike Ranmal, Kanhadade loses to the *yavana* forces due to an act of treachery; the enmity is resolved at another narrative level as the sultan, we are made aware, is an incarnation of Shiva, and his daughter, Piroja, has in fact been a virtuous Kshatriya woman in many of her previous births.

local levels, reverberated in the changing political climate and impacted the political status of their leaders. The literary innovations such as the multilingual *Raṇmallachanda,* or adaptations of conventional genres such as *mahakavyas,* epics, and *masnavis,* that developed in parts of central and northern India during the fifteenth and sixteenth centuries, are indicative of the immense cultural potential that such hinterland courts had, but that have often been ignored in historiographies that focus on conventional sources emanating from large empires.

While men like Ranmal lacked formal courtly paraphernalia, their fortified frontier provinces emerged as spaces where ideas of resistance, heroism, and kingship at the local level could be reimagined during the fifteenth century. In times of transformations, as Sridhara Vyasa's poem suggests, this imagination was able to incorporate multiple possibilities. The poet constructs a heroic personality for his protagonist that is a bricolage of conventional and unconventional elements including the juxtaposition of multiple languages such as Sanskrit, Dimgal, and words from the Persian register. Ranmal is compared with Rama, but is also a warrior in the likeness of Ravana who is helped by little more than his own skills and strength, in his fight to protect his small territory from the enemy. Similarly, while the more normative attributes of an Indic king are alluded to in the Sanskrit preface, the bulk of the narrative remains about the violent battle, and the accompanying destruction of the enemy forces. The gory descriptions of war and the onomatopoeic verses serve to create an aural and visual sense of a fierce battle that Ranmal, the solitary hero, fights alone to protect his lands and honour. In reality a local chieftain, he imagines a domain that is all-encompassing, and himself as Timur, who is reputed for shaking the foundations of Delhi. Ultimately, the opposition between Ranmal and his enemies, the *yavanas*, is presented in complex terms. On one hand, the poet depicts Ranmal's sultanate rivals as being formidable and fierce warriors, much greater in number than the chieftain's own army. He also describes the sultanate soldiers in ethnic, rather than religious terms. On the other hand, however, the poet appears to place emphasis on religious binaries that enhance the chieftain's persona as an elite Indic warrior. Further, rather than focusing on his achievements as a patron or administrator, Ranmal is lauded as a hero for his prowess in battle. His lineage thus need not be from a pure bloodline of Kshatriya rulers, but may draw its inheritance from Puranic and local heroes alike.

The languages in which these ideas are expressed also played a crucial role in the way the chieftain's persona was constructed by the poet. In the short

Sanskrit preface, the poet gestures towards the classical Indic courtly ethos that was associated with royalty. Ranmal is not quite a great king and lacks any royal titles. But the poet does speak of him as the destroyer of great kings and adapts his 'building' agenda to his own immediate needs. Drawing from the prestige of the cosmopolitan language, these verses tantalisingly hint at the possibility of royal greatness, but their claims are also circumscribed by the protagonist's actual political and social constraints. As has been well established, Sanskrit as a language of power was in decline by the second millennium of the Common Era, and many other language choices were becoming available to patrons in Gujarat. Yet, as we shall see in the following chapters too, Sanskrit, particularly from the mid-fifteenth century to a few years after the end of Mahmud Begada's reign, continued to carry import in the ways in which the chieftains and even the sultan chose to articulate their royal aspirations.

It is noteworthy that the primary language that the poet chooses to use is not the Gujarati that was emerging in the region from the early decades of the fifteenth century, but the trans-regional Dimgal style that was well-known all over western India among warrior lineages, both elite and non-elite. Here, too, the poet merges universal/cosmopolitan allusions with regional ones. But in doing so, he appears to create a work that would not only establish his patron's local prestige, but connect him to the wider warrior ethos that was evolving all over western India. While Ranmal himself did not make it into the seventeenth-century Marwari historian Nainsi's account of the Rathods, his ancestor Sonugji and their establishment at the Idar fort did, and Ranmal and his memory certainly found their way to Alexander Forbes and Shayamaladas's nineteenth-century histories based on bardic narratives.

Chieftains such as Ranmal dotted the landscape of northern and western India during the fifteenth century and became crucial players amongst rapidly shifting loyalties. Like Ranmal's fort kingdom, their frontier kingdoms may not have had elaborate courtly accoutrements, but these men often patronised poets and panegyrists whose literary works articulated their local aspirations and stretched their achievements beyond their historical realities. Each local context then provided its own unique configurations of ideals that interacted with the trans-local processes of regional state formation. Moreover, like Idar, many of these places continued to remain vital to the regional kingdoms, and later the establishment of Mughal rule in these regions. While Ranmal's legacy survives in *Raṇmallachanda's* single manuscript and a few local legends, the Gujarati expression 'I have conquered Idar-fort' or '*idariyo gadh*' even today signifies the accomplishment of an impossible task.

Narratives like *Raṇmallachanda,* epics with a strong oral character, popularising war and the valour of the martial hero, continued to circulate in the region long after the fifteenth century, as we shall see in chapter 5. However, during this period the local warrior chieftains, whose marital and kingly identities were still evolving, were also laying claim to more classical linguistic and cultural resources that were simultaneously reminiscent of the bygone Chaulukya–Vaghela literary universe and anticipated newly emerging regional aspirations. It is to these that I turn in the next chapter.

3

Gangadhara's Oeuvre

Cosmopolitan Poetry for Local Kings

Oral narratives and written works inspired by oral traditions were crucial to the process through which local Gujarati chieftains imagined and represented their political aspirations during the ferment and flux of the fifteenth century. Such works, expressed in the regional language, were one means of self-fashioning for chieftains and for their fortified kingdoms, but other artistic narrative forms proved useful as well. Two significant works in Sanskrit, one from the court of the Chauhans of Champaner and another from that the Chudasamas of Junagadh, along with a variety of inscriptions on stone, suggest that, in their quest to affirm their political and social positions in the wake of the growing imperial power of the sultans at Ahmadabad, the warrior chieftains drew on classical courtly models of kingship that had evolved all over north India from the seventh century, or post-Gupta period, onwards. They did this by deploying the aestheticised Sanskrit literary tradition.

This chapter focuses on these two Sanskrit narratives, both of which were composed by a poet named Gangadhara who travelled to Gujarat sometime during the mid-fifteenth century from Vijayanagara in south India. The first of these is a play entitled *Gaṅgadāsapratāpavilāsanāṭaka* or 'the play on the glory of Gangadas'[1] about the then-ruling chieftain of Champaner in northeastern Gujarat. In this composition, which follows the conventions of classical Sanskrit drama, the poet narrates the Chauhan king's campaign against, and subsequent victory over, the Ahmadabad sultan. The second work is *Māṇḍalikanṛpacarita*,

[1] Gangadhara, *Gangadāsa-Pratāpa-Vilāsa-Nāṭakam*. The title can also be translated as 'The pleasures of Gaṅgadāsa and Pratāpa (devī)' as the wife of the chieftain was called Pratapadevi'. Henceforth *GPVN*.

or 'biography of king Mandalik', a *mahakavya* or epic poem eulogising the Chudasama king, Mandalik, of Junagadh in the Saurashtra peninsula.[2] In both works, Gangadhara displays his competence as a poet trained in the classical Sanskrit literary traditions, and fashions his patrons as ideal rulers in the style of older Puranic kings. Yet, in their contents and concerns, the compositions remain securely rooted in their specific spatial contexts of Champaner and Junagadh, two significant kingdoms that were located on the periphery of the Muzaffarid sultanate's heartlands, and in the historical moment of their interactions with the regional sultans who, by first half of the fifteenth century, had become the indisputable masters of the region.

Before making the journey to Gujarat in search of new patrons, Gangadhara had served at the court of the Vijayanagara king Pratapadevaraya, or Devaraya II (r. 1426–1447). He first went on a pilgrimage to the holy city of Dwarka, whence he proceeded to serve Sultan Muhammad Shah (r. 1442–1451) who ruled from his capital at Ahmadabad. At the court in Ahmadabad, Gangadhara encountered Sanskrit scholars, whom he overpowered with his excellent poetic skills. The writer himself, in fact, refers to this as a *digvijaya* – conquest of all directions – indicating a complete victory in the style of traditional Indic kings. After impressing the Gurjara sultan with his poetic abilities, Gangadhara continued southeast in his peregrinations to the kingdom of Champaner. While he does not specifically mention doing so, it is most likely that he would have visited the Junagadh court right after his visit to Dwarka in the Saurashtra peninsula. In this roving way, Gangadhara, the poet from the south, found patronage for his skills in Sanskrit, a cosmopolitan language, in the regional Islamic sultanate court as well as a number of local Rajput courts all over Gujarat.

The poet chose to compose biographical works in Sanskrit, although several language choices were available to Gujarati chieftains. If local chieftains already had access to locally recognised bards who composed eulogies for them in the regional languages and styles, patronising Sanskrit poetry must have served a distinct purpose. By focusing on the two Sanskrit narratives, *Gaṅgadāsapratāpavilāsanāṭaka* and the *Maṅdalīkanṛpacarita*, I explore how the cosmopolitan language of Sanskrit and the corresponding idiom of aesthecised poetry, or *kavya*, were put in the service of local kings in a period when vernacularisation was concurrently under way.

[2] Velankar, '*Māṇḍalīka*,' and Gangadhara, 'Śrī-Gaṅgādharakavi-Kṛt Śrī Māṇḍalīka-Mahākāvyam' Henceforth *MNC*.

Over the past few decades, Sheldon Pollock has demonstrated the close relationship between language and political power, specifically focusing on the role of Sanskrit in the royal courts of South and Southeast Asia prior to the first millennium of the Common Era.[3] In the post-1000 period, however, Pollock suggests that the prestigious position of Sanskrit was gradually eroded by the different regional vernaculars developing from this period onwards. While these languages showed a keen awareness of regional specificities, they nevertheless drew from the literary tropes offered by Sanskrit, particularly the genre of aestheticised poetry known as *kavya.* While Pollock's formulations are extremely significant in the study of the literary cultures of the subcontinent, more recent scholarship has shown that Sanskrit was not relegated to the background during the second millennium, but, in fact, came to serve a variety of different functions and was to become one among the prestigious language choices in this period. [4] In the case of fifteenth-century Gujarat, Sanskrit, available at a premium, continued to serve as a language of significance that could be harnessed by local chieftains seeking to secure their positions within their patrimonies. Sanskrit was also used in conjunction with other languages of repute in use in the region, such as Arabic, Persian, and Gujarati, particularly in the writing of inscriptions. Further, the chieftains or rajas of Gujarat also continued to draw prestige for their Kshatriya warrior aspirations through the partronage of Bhats and Charans, the traditional genealogist historians who sang in their own specialised dialects. As we have seen, the *Raṇmallachanda* by the Brahmin poet Sridhara Vyasa, drew on these oral traditions, combining them with verses from classical Sanskrit to enhance the patron's reputation. The Sanskrit works produced in the region were thus located in a courtly milieu in which a variety of languages and genres were available for patronage.

The itinerant poet, Gangadhara, used his literary skills and imagination to fashion and articulate for his patrons a rhetoric and ideology of kingship that combined the idealised monarch of the Indic tradition with a keen sense of contemporary political exigencies. While Gangadhara's work evokes older Puranic models of kingship, particularly in its employment of the Sanskrit

[3] For Sheldon Pollock's formulations on these issues, see for instance, Pollock, 'India in the Vernacular Millennium, 41–74; 'The Cosmopolitan Vernacular,' 6–37; and *The Language of the Gods.*

[4] One example of a detailed study on the changing role of languages, Sanskrit, Persian, and the regional vernaculars, comes from Sumit Guha's work on the Deccan. See Guha, 'Speaking Historically,' 1084–1103; and 'Transitions and Translations'. For a discussion on the emergence of regional Sanskrit, see Bronner and Shulman, 'A Cloud Turned Goose,' 1–30.

kavya tradition, the models are in fact reconfigured to suit the political realities of the local kingdoms of Gujarat. Although an outsider, Gangadhara displayed a strong geographical sensibility in his work, layering immediate physical domains and imagined ones, creating a constant interplay between the local and the cosmopolitan, the particular and the universal.

Local Kingdoms and Sultans in the Mid-fifteenth Century

By the mid-fifteenth century, the Muzzaffarid sultans were recognised as the undisputed overlords of the region. Their imperial position and authority are visibly acknowledged in inscriptions from all over Gujarat, including those patronised by local non-Muslim lineages.[5] However, the Rajput chieftains' access to material resources, such as forests, as well as pilgrimage and trade routes, made their fortified kingdoms crucial to the Ahmadabad sultans' quest to maintain control over the wider region. Their hold over these resources, through local networks, made the fortified kingdoms formidable nodes of power that the sultans were constantly forced to harness, accommodate, and subdue, by force if necessary, in order to increase their advantage in the political landscape that had developed in the aftermath of Delhi sultanate rule.

Located at a height of 2,500 feet above the surrounding plains, some forty kilometres northeast of Baroda, Champaner separates present-day Gujarat from Rajasthan, Madhya Pradesh, and Maharashtra. In medieval times, the city was an important location, giving those who ruled over Patan and Ahmadabad access to, as well as protection from, the Malwa region. As oral traditions and excavations demonstrate, the Pavagadh hill at Champaner was also the seat of a complex religious landscape. It had long been a site for the worship of goddess Kali but appears to have had a number of Shaiva as well as Jain shrines.[6] As an active pilgrimage centre it would have also been a valuable source of revenue for rulers and, as excavations have shown, it was the site of a large

[5] Sheikh, 'Languages of Public Piety,' 186–209. See also, Jamindar, 'Contribution of the Sanskrit Epigraphs,' 195–204.

[6] Pavagadh remains an active pilgrimage site for the worship of the goddess Kali in modern day Gujarat. A number of traditional *garba* songs from the region, to which women danced in celebration of the Goddess, are also dedicated to Kali who resides at Pavagadh. However, the remains of a Lakulisa–Mahadeva temple, as well as an actively worshipped Jain shrine, are also to be found on the hill. The numerous *dargahs* and mosques that survive from the medieval city of Champaner–Muhammadabad at the base of the hill further contribute to the complex religious geography of the site.

city built by Sultan Mahmud Begada (r. 1459–1511), the most influential of the Gujarati sultans in the late fifteenth century.[7] Junagadh, in the Saurashtra peninsula, was also a significant economic and strategic location for control over Gujarat, with access to important pilgrimage sites like Girnar, Dwarka, and Somanatha. Long before the rule of the Muzzafarid sultans, the wealth of these places, particularly Somanatha, had been a point of contention between the peninsular chieftains and those ruling in the east from Patan.

Hill forts like Idar, Champaner, and Junagadh were strategically important for the sultans to be able to rule over the entire region. Until Mahmud Begada managed to capture Champaner and Junagadh in the late fifteenth century and established new towns there, vain attempts to gain control over the two forts had been made by almost all his predecessors. Sultan Mahmud's reign marked an important shift in the nature of the polity in Gujarat, as older models of alliance politics were integrated into the larger sultanate polity.[8] But, prior to Mahmud's takeover in the fifteenth century, chieftains like the Rathods of Idar, the Chauhans of Champaner, and the Chudasamas of Junagadh remained extremely powerful in their local domains; even after his reign, they reemerged as forces to be contended with.

Within Saurashtra, for instance, the Chudasamas of Junagadh were the most powerful among the lineages active in the region. Like the other clans, including the Gohils and Jhalas, the Chudasamas had migrated into the peninsula in the early medieval period. The Chudasamas had also long been associated with the *abhiras*, or pastoralists, with close links to the Sammas of Sindh, who were Muslims, as well as to the Jadeja chieftains of Kachchh, who claimed Rajput descent. The Chudasamas were a branch of the Samma lineage that acquired the principality of Vanthali from the local ruler and subsequently occupied the already fortified city of Junagadh.[9] From there they were able to control a considerable portion of Saurashtra until the sultans from the east defeated them in the late fifteenth century. As Samira Sheikh has discussed, prior to this defeat, the Chudasamas had come to acquire an elaborate court

[7] Excavations were first conducted at the site of Champaner in the 1940s by the German scholar Hermann Goetz. Later, beginning in 1969, a six-year-long archaeological project was led by Professor Mehta of the University of Baroda. For details, see Mehta, *Champaner: A Medieval Capital.*

[8] Sheikh, *Forging a Region*, 106–119. For details on the Chudasama's reinvention of status and rise to prominence, see Sheikh, 'Alliance, Genealogy and Political Power,' 29–61.

[9] Sheikh, 'Alliance, Genealogy and Political Power,' 32–33.

and aspired to a prestigious Sanskritic identity, giving up the more heterodox traditions that the Jain and other historical chronicles attribute to them.[10] A number of hero-stones, or *paliyas*, in the region mention the Chudasamas as rulers; inscriptions at temples and step-wells patronised by merchants, courtiers and elite women testify to the same. In these inscriptions, the Chudasamas are linked to the Puranic dynasties of the moon; later inscriptions, as well as the *Māṇḍalikanṛpacarita,* link them to the Yadava family of Krishna, legitimately incorporating them into the Vaishnava fold.[11]

Less is known about the ancestry of the Chauhans of Champaner. A late nineteenth-century tradition claims they belonged to the Khichi branch of the Chauhan lineage at Ranthambhor, who had migrated to Gujarat from Rajasthan soon after the conquest of Khichiwada by the armies of 'Ala' al-Din Khalji.[12] While it is not entirely clear how they acquired the Champaner territory, a Sanskrit inscription from *c.* 1469 gives a genealogy of nine predecessors of Gangadas, indicating their long-standing presence in the region. The inscription is composed in a mix of Sanskrit and Old Gujarati and specifies that it was issued during the victorious reign of 'the great king' (*mahārāja*) Jayasimhadeva, for the benefit of his mother. It notes:

> In the lineage of Pṛthvīrāja, the chief of the Chauhans, many kings have ruled (Old Gujarati: *ghaṇa rājā hoā*). In the family of Hammiradeva, the ornament of his *kula*, was Raja Shri Ramadeva, Shri Changadeva, Shri Chachimgadeva… Shri Palhanasimha, Shri Jitakarna, Shri Kumpuraula, Shri Virdhavala, Shri Savarāja, Shri Raghadeva, Shri Triṁbakabhūpa, Shri Gangarajeshwara. His son, renowned for increasing the religious merit of his ancestors, worshipper of Shri Shakti, and a perpetual bestower of cows and gold (Sanskrit: *nitya suvarnadhenudānakartā*) as well as the giver of grants (*śasana*) to Brahmins, donor of elephants, the illustrious king over kings (*rājādhīrāja*) Shri Jayasimhadeva in the village Ayasuamanu, built [this] well for the spiritual benefit of his own mother, Shri Phanmadevi …[13]

---

[10] Sheikh, 'Alliance, Genealogy and Political Power,' 36.

[11] Sheikh, 'Alliance, Genealogy and Political Power,' 36–38.

[12] Watson, 'Historical Sketch of the Hill Fortress of Pāwāgadh,' 1. Several lineages of Rajasthan and Gujarat trace their migrations from their original homelands to 'Ala' al-Din's incursions to the region. However, many of these are later recordings and it is difficult to establish the veracity of this tradition.

[13] For full text of the inscription, see Watson, 'Historical Sketch of the Hill Fortress of Pāwāgaḍh,' 2–3.

While Jayasimhadeva, the son of Gangarajeshvara (Gangadas), thus embodies all the qualities of an ideal ruler, it is noteworthy that the inscription links the Chauhans of Champaner to historical kings like Prithviraja and Hammira, who were popular in the wider region of western India, rather than to a divine lineage. It may be recalled that in *Raṇmallachanda,* the protagonist, Ranmal, also sought links to the same locally renowned historical figures, suggesting that such connections enhanced the prestige of these upwardly mobile men within the social world of warrior elites. The *Mir'āt-i Sikandarī* also depicts the Chauhan rulers of Champaner as actively involved in the politics of the region and as an obstruction to the sultans' efforts to consolidate their rule. Around 1416, Trimbakdas, the Raja of Champaner, seems to have formed a confederation with other chieftains of the region, including Raja Punja of Idar and Satarsal of Jhalawar, to invite Sultan Hoshang Shah of Malwa to invade Ahmadabad while its ruler, Sultan Ahmad was away from the capital dealing with other rebels.[14] Sikandar also writes that when Sultan Muhammad II (Ahmad's son) marched against Raja Gangadas (son of Trimbakdas) of Champaner, the latter was defeated, despite putting up a fight, and fled to the upper part of the fort: 'When the garrison of the castle became strained, the Raja sent ambassadors to Sultān Mehmūd of Māndu offering to pay him a lakh of *tānkās* for every march he should make to his assistance' – an episode, as we shall see, alluded to somewhat differently the *Gaṅgadāsapratāpavilāsanaṭaka.*[15]

Drawing on B. D. Chattopadhyaya's analysis of the societal processes of local state formation and on 'Kshatriyayisation', I thus suggest that these processes continued in western India even after 1200 and contributed to defining the manner in which the chieftains chose to portray themselves amid the fluctuating politics of fifteenth century Gujarat. By this time, the rulers of Champaner and Junagadh had held their patrimonies in the region for several generations, and as inscriptions and textual production show, they patronised scribes and men of literature, even coming from afar, to write of their lineages and rule. These chieftains gradually developed large fortifications that housed wid-ranging populations including priests, warriors, traders, and craftsmen, and were deeply involved in the politics of the region. The resources they controlled were valuable to the sultans, who were trying to consolidate their

[14] Sikandar, *Mir'āt-i Sikandarī,* trans., 14–15.

[15] Sikandar, *Mir'āt-i Sikandarī,* trans., 24.

rule as well as fight their extra-regional rivals. It is in this context that the choice of Sanskrit and the articulation of kingship within the cosmopolitan idiom of Sanskrit *kavya* acquire particular interest.[16]

The Narratives

The *Gaṅgadāsapratāpavilāsanāṭaka* exists in a single manuscript.[17] On the basis of the script used, its editor, B. J. Sandesara has suggested that it may have been copied sometime in the sixteenth century from an earlier manuscript.[18] The original play, on the other hand, is believed to have been composed much closer to the actual historical event in 1449, possibly between 1450 and 1460. The accuracy of this estimate is supported by the fact that after the reign of Gangadhara's Vijayanagara patron, Pratapadevaraya, the fortunes of Vijayanagara seem to have declined: it is therefore possible that the poet left this court in search of better prospects in other parts of the subcontinent.

The *Gaṅgadāsapratāpavilāsanāṭaka* is a play in nine acts that makes use of both prose and poetry. It is composed primarily in Sanskrit but the Sanskrit is interspersed with a form of Prakrit, used traditionally in Sanskrit classical drama by the court jester (*vidusaka*) and female characters. In addition, the soldiers of the sultan's army use a language that appears to be some form of Hindavi, which the poet associates with Muslim soldiers.[19] However, in keeping with convention, the sultan speaks Sanskrit, as do the other prominent male characters

---

[16] These social groups are often referred to in texts from these courts in formulaic terms as 'eighteen varna' or castes.

[17] The manuscript of the *Gaṅgadāsapratāpavilāsanāṭaka* is in the British Library. British Library MS 2388. It is missing a few pages and lacks a colophon with the exact date and place of production; it only tells us: 'This book belongs to the excellent Vaidya Bhamaji (f. 136). No commentaries on the text have yet been discovered, nor has the text ever been translated, although B. J. Sandesara has discussed some portions of it; see Sandesara, '*Gaṅgadāsapratāpavilāsa* by Gaṇgādhara,' 193–204; and 'Detailed Description of the Fort of Chāmpāner,' 45–50. Sandesara subsequently edited the play, which was published by the Oriental Institute in 1973.

[18] Sandesara in introduction to *GPVN*, ii.

[19] I am grateful to Francesca Orsini pointing out the link with Hindavi in this part of the text. One example of their speech is as follows:
'aṣkaundālam dekhataṅ kimu laḍho chohmi khudālammkā
baṅdā tīra kamāṇā lekara hiṅdū diwānā ihāṅ,
āyā jāya kahāṅī? tāla pagadoṅ ghālo galāṅ pāgaḍī
bistākī kartā khudālam age dartā nahin amhakuṅ.' GPVN, VII, 53.

in the play. The setting for the performance itself is the festival dedicated to the goddess Mahakali. While the political conflict between the Chauhan king and his rival, the sultan of Ahmadabad, form the basic core of the narrative, it also follows the conventions of courtly Sanskrit drama by including elaborate performances of praise for the palace and the ruler as well as displaying a variety of emotions (*rasas*). The *Gaṅgadāsapratāpavilāsanāṭaka* also features another important element of the genre: the play within the play.

Briefly, the plot of the *Gaṅgadāsapratāpavilāsanāṭaka* is as follows: The sultan has demanded the Chauhan chieftain's daughter in marriage, but the latter is unwilling to stake the honour of his lineage by acceding to the request. Meanwhile, news arrives that the sultan of Mandapa (Mandu) has agreed to assist Champaner against his abiding rival, the Gujarat sultan. This brings great joy to everyone present: elborate prayers are offered to the family goddess and several Vedic rituals are performed. The festivities continue, and a set of actors, who, like the poet himself, hail from the south, perform a play in honour of the chieftain, depicting an affectionate exchange between him and the queen, Pratapadevi, in their youth. While the king and the queen are enjoying the play, a chamberlain brings the news that one of Gangadas's generals has arrived at court with the slain heads of some men from the sultan's army, the *yavanas*, as Muslims are often called in this period. The battle has begun and a victory has evidently been achieved, as the sultan's attempt at reconciliation in a later act will also suggest. A message is sent to Gangadas stating that the reason behind the sultan's attack on Champaner is that Gangadas has been sheltering certain recalcitrant, trouble-making landholders or *garasiyas* in his court.[20] It would be wise, the message suggests, for Gangadas to accept the sultan's suzerainty instead of acting in favour of his enemies. This message is sent to the Champaner court by two Rajput allies of Muhammad Shah. However, for Gangadas, his independence is so precious that he insults his fellow Kshatriyas who have accepted the sultan's authority. A confrontation is inevitable. Gangadas now takes up arms himself, and, in the ensuing battle, the Sultan's forces suffer several reverses that force them to flee. Gangadas decides not to pursue the retreating army because it would be dishonourable to do so.

[20] *Garasiya* (called '*grāsino rājānaha*' in the text) is a term that came to be used in the period for landholders. It did not specify the ethnic or community origin of the landholders (although some like the Kolis or Bhils were usually singled out). This term could be used for landholders of different levels. See chapter 2 for more on this term.

The disheartened Sultan, however, is cheered when one of his Kshatriya allies, Virama, who we are told is the son of a certain Punja,[21] presents him with a detailed map of the Pavachala fort in Champaner. The Sultan decides once again to besiege the fort but again is forced to retreat. We are also made privy to the fact that he is worried about a simultaneous attack on his armies by his rival, the sultan of Mandapa, who we already know is allied with Gangadas. The Sultan launches a new strategy of attacking the tribal areas around the Champaner fort which, once sacked, will lead to its fall 'like a ripe fruit'.[22] Both parties seem to suffer equal reverses, and the trouble-making *garasiya*s sheltered by the chieftain are killed as well. However, when the announcement comes that the sultan of Mandapa is indeed on the outskirts of Muhammad Shah's territories and moving forward with a large army, the Sultan deems it wise to give up the siege of Champaner. Gangadas once again refrains from pursuing the retreating army, as his code of honour does not permit him to attack an army that has turned back. The final act returns to the Champaner court, and, while the last few folios of the manuscript are missing, the play seems to end with the chieftain and his queen offering prayers to the goddess Mahakali, who in turn grants them her blessings.

The other text under examination, the *Māṇḍalīkanṛpacarita*, is a Sanskrit epic poem in ten *sargas*, or chapters, composed as a traditional *carita* or biographical eulogy.[23] It narrates the life and exploits of Mandalik, the Chudasama chieftain of Junagadh. The narrative begins with a description of the city of Jirnadurga, or Junagadh, and its formidable fort, which was ruled by the Chudasamas. This is followed by a detailed genealogy of the lineage, spanning the five generations preceding our hero, Mandalik. It is explained that Mandalik's father, Mahipala, obtained a son after seeking the favours of the deity Radha-Damodara, another term for the Puranic diety, Krishna. The

---

[21] *GPVN,* VI. Various Persian accounts tell us that Muhammad Shah conquered Idar in 1441. The Raja of Idar also gave his daughter to the sultan in acceptance of sultanate suzerainty. Punja was in fact the name of the Idar chieftain that these accounts mention. It is possible then that Virama is in fact the Idar chieftain's son. The sultan also attacked Bagar in the same year; see Bayley, *The Local Muhommadan Dynasties of Gujarat*, 130. The Sultan's allies may have been the chieftains of these kingdoms.

[22] *GPVN,* VIII, 62.

[23] Even though its author provides no information about himself except that he 'was the conqueror of the poets of the *Kali* age,' it is indeed quite possible that the itinerant poet from Vijayanagara, who had travelled to the courts of Ahmadabad and Champaner, stopped at the Junagadh court on his way from Dwarka in order to continue his poetic conquest of the directions or *digvijaya*; *GPVN,* I, 18.

child, therefore, is associated with Vishnu and is projected as his incarnation – as Krishna – throughout the narrative.

Following the genealogy, the biography takes us through the childhood of the prince, who grows up to be an extremely religious, intelligent, handsome, and brave youth, who surpasses his teachers in everything. When Mandalik becomes eligible for marriage, a suitable bride is found for him: the daughter of the Gohil chief, Arjuna, who has been brought up by her paternal uncle, Duda. The Krishna-like Mandalik is then installed as the crown prince, and, under his administration, the city of Jirnadurga becomes a utopian place of virtue, prosperity, and happiness. Chiefs from the neighbouring provinces also offer their allegiance; only Sangan, 'king of the Western Ocean', remains defiant. This chieftain can be identified as a pirate of the Vadhel clan who took control over parts of the coast of southern Saurashtra.[24] Mandalik is able to quickly set Sangan straight, acquiring a rich tribute of gems and horses in the bargain. He also conquers and kills Duda, his Gohil father-in-law, as a favour to the *yavana* king, the sultan of Ahmadabad.

After this victory Mahipala hands over the kingdom to his son and retires from active political life. Once on the throne, Mandalik asks his minister to find him another suitable wife. The minister presents a list of about fifteen princesses from all over the subcontinent. But the minister feels that the princess most suitable for the young king is Uma, the daughter of the Jhala chieftain Bhima. She is suitable both in terms of her own virtues as well as her lineage. The poet describes the marriage procession and ceremony in great detail. This is followed by a description of Mandalik's benevolent rule, wherein it is reiterated that the Jhala and Gohil chieftains serve the king in a subordinate position.[25] A considerable portion of the narrative that follows describes the approach of spring and the king's romantic dalliances with the queens in the pleasure gardens, in imitation of classical *kavya* style and Sanskrit court drama. After this interlude, the scene shifts back to the world of military and political activity: Mandalik's minister informs him that all his neighbouring chieftains have accepted shelter 'at his feet' except Sangan, who is once again challenging his authority. The protracted battle between the two is described in detail and involves Sangan seeking aid from a Persian chief, or *parasika*. Mandalik eventually defeats his enemy and acquires large booty. The *Māṇḍalīkanṛpacarita* ends with a further eulogy of Mandalik that compares him with Vishnu's last incarnation, Kalki, the saviour of the dystopian *Kali* age.

---

[24] Sheikh, *Forging a Region*, 117.

[25] The Jhalas and Gohils were also locally powerful clans based in Saurashtra.

The Rhetoric of Kingship

Given that both the Chudasama and the Chauhans aspired for higher social and political status in the region, the patronage of Sanskrit panegyrics may have been one among many routes to fulfilling this aspiration. *Kavya*, Daud Ali has convincingly argued, was crucial to the production and reproduction of courtly culture.[26] The transmission of the *kavya* tradition was accompanied by elaborate gestures and had a 'perfomative' or 'spectacular' character to it. Such signs and gestures were familiar to all those men and women who were part of the courtly society. This meant that even if the language was not always understood by all members of the audience, they had the shared ability to interpret the indicators of this life. Ali thus argues that drama and poetry produced in this tradition played an important role in shaping the ideologies and values of the people who were part of the courtly world.[27] Moreover, this tradition, as it was associated with elite groups, was aspirational, and in the post-Gupta period, came to be emulated by several large and small courts all over India to suit their own needs. Even the *Gaṅgadāsapratāpavilāsanāṭaka* and *Māṇḍalikanṛpacarita* are not static reiterations of the formulaic values of kingship in which the regional chieftain is merely fitted into a pre-existing framework. Instead, both these works negotiate universal ideals of kingship. These, in turn, are reconfigured by the needs of the local polities.

Gaṅgadāsapratāpavilāsanāṭaka and *Māṇḍalikanṛpacarita* use highly stylised idiomatic language and take place in what appears to be an elaborate courtly setting with all its accoutrements. Gangadhara endows his protagonists, Gangadas and Mandalik, with opulent palaces and courts within the precincts of their forts. These forts, as we shall see, are replete with signs of prosperity, including numerous temples dedicated to Puranic deities, lakes and wells overflowing with water, ample food provisions, and weaponry. In Gangadhara's

[26] Daud Ali is specifically concerned with the courtly sources of beauty, refinement, and love, which he points out were most volubly attested by literary texts that were produced and heard widely at the households of men of rank. These included a wide variety of praise-poems or eulogies, particularly in the form of inscriptions, as well as exchanges of letters, manuals on style and performance like the *Nāṭyaśāstra*, as well as shorter proverbial verses and stories with morals like the *Pañcatantra*, and manuals on love and sexuality like the *Kāmasūtra*. See Ali, *Courtly Culture*, 78. For more descriptive accounts of the history of *kavya* see Keith, *The History of Sanskrit Literature*; Macdonell, *The History of Sanskrit Literature*; Warder, *Indian Kāvya Literature*.

[27] Ali, *Courtly Culture*, 75–85.

telling, Gangadas and Mandalik's kingly duties are likewise more varied than those of simple warriors: they include maintaining moral, political, and social order in their kingdoms. It is the rule of these virtuous kings (and in the case of Mandalik, the rule of his ancestors as well) that makes these places utopias of prosperity and virtue. Already upon Mandalik's coronation to the position of crown prince, all the people in his father, Mahipal's kingdom were happy and conducting their duties with utmost honesty. There was no thief in the kingdom, except the great sun who 'robbed the darkness of its treasures'.[28] No one recited harsh words except the students of *tarkashastra* (a branch of the *Nyaya* school of philosophy) and prince Mandalik himself only spoke sweet words.[29] Nobody told lies, apart from the 'deceitful lover', and if anyone did utter a falsehood it would only be for the benefit of others and not with a selfish motive.[30] The merchants of the kingdom were also skilled and powerful, while the best of the Brahmins were happy and satisfied.[31] Mandalik's own good qualities are all-pervasive, preventing the populace from deviating from the path of virtuousness. In sum, the poet indicates, in no uncertain terms, that Mandalik's rule and protection has brought unprecedented good to the people. These images of the kings' virtues are, in many ways, enduring, and belong to no particular instance in time, but rather draw from the tradition of *kavya* literature. Using this ornate *kavya* style of prose and poetry, *Gaṅgadāsapratāpavilāsanāṭaka* and the *Māṇḍalikanṛpacarita* portray their patrons as idealised Kshatriya kings. Both Gangadas and Mandalik are aware of this role and constantly reiterate its constituent values. When Duda, the Gohil chief, asks Mandalik to withdraw from the battle and 'live long to enjoy the pleasures of having a son',[32] he replies:

> It is a merchant's ambition to enjoy the pleasures of a home in the company of a wife and relatives; a king aspires for the higher joys of heaven obtainable by those who die on the battle-field.[33]

For the same reason, in the play set in Champaner, on the occasions when the sultan's army flees the battlefield, Gangadas chooses not to follow them because

[28] *MNC*, III. 3, 47; and Velankar, 'Māṇdalīka', 43.
[29] *MNC*, III. 4.
[30] *MNC*, III. 6.
[31] *MNC*, III.7.
[32] Velankar, 'Māndalīka,' 45, and *MNC*, III.58.
[33] *MNC*, III.63 and Velankar, 'Māndalīka,' 45.

attacking a fleeing army would not be an appropriate act for a Kshatriya.[34] By allowing his militarily superior rivals to run away without an actual fight, he succeeds in establishing the superiority of Kshatriya values.

Such ideal kings also need excellent lineages. As mentioned previously, the *Māṇḍalikanṛpacarita* provides a genealogy that covers five generations prior to Mandalik's birth. His ancestors, it suggests, belong to the lunar lineage (*chandra vamsha*) and are of the *yadava* family or *kula*. All of them are great warriors, have subdued neighbouring chieftains, and have also been the destroyers of the *yavanas*. In addition to this, they have been of an extremely virtuous and religious disposition and have always been generous to the Brahmins. Mandalik, who is himself a partial incarnation of Damodara, or Vishnu, shares all these qualities with his ancestors, making him a fitting descendent for this illustrious line of kings. While the play does not provide a conventional genealogy for Gangadas, he is also mentioned more than once as the descendent of the great Chauhan Hammira of Ranthambhor, and ism represented as a virtuous and religious benefactor of the Brahmins. His virtuousness is, in fact attested to, by a disembodied voice from the sky. When the Sultan receives the news that the women of his harem have been captured by the Chauhan chieftain, he is angry and alarmed. But the voice (meant to be divine) reassures him that:

> These dancing girls were brought before Gangadas while he was sitting with Pratapadevi, Namalladevi, and other queens. The king who did never cast a glance at other women was displeased; he gave jewels and ornaments to the girls and returned them safely in palanquins to the sultan's camp.[35]

Both narratives, then, construct the personalities of their protagonists within a formulaic Indic idiom that later came to be associated with a legitimate Rajput high culture; thus entirely negating the more ambiguous origins of these groups. It is also worth digressing to note here that the capture of women, along with horses and elephants, as spoils of war by the victor was a common feature in elite Rajput narratives, particularly from the sixteenth century onwards. The women therefore held crucial value in the ways in which these warrior elites negotiated power between rivals in times when these groups were asserting their

[34] *GPVN*, VIII, 71.
[35] *GPVN*, VIII, 70.

status.[36] While this feature was less common in fifteenth-century narratives, as a narrative device, the capture of women plays two roles. As seen in the *Gaṅgadāsapratāpavilāsa*, the protagonist's capture of women affirms his military prowess and dominance over the Sultan's forces. But it also gives Gangadas the opportunity to demonstrate his moral superiority, as he can magnanimously return the women to the Sultan.

The depictions of Gangadas and Mandalik's positions as kings are thus located firmly within the political contexts of Champaner and Junagadh. At first glance, while the *Gaṅgadāsapratāpavilāsa* and the *Māṇḍalīkanṛpacarita* seem to contain most of the essential elements of the courtly *kavya* tradition, they present unusually detailed depictions of the political activity surrounding the Champaner (*Campakapuri*) and Junagadh (*Jirnadurga*) kingdoms. Gangadhara also mentions specific personal names of military commanders, courtiers, subordinates, and so forth, along with the details of the events that he chooses to portray. His narratives thereby engage with the complexities of the context within which they are produced, making them accessible to the audience that was consciously aware of and actively involved in that context. The universal and timeless ideals of kingship find themselves modified by the needs of this localised environment.

Thus, while the initial reason for the Gujarati Sultan's attack on Champaner appears to be Gangadas's refusal to give him his daughter in marriage, the *real* reason is revealed to the audience only in a later act of the play. The two 'Kshatriya' allies of the sultan have written a letter to the Chauhan chieftain, stating:

> Do not shelter the *garāsiyās*, who are the enemies of the sultan and are making trouble in his territories... do not initiate enmity... a clever man knows these times well, this is not the time of the Kshatriyas, it is the *Kali* age of the *yavanas*.[37]

They advise Gangadas to marry his daughter to the Sultan, and wash the Sultan's feet in submission thus relinquishing his honour and pride and accepting his suzerainty instead of challenging him by giving refuge to the troublemakers.[38] In short, the Sultan's allies, warrior chieftains like Gangadas

---

[36] Sreenivasan, 'Drudges, Dancing Girls, Concubines, 136–161. Sreenivasan has discussed the different and changing ways in which captured women were incorporated into Rajput courts and households into the nineteenth century.

[37] *GPVN,* IV, 40.

[38] *GPVN,* IV, 40.

himself, counsel Gangadas to give up the older model of alliance politics for the new sultanate polity. Marrying his daughter to the new overlord would also imply giving up his own autonomy.

The tensions between the old and the new models, articulated in terms of the crisis of the Kshatriya ideal of honour, emerge again at the end of the play. When the battle between the sultan and Gangadas is at its height, some of the *garasiyas* are killed by Muhammad Shah's soldiers.[39] The families of the deceased men are desperate with rage; the sons of these brave warriors have left the fort to fight the sultan while their devoted wives have walked into their funeral pyres as the war trumpets sound in the background.[40] Gangadas is disappointed on hearing the news. He articulates in no uncertain terms that the *garasiyas* were the cause of his rivalry with the sultan. He is upset that he has not been able to save the lives of those who sought protection under him and chides himself for not living up to his Chauhan lineage, which is well-known for granting refuge to those who need it.[41] He now forbids his officers from using the services of the remaining *garasiya* in the battle against Sultan Muhammad; it is his duty, he asserts as their protector, to keep them away from danger. The surviving *garasiyas*, however, are eager to fight as they have pledged their lives in gratitude to Gangadas. Despite these emotional exchanges, the death of the *garasiyas* creates a sense of futility around the enmity between the sultan and Gangadas, and has reestablished the partial superiority of the sultan. The poet finally resolves the matter by bringing the play to a close and by shifting the focus on to another field of competition: Muhammad Shah must leave the battlefield because his other major rival, the sultan of Mandapa, is now about to seize Ahmadabad with an army of a hundred thousand cavalry, two hundred thousand foot soldiers, and a thousand elephants.[42] Sultan Muhammad's ally, Virama, goes on to provide a justification for the action by pointing out that the protection of one's own territories should be a king's foremost task.

A similar tension between alliance polilitcs and integration into the sultanate is also expressed in the *Māṇḍalikanṛpacarita*. The sultan of Ahmadabad sends an envoy to Mahipala, Mandalik's father, complaining that Duda, the Gohil chieftain who is his son's father-in-law, is wreaking havoc within the sultanate territories.[43] The envoy warns the king about the Gohil and his associates and

---

[39] *GPVN,* VIII, 67.

[40] *GPVN,* VIII, 67–68.

[41] *GPVN,* VIII, 68.

[42] *GPVN,* VIII, 70.

[43] Velankar, 'Māṇḍalīka,' 44.

states that they would disregard their matrimonial ties with him in due course as well.[44] Mahipala reassures the envoy that he considers the sultan's enemy to be his enemy. Yet in reality he is troubled by the thought of fighting his relative in support of the *yavana*, noting that a battle with the *yavanas*, who had increased their strength owing to this *Kali* age, was not a happy thing. Already the king of the *yavanas* had deprived several kings of their kingdoms. However, the *yavana* king had shown no open enmity towards the royal family of the *yadavas* (namely his own clan of Chudasama) and so he feels it is wise not to voluntarily initiate a situation of hostility.[45] His minister also counsels him to the same effect:

> That *yavana* king, who on the strength of his army of elephants and thousands of horses had conquered the world, has courted your friendship. What greater good and safety do you ask for? It would therefore be best for you to do what is pleasing for him. On the other hand, if I were to recount the misdeeds of Duda I am afraid that I would incur the displeasure of the prince. These chiefs always seek shelter under you when they are attacked by the *yavanas* and yet claim as their own the lands bordering your kingdom.[46]

Hearing the pragmatic advice given to his father, Mandalik rises to the occasion and eventually overcomes his moral dilemma. He kills his father-in-law in the interest of Chudasama authority in Saurashtra, as well as his relationship with the more powerful sultan.

Tensions with rival claimants over resources in the region are also at play in Mandalik's encounters with Sangana, the king of the Western Ocean, who defies the Chudasama claims of complete authority over Saurashtra. At Mandalik's anointment as the crown prince, the kings of the bordering territories send gifts, accepting his supremacy and he suitably honours them in turn.[47] As we have seen, unlike the others who had accepted his supreme position, Sangana disregards the news brought by the Chudasama envoy. Mahipala, though angered, only smiles, but his son Mandalik pledges to fight the insubordinate chief.[48] The battle is described in some detail, at the end of which the prince manages to break Sangan's weapon and causes him to fall from his horse. Despite the clear advantage he has over his enemy, Mandalik

[44] Velankar, 'Māṇḍalīka,' 44 and *MNC*, III.47–51.
[45] *MNC*, III.34, III.35, 45, and Velankar, 'Māṇḍalīka,' 44.
[46] Velankar, 'Māṇḍalīka,' 45, and *MNC*, III.40, 49.
[47] *MNC*, III, 10.
[48] *MNC*, III, 13.

now spares his life (*jivanadānadadāmi*, literally, 'I grant you the boon of life'),[49] only collecting a tribute in the form of horses and gems.[50] The tension between the two rival claimants to authority in the region does not end here. Sangana once again appears in the later part of the narrative, in which he not only disregards the kindness Mandalik has shown him in sparing his life, but also demands that the Chudasama chieftain submit to his authority.[51] The subsequent battle is described in even more riveting detail than the one prior. The armies shower volleys of flaming arrows at one another, but Sangan's are easily diffused as if by a cold rain.[52] Mandalik triumphs again, winning large quantities of gold, silver, pearls, and jewels as well as horses and camels. These spoils are distributed among subordinate kings, artisans, and bards.[53]

The narratives thus show an acute awareness of the region's political processes and realities. In this regard the poet depicts the multiple spheres of rivalry and negotiations that the protagonists have to face *vis-á-vis* the Sultan, the *garasiyas*, the Gohil and tribal chieftains and the pirate chieftain Sangan, as well as the tensions between the sultans of Gujarat and Malwa. In these depictions we can discern the pressures to forge ties, and the struggles to establish hierarchies that would have existed between the different players. It is within these multiple spheres of rivalry that the Sanskrit poet is able to construct an idealised Kshatriya persona for his Chauhana and Chudasama patrons. Predictably, his protagonists are virtuous, brave, and just protectors of those who seek shelter with them; they also belong to prestigious lineages. All of these qualities later came to form the essence of a Rajput high culture. Ultimately, the poet Gangadhara presents a nuanced picture of the kind of political and social negotiations that his patrons may have been undergoing. Despite their use of courtly-drama and epic-poem form, Gangadhara's works are a commentary on Gujarat's history, and shift back and forth between the universalised and timeless realm of *kavya* and the specificities of the region's contemporary politics.

Gangadhara provides no background for the political conflicts in the play and the epic-poem or *mahakavya*. In the play, *Gaṅgadāsapratāpavilāsa*, he also does not give an explanation of the role of the *garasiyas*, nor one for the more long-term rivalry between the Gujarati and Malwa sultans. He is similarly

49 *MNC*, III, 23.

50 *MNC*, III, 22.

51 *MNC*, VIII.

52 *MNC*, IX, 10.

53 *MNC*, IX, and Velankar, 'Māṇḍalīka,' 51.

opaque in *Māṇḍalikanṛpacarita*, providing no substantive detail regarding the history of Mandalik's relations with others in the region, including the sultan. Gangadhara instead assumes his audience's familiarity with these factors. Thus, understanding these narratives essentially requires prior knowledge of the region's geography and politics. The events Gangadhara describes firmly situate his narratives within their local contexts. His works thus establish their patrons' glory within their own social and political domains, rather than facilitating its spread to other parts of the subcontinent. And, despite the use of the different universalised idioms of kingship, neither Gangadas nor Mandalik aspire to 'the conquest of all directions', or *digvijaya*, an essential element of a typical Indic king's aspirations to expand his realm. Their aspirations are instead limited to protecting their sovereignty and status within their own patrimonies; the conquest of the Sultan's territories is hardly contemplated. The merger of the dharmic norms of kingship with their localised manifestations would help facilitate the process by which chieftains became more accepted as 'rajas' or kings within the areas in which they sought supremacy.

Political Geography and Significance of Place

Gangadhara's Sanskrit narratives strive to portray the intricate details of the region's political history, while also projecting his patrons as idealised Kshatriyas; they display complex interactions between local and cosmopolitan geographies, between real and Puranic topographies, and between local and transregional geopolitics. Once again, through Sanskrit, Gangadhara seem to be evoking *both* a local and cosmopolitan geography for his *local* audience.

One form of geographical knowledge that Gangadhara displays in his work is that of local topography, particularly that of Champaner and its adjoining hill, Pavakacala or Pavagadha. The *Gaṅgadāsapratāpavilāsanāṭaka* begins with the *sutradhara*, the stage manager who traditionally recites the prologue, extolling the virtues of this hill, which is the abode of Mahakali. It is also the place that Lord Shiva visits after having left his snow-clad mountain in the agony of separation from his beloved.

> It [the hill] is the support of the weak… it is the place where the residents of all three worlds find friendship… where the earth is pure and radiant, touched by the soft breeze and the skies are bright and clear…[54]

[54] *GPVN*, I, 1–2.

The virtuous people of Champaner live around this heavenly Pavakacala, or 'auspicious mountain'. Later in the play these poetic effusions merge with the strategic requirement of the conflict. When, in the seventh act, the Sultan is disheartened by his losses at the hands of Gangadas's army, one of his Rajput allies, Virama, presents him with a painted cloth, or *patta*, containing a detailed map of the fort and its surroundings in order to facilitate their movements through it. The source of this information is a treacherous Brahmin who regularly visits the fort in order to receive the generous donations that Bhamaba, Gangadas's mother, makes to the priestly caste.

The map combines Puranic/sacred geography with exact topography. It shows that on summit of the hill there is a Shiva temple made of gold and silver. In the distance, between the east and north, we are told, there is a lake named *Ramanaganga* built by Rama.[55] The deep lake to the south has been created by Sita and to the west of it is another lake created by Bhima named *Bhimagaya*.[56] To *Bhimagaya's* west there is a large lake with white waters, created by Gangadas; it is surrounded by temples dedicated to the deities Ganesha, Durga, Dinkara, Kṣetrapala, and the Jina.[57] The clouds that are ever-visible on the top of the hill are from the smoke of the sacrificial fires. The fort is also dotted with the dwelling places of the other members of the royal family; the unfurled victory flags are a reminder of the ongoing festivities.[58] The place is prosperous beyond belief and replete with food, wealth, and wells. The subordinate kings also live happily within this citadel that is forever watched over by the gods. To the south of the king's own palace are the stables and living space for cows and other cattle. The goddess Mahakali is constantly protecting Gangadas from the summit where she sports with the gods.[59] To the left of her temple is the temple of the desire-fulfilling *Jareshavara*.

Virama's painted cloth and elaborate descriptions thus take the audience (and the Sultan within the play) through the particulars of the hill fort's geography, and elevate them with references to Puranic mythology. The poet not only describes the location of a specific palace, temple, or body of water, but also makes a point of emphasising the prosperity that surrounds them; an important consideration when reciting or performing the play before the audience of royals that may have been attending the celebrations related to the goddess festival.

---

55 *GPVN*, VII, 7, 57.

56 *GPVN*, VII, 9–10, 57.

57 *GPVN*, VII, 11–12, 57.

58 *GPVN*, VII, 14, 57.

59 *GPVN*, VII, 30, 59.

Thus, the Vijayanagara poet's knowledge of local politics is matched by his knowledge of local geography. The idealisation of his protagonists is matched by the idealisation of the local landscape.

Another form of geography enters the narrative through the poet's imagination of various links that his patrons in the little kingdoms of Gujarat have with other subcontinental rulers or polities. While Champaner was an important actor within the politics of the emerging region of Gujarat, it was much smaller and less powerful than other regional polities, such as Malwa, Vijayanagara, or the kingdoms of the Deccan. Yet, in a particularly interesting act of the play, the poet again appears to equate the little kingdom of his Chauhan patrons to the wider network of regional polities that existed in that period. Just before the poet introduces his audience to the real cause of the rivalry between the raja and the sultan, he dedicates almost an entire act to the former's interaction with his courtiers within his palace interior. As Gangadas sits on his throne in full courtly regalia, surrounded by musicians, female attendants, and ministers, he receives his envoys, or *dutas*, who have brought news from every direction. Each envoy has returned with detailed reports after visiting the courts of the king of Simhaladesha, the Gajapati king in the east, the king of Champaranya in the north, and the sultan of Delhi. They bring news of utter political mayhem in these places, where treason and war have undermined the rulers' positions. Compared to these chaotic situations, Gangadas's kingdom in the west is seen as a haven of peace and prosperity.

Once again, the cosmopolitan political geography that is evoked is a mixture of poetic conventions and political reality, possibly with a good dose of the itinerant poet's wondrous experiences thrown in, and is worth describing in some detail. The fourth act of the play opens with Ranachanga, one of Gangadas's military commanders, entering the court after slaying the Sultan's commander, Naroj, and five thousand of his soldiers. His triumphant entry into the court is followed by the arrival of the envoys, as if to emphasise the vast reach of Gangadas's rule. The envoys narrate their observations in great detail, giving a distinct sense of the nature of each of the places described. Thus, the messenger reporting from the city of the Simhala lord describes a rather complex process by which precious gems are produced there: in this city, there is a lake named *mantharavahini* in which there are lotuses of a number of hues. When the king bathes in the lake alongside his wife, drops of water splash into the flowers.[60] These drops of water, along with a number of other factors, including the impact of the gem goddess, turn into solid gems of the

[60] *GPVN,* IV, 36.

colour of the lotus in which they were born: the red lotuses produce rubies, blue ones produce sapphires, and the yellow flowers produce gold-coloured gems; the drops which have solidified with two or three filaments bring forth cat-eye gems. The courtiers are struck by this unusual phenomenon, but the messenger reassures them that he is merely reporting what he has experienced himself (*pratyakṣamanubhūta*) rather than from inference (*anumānena*), or through the words of a loved one (*āptavacanena*).[61]

Next, the king Gangadas inquires about the events in the east. Here, reports the messenger, the Lord of the Elephants, Gajapati, has been poisoned by a minister with the intention of usurping the throne. He also describes in some detail the preparatory rituals associated with the pleasures of the deity, Lord Jagannatha (though these are, according to him, indeed beyond this world or *lokottarameva*). The next messenger brings news from the north, in Champaranya, where the wise king has gradually managed to increase the size of his already large army.[62] In this region, another kind of precious stone seems to hold significance. This is the *shaligrama* stone, which is the black, and usually spherical stone considered to be the aniconic form of Vishnu. The next messenger reports on Delhi (*ḍhillīpuram*), where the sultans rule. The line of the sultans is coming to an end, he informs the king. The continued hand-to-hand fighting is causing their destruction, and the goddesses of death (*yoginis*) are hovering there in groups eager to drink the enemy's blood.[63]

After receiving animated reports from the three directions and Delhi, the king wants to know about the happenings in the west. The messenger reports:

> ... hundreds of kings who have taken shelter under him [Gangadas], along with their sons and grandsons, remain extremely satisfied and happy. Burning with the desire of swallowing the *gurjara-maṇḍala* at every occasion, *mahammad suratrāṇa* [Muhammad Sultan] bites his lip [in defeat].[64]

The Chauhan kingdom is thus presented as being equal, if not superior, to a number of other important kingdoms in the subcontinent, including Ahmadabad and Delhi.

---

61 *GPVN,* IV, 36–37.

62 The messenger uses an interesting analogy here: he says that the king first gained control over the source of the flow of the water and having freed this flow, he then managed to acquire the ocean, meaning that with the help of a small army he was able to obtain more soldiers, thus enlarging the size of his core army. *GPVN*, IV, 22, 38.

63 *GPVN*, IV, 26, 39. This could also be a reference to Delhi's other name, Yoginipura.

64 *GPVN*, IV, 39.

In the *Māṇḍalikanṛpacarita,* the interplay between cosmopolitan and local geography is played out distinctly in favour of the local. Mandalik is eulogised as an ideal, almost godlike, being. His intelligence and knowledge far exceed those of his teachers' and his physical beauty surpasses even that of the gods. He frolics with his queens in the gardens of spring and protects his subjects like a brave warrior and benevolent father. These characteristics, and the manner in which they are described, can be attributed universally to any royal protagonist of a *kavya* composition. Yet the actual military and political achievements of this fantastic and universalised king are restricted to the realm of the domestic or local. Despite the repeated mention of him and his ancestors as the 'destroyer of the *yavanas,*' Mandalik only conquers chieftains of the local lineages, like the Gohils, the Jhalas or Sangana, the chieftain from coastal Saurashtra. It is against these chieftains, who shared political space within Saurashtra with the Chudasamas, that Mandalik conducts his military expeditions and gains ritual submission. This prominence of the local within the universal becomes even more obvious in the description by Mandalik's minister of all the princesses that he can potentially wed once he has been crowned king. The minister notes:

> … the daughter of the king of *simhaladvipa* is a *padmini*, she has lotus-like eyes … [but] she is of low birth[65]… the daughter of the *karnata* king is proficient in playing the *vina* and in other musical arts, [she] is endowed with all the auspicious bodily marks and has beautiful eyes [but] she is not appropriate as she has a dark complexion[66]… the daughter of the king of *madhyadesha* is proficient in painting [but] her thighs are thickly covered with hair[67]… the daughter of the king of *mahārāṣṭra* is well dressed and has a cuckoo-like voice (but) is much too clever and witty…[68]

The minister describes the princesses of Trilinga, Kalinga (Orissa), Kanyakubja (Kanauj), Kamarupa (Assam), Gopachala (Gwalior), Medapata (Mewar), and several other kingdoms all over the subcontinent in a similar vein. The criticisms finally end when he comes to the daughter of the Jhala chieftain, Bhima. She is not only beautiful, virtuous, and skilled in every art, but also of noble lineage. This princess and her father are both mentioned by name. We are also given details about Bhima's capital and the chieftain's current whereabouts. The cosmopolitan poet thus claims a position for his

65 *MNC,* IV, 8.
66 *MNC,* IV, 9.
67 *MNC,* IV, 15.
68 *MNC,* IV, 19.

apparently 'regional' level protagonist within the wider political networks of the subcontinent. In Gangadhara's imagination, Mandalik obviously has access to the daughters of all these different kings. The act of rejecting them establishes his superiority over their fathers' kingdoms. The choice of marrying the Jhala princess, on the other hand, confirms his position within the local political scenario.

The interplay between the local and the cosmopolitan is also evidenced by in the intended and imagined audiences for these works. On the one hand, as I have argued, the thickness of local details and implications in *Gaṅgadāsaprāpavilāsa* and the *Māṇḍalikanṛpacarita* demand a local audience who will understand them without need for further explanation. But Gangadhara brings to his local patrons and audiences not only a vision of the wider political world but he also imagines an audience that lies beyond the immediate one comprising the 'entire group of kings who has come to the shrine of Mahakali, to worship the goddess in the autumn season.'[69] The last act of the play begins with another travelling poet, or *vaitalika*, singing the praises of the victorious Gangadas. He is joined by the glory, or *kirti*, of the Chauhan king and the infamy, or *apakirti*, of the Ahmadabad sultan, personified as two women; the first of the two being of noble birth. It is noteworthy that noblewoman *kirti* speaks in Sanskrit, while the *vaitalika* and *apakirti* use Prakrit and are therewith assigned a lower status in the play. But the *vaitalika's* ability to comprehend Sanskrit also allows him to be the transmitter of Gangadhara's tale in the language of the people.

The two women are introduced to each other by the *vaitalika* and soon discover that they share a birthday, that is, they are both born on the day that Muhammad Shah, with his mighty armies, was defeated by Gangadas. Gangadas's *kirti* and the Sultan's *apakirti* are now eager to travel the world. The bard, whom they consider their brother, has promised to take them from 'country to country (*deśa deśāntaram*), island to island (*dvīpa dvīpantaram*), pilgrimage to pilgrimage (*tīrtha tīrthāntaram*), city to city (*pura purāntaram*), royal court to royal court (*rājasabhā rājasbhāntaram*), from one gathering of noblemen to another (*sajjanasabhā sajjanasabhāntaram*), forest to forest (*vana vanāntaram*)'[70] and to any other place beyond these that they may wish to go to. The poet thus imagines a world pervaded by the story of Gangadas's victory and the Sultan's loss. In bringing the *vaitalika* together with the personified forms of glory and infamy, he also brings about the merger of the written with the oral. Gangadhara thus hopes for the spread of his written tale through the

---

69 *GPVN,* I, 4.

70 *GPVN,* IX, 73.

oral version that the bard, or *vaitalika*, will sing on his travels along with his two imaginary sisters. After all it is through the *vaitalika* that the Vijayanagara king Mallikarjuna learns about Gangadhara's travels to Champaner, and Gangadas's wealth and generosity.

Thus both in the *Gaṅgadāsapratāpavilāsanāṭaka* and *Māṇḍalikanṛpacarita*, the Sanskrit poet imagines multiple geographies. However, whether it is the topography or the wider political networks outside and within Gujarat, the king and his kingdom are primarily situated within their local contexts. And so while universal values of kingship are evoked, in the poet's imagined geography, they are woven into and reconfigured by the 'place' to which they belong.

Conclusion

The foregoing discussions show how the poet Gangadhara represented his regional patrons from Champaner and Junagadh in his Sanskrit compositions. In both the *Gaṅgadāsapratāpavilāsanāṭaka* and *Māṇḍalikanṛpacarita*, the poet projects his patrons as universalised Kshatriya kings and yet he situates them within their very localised political and geographical context. From this combination of cosmopolitan idiom and local reality emerges a rhetoric of kingship that appears to have been created for the local milieu of immediate rivals and audiances. The image of the morally superior Kshatriya king makes for an effective foil against the *yavana* sultan as well as against those regional rival Kshatriya chieftains who may have chosen to support him. Gangadas and Mandalika's situation as the most successful kings within their local political scenario in turn establishes their moral and political superiority.

It can also be suggested, therefore, that Gangadhara's compositions belong to the body of 'regional' Sanskrit texts that had an immense significance despite the emergence of the regional vernaculars. In Gujarat, as the existence of Udayaraja's *Rājavinoda,* discussed in the next chapter, demonstrates, Sanskrit was also patronised by Sultan Mahmud Begada (and his predecessor Muhammad, whose court Gangadhara may have travelled to), despite the growing significance of Persian and Gujari as the languages of the regional court. As Yigal Bronner and David Shulman have suggested for another context,[71] not only did such texts often use a form of Sanskrit that was

---

[71] Bronner and Shulman, 'A Cloud Turned Goose,' 1–30. Recently, Chitralekha Zutshi has made a similar argument about Persian in the regional context. She argues for the vernacularity of Persian in historical Kashmiri narratives which, despite using the

modified by the grammar of the regional language but they were also shaped by the region's geography and historical specificities. As works that were firmly set in their local surroundings, the *Gaṅgadāsapratāpavilāsanāṭaka* and *Māṇḍalikanṛpacarita* would have established their patrons' glory within their own social and political domains rather than spreading their fame far and wide. In this regard, these narratives can be viewed as carrying the aspiration of regional elites to reinforce their political and moral values within the fluid politics of the region. For their composer, Gangadhara, an itinerant poet originally hailing from Vijayanagara, creating such works must also have afforded the possibility of traversing several domains through which he could display the versatility of his poetic skills.

With Ahmad Shah's reign which began in 1411, the sultanate's rule was firmly established in Gujarat. Urban centres like Cambay and other port towns continued to flourish under the sultans, while Ahmadabad, the capital founded by Ahmad Shah, also emerged as an important new city in this period. The sultans continued to face challenges at the hands of the local hereditary chieftains and rival sultanates: *Mir'āt-i Aḥmadī* mentions that Ahmad's successor Sultan Muhammad Shah was also forced to march against Idar, Bakhda, and Champaner, while his son and successor Qutb al-Din successfully overpowered the sultan of neighbouring Malwa.[72] But by the mid fifteenth-century the Gujarat sultans had developed a reputation for prosperity, piety, and the ability to harness military resources and emerged as the most prominent political presence in north India.

The regional sultans of Gujarat simultaneously emerged as great patrons of language and learning during this time. As pious Sunni Muslims, they encouraged the presence of *'ulama* in the region. Unlike the rulers of many of the regional sultanates, the Muzzaffarid sultans were recent converts to Islam and thus all the more anxious to prove their orthodox credentials.[73] The pacification of Gujarat also involved sending *'ulama* to different parts of the region, and several Sunni *'ulama* also served administrative and judicial functions. In addition to the promotion of Sunni Islam, Gujarat under the sultans also saw the migration of a number of Sufi orders into the region. Members of Sufi orders were actively involved in the politics of the time but were also prolific writers and scholars. As the sultans' reputation for patronage grew,

---

cosmopolitan language, were explicitly concerned with specific space and place. See Zutshi, *Kashmir's Contested Pasts.*

72 Sikandar, *Mir'āt-i Sikandarī,* trans., 41–42.

73 Sheikh, *Forging a Region,* 204.

scholars from different parts of the Islamic world chose to migrate and settle in Gujarat, consequently creating a vibrant intellectual atmosphere, particularly in the urban areas. Sultan Ahmad himself was the author of a collection of Persian verse; he also managed to gain the blessings for his newly founded city of Ahmadabad from Burhan al-Din Qutb Alam (the pole of the world), the Bukhari Sufi, by composing a *qasida*, or ode, in praise of the spiritual master.[74]

While Persian and the regional language Gujari remained the primary public and courtly languages for the regional sultans, a multilingual literary landscape emerged in Gujarat during the fifteenth century. This multilingual landscape was what made it possible for the local courts, such as the ones at Idar, Champaner, and Junagadh, to emerge as patrons in their own right, albeit not on the same scale as the sultans. Yet they were able sponsor the production of texts that allowed them to represent their political ideals and positions to suit their desires for social and political mobility. These values, as we have seen in the case of Ranmal and the chieftains of Champaner and Junagadh, drew from a reservoir of rhetorical resources, combining the elements of classical 'Khastriya-hood' and the more fluid warrior ethos that was represented in the oral traditions. Still, patronage of panegyrics that had grand valences in addition to narrower, geographically specific qualities, would have to find a way to coexist with the discourses that sultanates were weaving about their own aspirations. It is to the sultanate's connection with Indic kingship traditions and the classical language of Sanskrit that we turn in the next chapter.

[74] Khan, *Mir'āt-i Aḥmadī: Supplement,* 25.

4

Rājavinoda
The Sultan as Indic King

Conventionally, Indic traditions considered the king and the deity homologous, whereby the king shares in the god's divinity as the earthly lord. In that respect, the following passages equating a king and the Puranic diety Vishnu are not particularly unusual; they follow the pattern of many descriptions of pre-modern Indic sovereigns composed in Sanskrit:

> To the sound of drums and anklets, doe-eyed beauties enter the place of musical performance.[1]
>
> Erasing the darkness with their shining ornaments,
>
> Women holding strings of evening lamps, offer songs of devotion to the king.[2]
>
> The king, seated on the golden throne appears in the likeness of Vishnu.[3]

These short passages, however, are not from a longer description of an Indic monarch. They are from a Sanskrit epic poem written during the fifteenth century about the Muslim sultan, Mahmud Begada (r. 1459–1511), who ruled over the region of Gujarat, the most prosperous and powerful of the regional sultanates at the time, for fifty-two years. This is the *Rājavinoda*, 'pleasure of the king', also referred to as the *Śrīṁahamūdasuratrāṇacarita*, 'life of 'Sultan Mahmud', composed sometime in the mid-fifteenth century by a poet named Udayaraja. Contradicting the conventionally held view that the Sultan was a pious Muslim monarch, this biography, an epic poem or *mahakavya* in Sanskrit,

[1] Udayaraja, *Rājavinodamahākāvyam*, V, 1. Henceforth, *Rājavinoda*. Also see Shelat and Qureshi, *Mahākavi Udayarāja Viracitaṃ Rājavinodamahākāvyam*.

[2] *Rājavinoda,* V.5.

[3] *Rājavinoda,* V.6.

presents him as a paramount or universal ruler with links to a prestigious solar dynasty, or *suryavamsha*, a link traditionally claimed by the Kshatriya kings of the subcontinent.

By the end of the fifteenth-century, Sultan Mahmud Begada's reputation appears to have been well-established in and around his domains. A variety of sources document stories of his greatness as the most powerful of the rulers of the regional sultanate of Gujarat. His military achievements and administrative measures to bring the local chieftains under control are documented extensively in the Persian writings from the region. These accounts speak of Mahmud Shah's continuous military campaigns to subjugate the ruling chieftains as well as the ever-rebellious nobility, which, in Gujarat, included men of diverse ethnic origins. Sikandar Manjhu's *Mir'āt-i Sikandarī* notes, 'May it not remain secret that this Sultan was the best of the Gujarat sultans as a ruler, as a warrior, and a dispenser of justice.'[4] Superlative praise for Mahmud's many aptitudes is found in earlier accounts of his reign such as Abd-ul Karim Hamdani's *Tā'rīkh-i-Maḥmūd Shāhī*, composed in the second half of the fifteenth century, as well as in later works including the *Tā'rīkh-i-Firishtā*, in which he is depicted as both militarily successful and as a wise, just, and pious ruler.[5]

In these Persian works, Sultan Mahmud is represented as particularly dedicated to the Islamic faith and in favour of the Sufi saint Shah Alam, who

---

[4] Sikandar, *Mir'āt-i Sikandarī,* trans., 42. Mahmud was also associated with fabulous dietary and sexual habits. He was known to consume enormous quantities of food; Sikandar writes that in addition to his regular meal, which itself was huge, he would eat five *seers* of roasted rice. The Sultan would also ask for two plates full of samosas to be kept on either side of his bed, so he could eat some when he woke from his sleep. This would happen a few times each night. In the morning, after performing his prayers, he would drink a cup of honey, a cup of *ghee* (clarified butter), and eat a hundred and fifty plantains. He would often remark: 'Oh Almighty, who would have fed Mahmud, had you not granted him the throne.' His sexual appetite was similarly voracious: after cohabiting with several women, he would only be satisfied with one particular tall and young Abyssinian lady. This summary is based on Sikandar, *Mir'āt-i Sikandarī,* trans., 42 and the Hindi translation of the work. For Hindi, see, Sikandar, *Mir'āt-i Sikandarī*, Hindi trans., 75.

[5] Hamdani was originally from the Deccan but settled in Gujarat for some years during Begada's reign. See Mahamud, 'Introduction' to *Tā'rīkh-i-Maḥmūd Shāhī*, i–xi and Firishta, *History of the Rise of Mahomedan Power*, Vol. 4, 27–47. Mahmud, however, only finds passing mention in the sixteenth-century text, the *Tārīkh-i salāṭīn-i Gujarāt* by Mahmud Bukhari, which focuses mainly on Ahmad Shah and Bahadur Shah. See Tirmizi, 'Tarikh-i-Salatin-i-Gujarat,' 41.

had become very influential in the region during this period.[6] The Persian sources also suggest Sultan Mahmud's personal piety pervaded his political actions: the conquest of Junagadh, for instance, is recorded as having been strongly motivated by religion rather than by the desire for mere political and economic gains. Even after Junagadh's ruler offered submission, the Sultan is said to have spared his life only on the condition that he convert to Islam.[7] When he was advised by his nobles to launch an attack on the rival kingdom of Malwa, its ruler, following the death of its ruler, Sultan Mahmud Khalji, in *c.* 1469, Sultan Mahmud Begada is said to have responded, 'To desire the country of a Muslim brother, whether he be dead or alive, is inappropriate.'[8] In these stories, Mahmud is shown to have merged military might and religious devotion with political shrewdness. These facets of his character are mutually reinforcing, and so the *Rājavinoda's* portrayal him as an Indic king necessarily deviates quite sharply from those depictions in the Persian traditions.

Prior to the establishment of Mahmud's reign, as the Muzaffarid sultans were consolidating their rule in the region, literary works from the smaller local courts portrayed their patrons' complex social and political aspirations in a period shaped by ambiguous sovereignties.[9] By the second half of the fifteenth century, however, the regional sultanate's rule had been firmly established. Thus, a close reading of a narrative such as *Rājavinoda*, wherein a Muslim sultan chose to mobilise pre-existing notions of political power in order to fashion his own rule, gives us a striking picture of the diverse ways in which kingship was being articulated and represented in the regional context. *Rājavinoda* also points to the continuing political utility of Sanskrit in the fifteenth century, even for a king firmly established and represented in other literary traditions popular in the region.[10]

---

[6] Sikandar recounts a number of incidents when the saint performed miracles to protect the Sultan from enemies' attacks. Sikandar, *Mir'āt-i Sikandarī*, trans., 36–38.

[7] Sikandar, *Mir'āt-i Sikandarī*, trans., 69. Also Ahmad, *Mir'āt-i Aḥmadī*, trans., 47.

[8] Sikandar, *Mir'āt-i Sikandarī*, Hindi trans., 97.

[9] For details on such portrayals see chapters 2 and 3 in this monograph.

[10] In the context of Vijayanagara, also a fifteenth-century kingdom, Philip Wagoner proposes a theoretical model of 'Islamisation', which involved the indigenous political elite of a region participating in the more 'universal' culture in order to enhance their prestige. According to Wagoner, this was done primarily through the adoption of the secular rather than the religious culture of Islam and did not necessarily occur at the expense of the indigenous cultural traditions. This was articulated in the Vijayanagara kingdom through the adoption of a certain courtly etiquette, particularly in the courtly dress and headgear that was popular all over the wider Islamic world. It was similarly

The Regional Imperium, 1411–1511

Sultan Mahmud Begada, born Fateh Khan, ascended to the throne of Ahmadabad in 1459, marking the beginning of what contemporary and modern historians alike identify as the pinnacle of the regional sultanate's reign in Gujarat. By the end of his grandfather Ahmad Shah's rule, the Muzaffarid sultans' presence had been accepted in most parts of the region, as is attested by the numerous public inscriptions found all over Gujarat. As the early decades of the fifteenth century unfolded, the Muzaffarid sultans also emerged as the most prosperous and powerful of the regional rulers in the subcontinent, superseding rival kingdoms in north India and the Deccan in the south. While skirmishes with the local chieftains continued – Ahmad Shah and his immediate successors continued to face resistance from the fort kingdoms that surrounded the heartland – the sultans had initiated military and administrative measures that cemented a climate of stability in the region. Simultaneously, the sultans emerged as great cultural patrons, also opening up a new era of regional literary, architectural, and religious productions. These perhaps paradoxical but simultaneous aspects of their dispensation found

articulated through the adoption of the title '*hiṃdūrāya suratrāṇa*' or 'sultan among/of Hindu kings.' For Wagoner, the adoption of this title did not indicate a merely homologous connection with the Sanskrit or Telugu equivalent for king but signified a willingness on the part of the Vijayanagara ruler to participate in the political discourse of the Islamicate civilisation. The ruler could thus be considered a 'sultan' not solely in terms of political standing, but in actual form and substance. Wagoner finds that the kingdom of Vijayanagara, traditionally viewed by historians as the bastion of high 'Hindu' culture, was, in fact closely connected in its material and courtly cultures to the wider Islamic world. See Wagoner, 'Sultan among the Hindu Kings,' 851–80. Richard Eaton goes further to compare the Hindu kingdom of Vijayanagara to the Islamicate Bahamani Kingdom. Both, he demonstrates, were successor states of the Delhi sultanate. Consequently, their political ideologies appear similar as they had a shared history of association and separation from Delhi and were influenced deeply by the ideology propagated by the 'Mirror of kings' literature introduced in India through Turkish rule. See Eaton, 'The Articulation of Islamic Space in the Medieval Deccan,' 159–75. The similarities between the Islamicate Bahamani Kingdom and the Hindu kingdom of Vijayanagara thus reflect the dialogic, rather than purely confrontational, relationship of political Islam with indigenous political traditions, right from the earliest years of the Delhi sultanate. They also illustrate how the Islamicate cultural practices that emerged in the regional kingdoms provided another form of cosmopolitanism, which was to be adopted, just like Sanskrit, to assert power and authority. A similar dialogic relationship can be asserted in Mahmud Begada and the Muzaffarid's drawing on Indic vocabularies of kingship.

culmination in Sultan Mahmud's fifty-two-year reign, which followed Muzaffar Shah's establishment of the independent sultanate nearly sixty years earlier.

In the century that followed Ahmad Shah's rule, from its inception in 1411 to the end of Sultan Mahmud Begada's reign in 1511, the Muzaffarid sultans gained control of considerable military and material resources. While the Delhi sultanate remained powerful in name, by the fifteenth century, Delhi had been reduced to a provincial kingdom. In contrast, the regional kingdoms, particularly Gujarat and the Deccan, surpassed Delhi in military strength and economic resources. The sultans of Gujarat were able to link the diverse geographical areas and political nodes of the region and develop a culture nurturing new literary and architectural forms. They also facilitated more extensive trading networks than ever before.[11] In the years between 1411 and 1511 the Muzaffarid sultans held sway over the most successful of regional kingdoms, whose prosperity and reputation would far outlast its existence.

The Muzzafarid sultanate's success in the region was marked by the bringing together of a number of local chieftains under the new regime, particularly those in control of significant trade routes and forts such as Idar, Champaner, and Junagdh under the new regime. Sultan Mahmud defeated the Chudasama chieftain, Raja Mandalik of Junagadh, in a decisive victory in 1472. Several attempts by his predecessors to subjugate Mandalik prior to this had resulted only in limited success. Mahmud Begada had harnessed a vast amount of financial and military resources in order to achieve his victory, as the Raja was well-protected by the mountainous and forested lands surrounding his fort kingdom. Mandalik was eventually overpowered; he accepted Islam and was granted the title of Khan Jahan, according to the Persian histories of the sultanate.[12] The Chauhan kingdom of Champaner was also taken over by Mahmud some eleven years after the conquest of Junagadh, in *c.* 1483. As in the previous years, the Sultan's relationship with Champaner was closely tied up in regional rivalries with the sultans of Malwa. Since this hill kingdom lay on the strategic borders of both their domains, the conquest of Champaner marked an important victory against the rulers of Malwa as well. Mahmud established the city of Muhamammadabad at the base of Pavagadh Hill to

---

[11] Sheikh, *Forging a Region*, 185.

[12] This tale is quite different from the one of the virtuous and brave Kshatriya king of the *Māṇḍalīkanṛpacarita* composed only a few years earlier (Chapter 3). Sikandar, *Mir'āt-i Sikandarī*, trans., 57. Mandalik is said to have died in Ahmadabad. Sikandar also reports that Mandalik, on moving to the capital of the sultans, was deeply influenced by the spiritual powers of the saint Shah Alam.

commemorate his success. It was believed, Sikandar reports, that it was the conquest of these two forts, which his predecessors had struggled to subdue, that earned Mahmud the curious epithet of 'Begada' or 'Begadha'; *be* in Gujarati means two and *gadh* refers to fort.[13] But Junagadh and Champaner were not the only chieftaincies that Mahmud conquered. He also launched successful campaigns against the chieftains in the coastal areas of Diu and Jagat, parts of Sindh and Kachchh. Additionally, he was also closely involved in the wider politics of the region, aiding or fighting kingdoms in the Deccan, Malwa, and southern Rajasthan.[14]

Mahmud's grandfather, Ahmad Shah, had introduced a number of administrative and military innovations that enabled the sultans to become the most generous and powerful employers of military manpower in the region, thus ensuring a solid power base.[15] He introduced a regular system of payment for his soldiers in which half their salary was to be paid out as a land grant, or *jagir,* and the other half was to be given to them in cash, ensuring their own security as well as their loyalty to the crown.[16] Ahmad also initiated the process of incorporating the local chieftains into the administration through the *vanta*, or 'part', system of collecting revenues from directly administered territories.[17] The *vanta* was to be one-fourth of the territories that the chieftain had formerly controlled. The other three-fourths, assigned the title *tulput*, were acknowledged as 'property of the king'.[18] The chieftains – or *zamindars*, as

---

[13] This explanation for Sultan Mahmud's name comes from Sikandar Manjhu. Sikandar also mentions another, and more fantastic, belief about the title that was widespread when he was writing during the seventeenth century. In Gujarati, notes Sikandar, the term referred to a bullock whose horns stretch horizontally forward 'in the manner of a person extending his arms to embrace another'; the Sultan's moustache was so thick and long, it was said, that it resembled such a bullock's horns. Sikandar, *Mir'āt-i Sikandarī*, trans., 42. Ali Muhammad Khan, the author of the *Mirāt-i-Ahmadī* also mentions these legends related to the Sultan but his account is derived, as he himself acknowledges, from Sikandar's work. See his *Mir'āt-i Aḥmadī*, 45.

[14] For details of Mahmud's conquests, see Sikandar, *Mir'āt-i Sikandarī,* trans., 41–89.

[15] Sheikh, *Forging a Region*, 73.

[16] Khan, *Mir'āt-i Aḥmadī*, 39. Khan writes: 'If the complete salary is paid in cash, there will not remain any surplus with him [the soldier]. A soldier will be without any means. He will become careless in his defence of the kingdom. If half out of the revenue produce is assigned to him as salary, he will derive benefit in the shape of grass, fuel, etc. from that mahal … Half in cash will be conveyed to him every month without delay and waiting so that he may remain present wherever he may be for receiving it.'

[17] Sheikh, *Forging a Region,* 193.

[18] Forbes, *Rās Mālā,* vol. 2, 270.

they were known in the Persian writings – were responsible for the protection of their own villages and to make themselves available for the military service of the king when so required.[19] Those landowners who were able to retain control over their patrimonies, or *gras*, were usually forced to pay an annual tribute to the sultans. The sultans did not usually interfere with the internal administration of these territories, and the landlords were allowed to collect revenues from their lands.

Ahmad Shah's military and administrative reforms were consolidated by his son and successor, Sultan Muhammad II. It was on these foundations laid by his grandfather and father that Mahmud Shah Begada was able to build his successful reign. Mahmud encouraged courtiers to administer the territories granted to them as military assignments where they were expected to raise troops. Alternatively, a paid official would be stationed at the principal town or fort to administer it and collect revenues, with the support of troops from Ahmadabad.[20] This would ensure successful collection of revenues, at least in the areas in which the traditional chieftains had been alienated from their lands and integrated into the wider system of government. Mahmud introduced a measure of assigning the *jagirs* of the nobles and soldiers who were slain in battle, to their sons; if there were no sons, half the property was to be assigned to the daughters. In the absence of a daughter, settlements were to be made with the dependents of the deceased.[21] As with the measure of paying soldiers partly in cash and partly by the assignment of a *jagir*, this move was intended to reduce any dissatisfaction towards the ruler or prevent the noble from developing roots in the land. By the mid-fifteenth century, the administrative and military innovations the sultans introduced, along with the facilitation of what historian Samira Sheikh has called the 'religious marketplace', much of Gujarat had been settled and its diverse environmental and social elements combined into what emerged as the most prosperous and powerful kingdom with a distinct regional character.

From the inception of their reign, the sultans had patronised Arabic and Persian, consciously linking themselves to a wider cosmopolitan literary world within and beyond the subcontinent, where other Indo-Islamic sultanates were also becoming prominent.[22] Sufis, and other Muslim intellectuals and scholars,

[19] Forbes, *Rās Mālā*, vol. 2, 270–71.

[20] Sheikh, *Forging a Region,* 194.

[21] Sikandar, *Mir'āt-i Sikandarī*, trans., 45.

[22] Alam et al note that the regional sultanates that followed the dismantling of the Delhi Sultanate represented a kind of 'apogee' of Indo-Persian culture. Gujarat and Deccan's

migrated to the region, leading to the formation of a diverse intellectual community that composed works in Persian, Arabic, and Gujari, a regional language that gained prominence under the sultanate rule.[23] Not only did the sultans, styling themselves as pious Sunni rulers, offer their support to Sufis and religious scholars, but they also established cities and institutions that further enabled urban settlement and literary production during the fifteenth century.[24] As relatively recent converts to Islam, the sultans were eager to gain legitimacy from their association with these men of religion and competed with their extra-regional rivals to attract them to their courts.

However, the Muzaffarid dispensation also facilitated the multilingual and diverse society that was Gujarat. This was a region where overlapping linguistic spheres had existed from the Chaulukya period and these linguistic developments continued to flourish and expand during the fifteenth century. Devotional poets such as Narasimha Maheta composed his works in what is considered the earliest form of modern Gujarati; the Jains, still prominent in the region, continued to produce works in Apabhramsa and Sanskrit; and Sanskrit was also used extensively in the composition of the newly emerging genre of place- and caste-related Puranas.[25] Various performative and spoken dialects intelligible to specific religious groups, particularly mercantile communities such as Khoja Ismailis or different Vaishnava sects, were also in use during this time. The landscape of inscriptions which were extensively produced during this period reveals a great multiplicity in language use, including Arabic, Persian, Sanskrit, and Gujarati. Along with Charani-style productions, Sanskrit works were patronised by the emerging Rajput courts, so Gujarat and its various local power centres would have become quite attractive to scholars and poets looking for patronage for their art. Ultimately, however, it was the regional sultans who emerged as the greatest patrons in the region.

---

links to the Indian Ocean networks facilitated the arrival of new influences from Iran through merchants, soldiers, and statesmen who settled in these regions. The competition between these sultanates also led to a diversification of the Indo-Persian culture, compared to its rather monolithic expression under the Delhi sultans and the Mughals, according to the authors. See Alam, et al, *The Making of Indo-Persian Culture*, 25.

[23] For surveys of Gujari language and literature, see Dar, 'Gujarat's Contribution to Gujari and Urdu,' 18–36; Nayak, 'Gujarī Bhāshā, 268–85; Pathak, 'Gujari: The God-Given Great Gift to the World,' 98–104.

[24] For a detailed study of the migration of Muslim saints and scholars to Gujarat during the fifteenth century, see Balachandran, 'Texts, Tombs and Memory'.

[25] Majmudar, *Cultural History of Gujarat*, 342.

The Sultans in Sanskrit Inscriptions

The records of Sanskrit inscriptions from north India, and particularly from Gujarat, testify to the fact that the language continued to be in use after the establishment of Muslim rule in India.[26] Non-Muslim merchants, their wives, officials, and often even Muslim nobles, chose to use Sanskrit in their inscriptions. The epigraphic traditions of Gujarat had incorporated the Muslim rulers from the thirteenth century onwards. In numerous Sanskrit epigraphs from the time of the Delhi sultanate, Muslim rulers were mentioned with titles and adjectives that were part of the same pool of idiomatic resources that authors of poems and *prashastis* used.[27] Most commonly, the Perso-Arabic title 'sultan' was also modified to the Sanskritised, *suratrāṇa*, thus giving it the literal meaning 'savior of the gods'. In Gujarat, numerous inscriptions recording the deeds of locally powerful elites note the reign of the Delhi and Gujarati sultans by using such titles. Not only do these Sanskritise the names of the officials and rulers but they also use symbols, similes, and motifs that were common in other Sanskrit inscriptions, thus incorporating the new forms of authority into the ideological and literary conventions of the textual productions of the times.[28]

Take, for instance, an early Jain inscription in the Stambhan–Parshvanatha temple at Cambay or Khambhat during Khalji rule, dated *c.* 1301–10, which memorialises the construction of the temple dedicated to the Jain spiritual teacher, or *tirthankara*, Ajitadeva, by a merchant named Sah Jesal. The record mentions that the donation was made in 'the victorious reign of Alp Khan' (*śrīalpakhānavijayarājye*), the governor of Anhilvada and the Delhi sultan, 'Ala' al-Din Khalji. The Sultan's name and title are also Sanskritised as '*śri-alāvadīna-suratrāṇa*' and he is described, according to the coventions of the genre, as 'the one whose radiance pervades the earth' (*pratāpākrāntabhūtala*).[29] Similarly, in a memorial stone from Junagadh district, the Sanskritised name of the Tughluq official, Malik Muhammad Sadik (Skt. *māmalik-śrīmad-sadīk*) precedes that of the local Chudasama chieftain, a certain Mahipaladeva.[30] Sanskrit and Sanskritised terminology seems to have been adopted by the

[26] See, for instance, Prasad, *Sanskrit Inscriptions of the Delhi Sultanate*, and Chattopadhyaya, *Representing the Other?*, 48–60.

[27] Chattopadhyaya, *Representing the Other?*, 48–60.

[28] Chattopadhyaya, *Representing the Other?*, 50–51.

[29] Shastri, *Historical Inscriptions*, 4, no.1, 3–4.

[30] Shastri, *Historical Inscriptions* 4, no.3, 9–10.

Delhi sultanate officials based in Gujarat in their inscriptions as well. The Sanskrit portion of a bilingual inscription from Petlad records the grant of 20 *kubhas* of land and repairs of a step-well during the 'victorious reign' of Sultan Ghiyas al-Din Tughluq (Skt. *gayāsadīna*), the 'king among kings who ruled in Yoginipura (Delhi)'.[31] The grant had been sanctioned by a sultanate official at Anhilvada and locally executed by a certain Badr al-Din Abbuk Ahmad Koh, whose name was also inscribed in a Sanskriticised form on the epigraph. Such inscriptions that incorporate the Delhi sultanate rulers and officials in Sanskriticised forms can be found all over Gujarat.

By the early fifteenth century, the rise of the new regional sultanate, that of the Muzaffarids, was also reflected in the epigraphs of Gujarat. Of the 300 inscriptions that have survived and been published from Muzaffar Shah I's reign, 50 are in Sanskrit.[32] A few of these also form a part of the bilingual inscriptions that are found in a small but significant number on civic structures all over the region.[33] From the earliest part of their reign, the Muzaffarid sultans were incorporated in the same ways that their predecessors from Delhi had been: through the Sanskritisation of their names and lineages. For example, the Sanskrit portion of a bilingual Persian–Sanskrit inscription from Veraval recording the building of a city wall mentions the donor, Mahamalik Phajaral Ahamed (Malik Fazl allah Ahmad Abu Raja in Persian), and the reigning sultan, Muzaffar Shah, in Sanskritised form. Another inscription, dated 1457, mentions the victorious reign and title of then-ruler Qutb al-Din Ahmad I (r. 1451–1458) in Sanskritised form (*śrīkutabadīnavijayarājye*).[34]

The era of Sultan Mahmud's reign, and a few decades that immediately followed, yield not only brief inscriptions on civic structures, such as those mentioned above, but also a noteworthy number of relatively long Sanskrit incriptions in honour of major building projects. Many of these lengthier inscriptions can be dated to after the composition of the *Rājavinoda*, the Sanskrit epic-poem discussed in the following pages. These reflect the

[31] Shastri, *Historical Inscriptions* 4, no.2, 7–8. In Sanskrit: *yogiṇipurādhiṣṭha-mahārājādhirāja-śrīmat-suratrāṇa-śrīgayāsadīna-vijayarājyé.*

[32] Sheikh, 'Languages of Public Piety', 189.

[33] Sheikh, 'Languages of Public Piety,' 189. Sheikh finds that such bilingual inscriptions in Persian/Arabic and Sanskrit or Persian and Gujarati, were attached to civic structures such as walls or forts and water structures, especially step-wells.

[34] This inscription, which documented the construction of iron gates, was patronised by sultanate officials, but other Sanskrit inscriptions from this time, and from the reign of Mahmud Begada as well, were commissioned by civilians.

conventional use of Sanskritised names for the sultan and also display a degree of sectarian fluidity in their invocation of Puranic deities. One such inscription from 1497 records the building of a step-well (*vavi*), mosque (*masita*), and a mausoleum (*hajira*) near the sultanate capital of Champaner-Mohammadabad by a person named Sandal Sultani.[35] The Sanskrit is intermixed with Old Gujarati and Perso-Arabic phrases. Strikingly, the contents invoke the Puranic deities Ganesha and Sharada. The inscription also pays respects to Kali, the presiding goddess of Champaner, whose curse, it notes, will befall anyone who infringes on the terms of the grant. Another inscription in Sanskrit and Arabic from 1499 records the donation of a lavish step-well by a female courtier, Bai Harir.[36] The Sanskrit portion opens with invocations to the Creator (*ṣṛṣṭi kartā*), Varuna, 'the lord of the waters', and the supreme goddess (*śaktī'kundalīlīnī*).

The very first inscription from the Gujarat sultanate that offers information about Mahmud Begada's conquests and deeds is also in Sanskrit.[37] Closer in time to the *Rājavinoda*, the Dohad inscription from 1488 is believed to have been composed by the same author, Udayaraja, and indeed its twenty-six lines mirror the Sultan's Sanskrit biography.[38] This inscription, commissioned by the courtier 'Imad al-Mulk, and recording the construction of the Dahod (Dadhipadra, Dohad) fort, is a historical one describing the deeds and genealogy of the reigning sultan. The sheer number of Sanskrit inscriptions during the fifteenth century points to the continued value of the language during this period. While Persian was the predominant language of inscriptions, non-Muslims and Muslims, including sultanate officials, considered it important to record their donations and make proclamations in the vocabulary and idioms offered by cosmopolitan Sanskrit. On the one hand, this phenomenon was an extension of the convention of Sanskrit inscriptions incorporating rulers, their titles, and their lineages. But on the other, their fluid deployment of Old Gujarati and Perso-Arabic words, and the invocation of locally popular deities, signal that multilingual, Sanskrit-heavy inscriptions had a role to play in the administration and control of a region in flux.

[35] Sonawane, 'Māṇḍavī Step-well Inscription at Cāmpānera,' 223–27.

[36] For the Sanskrit portion, see Abbot, 'Bai Harir's Inscription at Ahmadabad,' 297–300, and Shastri, *Historical Inscriptions* 4, no.21, 53–54. For Arabic see Blochmann, 'Eight Arabic and Persian Inscriptions from Ahmedabad,' 367–68 and Chaghatai, *Muslim Monuments in Ahmedabad*, 70. For a detailed comparison with the Arabic portion see Sheikh, 'Languages of Public Piety,' 204–05.

[37] Sheikh, 'Languages of Public Piety,' 207.

[38] Gode, 'Dates of Udayarāja and Jagaddhara,' 101–15.

Sarasvati Moves to the Sultan's Court

The *Rājavinoda* is an epic poem in seven chapters, each with an individual title.[39] We know little about the poet Udayaraja, who only mentions the names of his father and his preceptor – Prayagadasa and Ramadasa, respectively.[40] However, we are told, that he has 'brought this pleasant offering of flowers of verses' as a gift for Sultan Mahmud Begada.[41] Playing on his own name, Udaya, or rising (usually of the sun), he reiterates in the end that he composed the work for the 'eternal rise or success' (*śaśvat udaya*) of the Sultan, but of course is it difficult to ascertain whether the 'gift' he composed in the hope of securing the Sultan's patronage actually led to him being granted an audience with the king. Because Udayaraja has also been identified as the composer of the 1488 Dohad inscription of 1488,[42] and because the events recorded in that stone inscription are not mentioned in the epic poem, the *Rājavinoda* can be given a later date.[43] If Udayaraja was indeed the composer of the Dohad inscription, then it is possible that he would have resided and worked in Mahmud's domains for several years.[44] Both the epic poem and, to some extent, the earlier eulogistic inscription, narrate the Sultan's genealogy and describe his virtues, achievements, and lavish court.

---

[39] The poem contains a total of 240 verses. At present, only one manuscript of the work exists. This manuscript was acquired by Georg Bühler in 1875 for the Government of Bombay and housed at the Bhandarkar Oriental Research Institute, Pune (BORI/MS 18/1874–75). The few modern scholars who have written about Udayarāja's *Rājvinodamahākāvya* have labelled it a 'unique' text, primarily due to its exaggerated praises of a Muslim sultan known for his dedication to Islam in the idiom of Hindu kingship. Gode, in his essay on the date of the poet Udayaraja, cites Bühler's note on the manuscript: 'The *Rājavinoda*...is quite a literary curiosity. The author...celebrates Mahmud popularly reported to have been the most violent persecutor of the Hindus and Hinduism as if he were an orthodox Hindu King.' Gode, 'Dates of Udayarāja,' 102. Another writer, S. A. I. Tirmizi, discusses the narrative in some detail but also ultimately critiques it as filled with 'the grossest possible exaggerations.' See Tirmizi, 'Sanskrit Chronicler of the Reign of Mahmud Begarah,' 45–60. The poem is not mentioned in modern general histories of Gujarati literature, which tend to view the sultanate rule as a period of declining Indic traditions.

[40] *Rājavinoda*, VII.41, 22. This is also the only entry found about him in Aufrecht, *Catalogus catalagorum*, 65.

[41] *Rājavinoda*, I.4, 29.

[42] Gode, 'Dates of Udayarāja', 101–15.

[43] See Sankalia, 'Dohad Stone Inscription,' 212–25.

[44] Sankalia, 'Dohad Stone Inscription,' 115.

The *Rājavinoda* itself is centred on the Mahmud Shah and his kingly activities, rather than a single battle or a series of events. The poet does not tell a story chronologically but instead captures different points in the life of the protagonist, as was often the case in epic-style *kavya* works.[45] In the *Rājavinoda*, Sultan Mahmud's court is the primary focus of the poet's representation of him. It is a near-divine space to which we are introduced right at the beginning of the composition; in fact, Sarasvati, the Puranic goddess of learning, has left her heavenly abode to reside in this magnificent court. It is she who narrates the virtues of the Sultan and his court throughout the poem, and it is at her bidding that the poet claims he has composed this very work.[46] Sarasvati is also invoked in the Dohad inscription as 'the goddess who resides in Kashmir' (*kāśmīravāsini devī*), and finds mentions in other inscriptions and texts from the Sultan's reign.

By the fifteenth century, the courtly ethos that developed with the emergence of new political systems beginning with the Gupta period around the fifth century, had become an integral part of the ruling houses all over India. The codes that defined the culture and practices of the court, however, were not static and were interpreted according to the political context. In the case of Gujarat, we find the use of courtly literature not only in the smaller chieftaincies but also in a sultanate, as evidenced by the composition the *Rājavinoda*. Dedicated to the regional sultan, it drew extensively from the courtly literary tradition of *kavya*. One of the most striking features of Udayaraja's panegyric honouring Mahmud is its portrayal of the grandeur of the Emperor's court. In the *Rājavinoda,* the Sultan's court is depicted as a semi-divine space in which the displays of erudition, wealth, and magnificence are of a fantastic nature. For Udayaraja, his patron's court is far superior even to that of Indra, the king of the gods. In fact, the *Rājavinoda* opens with a dialogue between Indra and Sarasvati, in which the goddess of learning and music, explains her decision to reside in Mahmud's court.

The goddess appears to have descended to earth from her heavenly abode. She is the daughter of the creator, Brahma, and her father is concerned about her whereabouts. Brahma has sent Indra, his disciple, to look for her. Indra, 'the thousand-eyed one', wanders from one street to another in her pursuit, and is surprised to find the goddess convening with the scholars at the court of Sultan Mahmud. Indra asks Sarasvati why she has given up the pleasures of eloquence

---

[45] Warder, *Indian Kāvya Literature*, vol. 1, 169.

[46] *Rājavinoda*, VII, 40.

in Brahma's heavenly world and has chosen instead to entertain herself on earth. The goddess responds with elaborate praise for Mahmud Shah's court, which is, she explains, not only the home of prosperity but also endowed with a 'council of the most learned of men'.[47] Moreover, she describes how poetry can be heard everywhere.[48] The rich artistic culture of the court is, in fact, emphasised throughout the poem. One chapter, entitled the 'occasion of music performance', is dedicated to pursuits of music and dance at the court.[49] Doe-eyed damsels enter the music hall to the sound of the drums, and various fragrant flowers and ever-burning incense infuse the atmosphere.[50] The lustre of the royal ceremony of arms is created by the rows of lamps lit in the evening – imagery reminiscent of a military and religious ceremony performed by Kshatriya kings in the monsoon season, before taking to the battlefield. Some of the women play the veena with proficiency; others play the flute. The sound of the soiree causes peacocks to dance vigorously.[51] Hundreds of learned and wise expert musicians, who appropriately sing of the king's glories and increase the joys of the courtiers, adorn the court.[52] The music is accompanied by elaborate dance performances by beautiful women who resemble the dancers from Indra's court.[53] The pleasing music and dance performances are followed by the Sultan's amorous sports with the beautiful maidens.

Not only, then, is Mahmud's court described in rich imagery and ornate language, it also appears before the reader as an aestheticised performance of pomp and show. The brilliance of Mahmud Shah's throne, Sarasvati tells us, surpasses not only that of Indra, the king of the gods himself, but also of the other gods like Vishnu, as well as Kama, the god of love. The goddess does not wish to return to the heavenly abode and has decided to permanently reside at the Sultan's court, which is the centre of poetry, music and scholarship. The goddess's change of residence, then by implication, is also a change in the location of heaven itself to the court of an earthly sultan.

[47] *Rājavinoda*, I.10, I.11.

[48] *Rājavinoda,* I.12.

[49] *Rājavinoda*, V. The Muzaffarid sultans, particularly Mahmud, were known to be great patrons of music. A number of Indo-Persian texts bear witness to this. For details of music patronage and textual production at the Gujarati court see Delvoye, 'Indo-Persian Accounts on Music,' 253–280; and 'Music Patronage in the Sultanate,' 342–60. Also see Kokil, 'Gujarātnā Sultānonā Samaymā Saṁgīt,' 394–400.

[50] *Rājavinoda*, V.2, 3, 12.

[51] *Rājavinoda*, V.11.

[52] *Rājavinoda*, V.14, 15, 13.

[53] *Rājavinoda*, V.18, 13.

In addition to being blessed by the goddess of learning, Mahmud Shah is also portrayed throughout Udayaraja's narrative as the paragon of a king: one who pursues the goals of life as defined by the Indic tradition. In this tradition, the king was, relative to his subjects, the man who most fully realised the three worldly goals of 'personal pleasure', 'the acquisition of wealth' and the 'upholding of the cosmo-moral order'.[54] It was only the most ideal of these kings, the paramount king, who realised these goals as does Sultan Mahmud. Under this king's command, we are told, that the cosmos is devoid of transgressions: the stars, moon, and sunrise follow the proper order of time, and the oceans do not flood. For the poet, not only does the Sultan partake of the divinity of Sarasvati and Brahma, but also himself, in his persona as an ideal paramount king, resembles a variety of other divinities. He shares each of their special qualities in the pursuit of the three goals of life. Likening the king to divine beings, often described as an incarnation on earth, is a notion that draws from the traditional Puranic idiom of divine embodiment.

Mahmud's portrayal as divine is further elaborated in the epic-poem's third chapter which, describes the Sultan's toilette and entry into the courtly space. This divine king, referred throughout this chapter as 'lord of the earth', is awakened every morning by the sweet sound of musical instruments, the neighing of horses, and pleasant songs and auspicious verses sung by his wives.[55] The Sultan's face, which resembles the reflection of the 'moon upon the ocean', is sprinkled with water and his body is anointed with the perfume from the 'deer's navel', or musk from the mountains in Kashmir.[56] The fragrance of camphor fills the air, while the betel leaf makes the Sultan's mouth fragrant. Udayaraja goes on to describe Mahmud Shah's physical features: his body appears to be home to the goddess of wealth who embraces his vast chest and resides in his four limbs.[57] The descriptions continue in a similar vein as the Sultan enters the court under a canopy and ascends the royal throne, where the subordinate kings recite his praises and the poets compose verses proclaiming his glory.

The *Rājavinoda*'s claims on Indic ideas of sovereignty surface in passages like these, replete with descriptions of Mahmud's physical attributes, his pursuits of pleasure at the court and the peace and prosperity that define his rule. Such representations of the court and the king's activities, along with the

---

[54] Inden, 'Hierarchies of Kings in Early Medieval India,' 130–34.

[55] *Rājavinoda*, III.1, 2.

[56] *Rājavinoda,* III.4, 5.

[57] *Rājavinoda*, III.10, 11.

depictions of the king's body, personal beauty, and exaggerated mannerisms were integral to the courtly traditions of India. The latter were best articulated in the *kavya* genre of elite Sanskrit poetry which had been patronised by the Indic courtly elite from the early centuries of the Common Era. The king's martial prowess and warrior-like traits were also equally significant in this convention in establishing his moral superiority over the rest of the society as well as his rivals. This combination of the aesthetic aspects of the king's court, his pursuit of pleasure, his sensual activities, and his martial qualities is what defined the nature of kingship in the classical Sanskrit literary world and had become widely accepted all over India from the fifth century onwards.[58]

In invoking this convention, that was well-known all over the subcontinent, the Sultan's panegyrist was conveying his regional patron's superiority over a number of spheres. By the time the sultans of Gujarat had consolidated their rule, the sultanate at Delhi had been reduced to just another kingdom among many. Yet the control of Delhi did hold a significant place in the subcontinent's political imagination and many regional rulers, including the Muzaffarid sultans of Gujarat, made unsuccessful attempts to gain control over it; Delhi thus continued to remain a symbolic rival for many of these rulers. Mahmud had also succeeded in taking control of the resources of his regional level rivals: the numerous warrior chieftains. Many of these strongmen, as we have seen, were of diverse origins and were also trying to establish their own social positions in the region by claiming idealised and conventionally accepted notions of Indic kingship through the patronage of poets and priests. The third and final set of rivals that the Gujarati sultan had to face was the rulers of neighbouring or distant regional kingdoms. In this context, there was no better means of addressing these multiple spheres of competition than by invoking ancient notions of authority that had been well-known from ancient times and through idioms and conventions of Sanskrit, the oldest language of power available on the subcontinent. Given the sheer number of language choices available in the region then, the patronage of a Sanskrit panegyric, rather than Persian or Gujarati, suggests that Mahmud also sought the prestige that this esteemed language, available at a premium, could grant him. The eclecticism in his self-representation as a ruler appears to be deliberate.

As has been established, *Rājavinoda* was not an entirely unprecedented literary development. By this time, we do have epigraphs patronised by the sultans of Delhi in which multiple elements of earlier long-standing Indic

[58] Ali, *Courtly Culture*, 96–99.

traditions, such as titles of kings or Sanskritisation of Muslim names, are clearly visible. However, such depictions were never on same scale as the *Rājavinoda*. What the *Rājavinoda* points to is the deliberate elaboration and flowering, in scale and scope, of this Indic tradition to establish power in several spheres. While it is the Mughals who have been celebrated in South Asian historiography for their large-scale mobilising varieties of Indic political and cultural traditions during the early modern era, what this poem indicates is that such practices were already at work in the regional kingdom of Gujarat during the fifteenth century.[59]

The Sultan's Lineage and Multiple Domains

As an ideal Indic king, Sultan Mahmud is no mere embodiment of superior physical and moral values but a holder of multiple titles and roles. The poet Udayaraja imagines him as a king whose influence spreads over a variety of domains, both real and imagined. First, Mahmud is the descendent of Muzaffar Shah, the 'lord of the *gurjara* country', and himself the emperor of the emerging region of Gujarat. In addition, Udayaraja places him at the apex of the different traditional hierarchies of Indic rulers as the 'king over high kings', (*maharajadhiraja*), asserting his independent status. Further, he is a 'paramount king', (*nripacakravarti*) having mastery over the entire Indian subcontinent.[60] As the ideal warrior and monarch, he has gained control over the different kingdoms through his own personal prowess. Thus, in this work the poet creates a sense of political geography in which the regional and specific interact closely with the pan-regional and universal elements of Sultan Mahmud's representation. This is most apparent through two key chapters in the narrative: the second, 'narration of the lineage' (*vamsanusamakirtana*), and the fourth, 'universal occasion' (*sarvavasara*), in which the rulers from different parts of the subcontinent visit Mahmud's court. The Sultan's universal status, however, is developed throughout the poem.

In the second chapter of his panegyric to Mahmud the poet provides a genealogy of the Gujarat sultans in thirty-one verses. Here the Sultan's and his predecessors' conquests are merged with references and comparisons to Puranic

[59] Another regional sultan who is known to have had a sustained engagement with Sanskrit is Zayn al-Abidin of Kashmir (r. 1420–1470). See Obrock, 'History at the End of History,' 221–236; Zutshi, *Kashmir's Contested Pasts*, 33 (33n); and Truschke, *Culture of Encounters*, 12.

[60] *Rājavinoda*, VII.39.

mythology. Each of the seven chapters in the poem also ends with a brief genealogy of the sultans: 'Lord of *gurjara* land' Muzaffar Shah, Muhammad Shah, Ahmad Shah, his son Muhammad Shah Gyasuddin. The list ends with the line, 'may his son, lord of kings, Mahmud Shah be victorious'.

Udayaraja's genealogy of the Gujarati sultans also begins with its founder Muzaffar Shah. The opening line links the rulers to the solar dynasty, thus granting them authentic Kshatriya status:

> The auspicious solar lineage emerged from the sun. This [lineage] was revered and considered exemplary by kings. Muzaffar Shah was indeed the first of these.[61]

This claim of the sultans' links with the solar lineage is not found very often in texts and inscriptions they patronised, though the Gujarati historian Sikandar does narrate the story of their ancestors having once been Hindu 'Tanks', a branch of Khatris who traced their descent from the dynasty of 'Rāmacandra whom the Hindus worship as God'.[62] The Tanks were expelled from their community, according to Sikandar, because they had taken to drinking wine. Muzaffar Shah's father and uncle were influential landholders and had the ability to summon thousands of horsemen and foot soldiers. Consequently, they managed to find service in Tughluq sultan, Firuz Shah's retinue, forge a marriage alliance with him, convert to Islam and eventually rise in the courtly ranks.[63] The regional sultans were thus indigenous Muslims whose conversion had been a recent event.[64] From Zafar Khan's early days in the province, he had been eager to display his commitment to the faith and encouraged the movement and settlement of religious leaders throughout the region.

---

[61] *Rājavinoda,* II.1.

[62] Sikandar, *Mir'āt-i Sikandarī,* trans., 1.

[63] Sikandar, *Mir'āt-i Sikandarī,* trans., 1–2.

[64] Parallels to this account of the rise of the status of Rajput warriors can be found in the accounts of the Kyamkhanis, a small Indian Muslim community from Rajasthan who rose to prominence after their conversion to Islam in the 1450s. As the Muzaffarids, the Kyamkhanis also benefitted from their ability to command resources in the military labour market and from their association with Islam, which facilitated their gentrification. Yet, Cynthia Talbot has demonstrated, in their historical accounts, composed in Braj Bhasha, the Kyamkhanis celebrated both their conversion to Islam and their Rajput warrior identities. Talbot argues that in doing so Kyamkhanis of the early modern era thus negotiated multiple social and cultural spheres, simultaneously participating in the local/vernacular as well as global/cosmopolitan arenas. See Talbot, 'Becoming Turk the Rajput Way,' 211–243.

Udayaraja does not mention these elaborate details and also refers to Muzaffar Shah, the first ruler of the dynasty, with the somewhat humble title of 'the noble king'. However, he also describes Muzaffar's establishment of his independent rule in Gujarat as a divine act. He notes that Muzaffar Shah left Delhi and established his royal power in the *gurjara* country (*gurjaradeśa*) in order to assist the diety, Krishna.[65] He similarly borrows from Puranic mythology to describe the same sultan's conquest of Kachchh and other parts of the region, comparing his fame to the monkey god Hanumana's leap to Lanka in the epic, Rāmāyaṇa.[66] Muzaffar Shah is even referred to as holding the title of the 'liberator of the Malwa king', whom he had initially defeated and imprisoned.[67] This Malwa king is Alp Khan, whose alliance he had sought after assuming the title of independence; this title then is reminiscent of the inscriptions of the Chaulukyas, who also seem to have been keen on expressing their victories over the neighbouring kingdom.[68] In repeatedly referencing their conquest of Malwa, the poet appears to be both affirming his patrons' superiority over their primary regional rivals as well as evoking the memory of their regional predecessors.

Next in the genealogy, Muzaffar's son, Muhammad, is praised for the strength of arms, and described as resembling 'the lustre of a thousand suns'.[69] In what is fairly conventional simile, Udayaraja writes that under his reign 'the sun of his munificence wipes out the darkness of poverty from the world'.[70] However, Udayaraja also refers to his march on Indrasprastha or Delhi in order to attack his

---

[65] *Rājavinoda*, II.2.

[66] *Rājavinoda*, II.3, II.4. Muzaffar Shah is not adorned with many elaborate titles in the Sanskrit inscriptions from his reign as well. The Veraval stone inscription of *c.* 1408 refers to him simply as 'respectable Dhafar Khan (from Zafar Khan) emperor Muzaffar' (*śrīdafarakhān mudāfarapātsāha*). See Shastri, *Historical Inscriptions* 4, no.6, 15. Similarly, the Dholka well inscription refers to him simply as 'respectable emperor Muzaffar' (*śrīmadaffarpātasaha*). However, this long inscription, which records the construction of the step-well, refers to the patron, a certain Sahadeva of the *ṭakṭa* lineage as being the Sultan's favourite. This Vaishnava family seems to have been involved in the administrative profession for at least three generations and an integral part of the Delhi and Gujarati sultanate governments. See Shastri, *Historical Inscriptions* 4, no.7, 16–18. In the Dohad Inscription of Mahmud, however, Muzaffar is called *nṛpabhūpati* (king, lord of the earth).

[67] *Rājavinoda*, II.5.

[68] See chapter 1.

[69] *Rājavinoda*, II.8. In the Dohad inscription he is only referred to in passing with the title of *mahīpati* (lord of the earth). See Sankalia, 'Dohad Stone Inscription,' verse 3, 223.

[70] *Rājavinoda,* II.6.

enemy, a certain Mallakhana,[71] and to his conquest of the formidable forests of Nandapada (Nandol),[72] once again interspersing the conventions of the Sanskrit poetry with elements of history. This juxtaposition continues throughout the genealogy. Ahmad, who arises from the 'ocean' that is Muhammad, is mentioned for his attack of Hushangshah's home at the Mandu fort and also for capturing the fort of the 'lord of Maharashtra' by force.[73] In addition to being a great warrior, this sultan was also deeply devoted to the people.[74] The generosity and military prowess dominate the poet's descriptions of all these great sultans of *gurajaradesa* or Gujarat' mentioned in the genealogy. After his son Muhammad Shah's 'lustre and glory pervaded the earth', the genealogy turns to the poem's protagonist: Muhammad's son, Mahmud.

Udayaraja unsurprisingly dedicates a large part of the genealogy, nearly half the stanzas, to the hero of the poem. As with his predecessors, exaggerated praises drawing from the conventions of Sanskrit *kavya* are used to describe the Sultan, yet in such descriptions, too, he emerges as superior to others in the lineage as he embodies the virtues of multiple deities. As the poet notes:

> In beauty he represents the god of love (*makaradhvaja*),
>
> In generosity Karna[75]
>
> In compassion he appears as the ideal divine king, Rama
>
> In the battlefield equals Bhima[76]
>
> In eloquence he is greater than the god of speech (*vākpati*), his charms are like those of the great lord Vishnu,
>
> The people are forever devoted to Mahmud Shah[77]

---

71 *Rājavinoda,* II.8. This could be a reference to the rebellion in Delhi following Muhammad Tughluq II's death through which Imad al-Mulk became the governor of the province. Muhammad Shah Gujarati, much against his father's wishes, chose to march to Delhi and, like other former nobles of the Sultanate, sought to capture the throne. For details of this expedition and how it eventually resulted in the sultan's death see Sikandar, *Mir'āt-i Sikandarī,* trans., 7–9.

72 *Rājavinoda*, II.9.

73 *Rājavinoda*, II.10-12.

74 *Rājavinoda*, II.13. In the Dohad inscription Ahmad is referred to as the 'knower of the essence of all religions and thought' (*sarvadharmavicārasārasarvajña*). He also seen as having conquered the lord of Malwa and capturing all his land and wealth. See Sankalia, 'Dohad Inscription,' verse 4, 223.

75 Known for his charitable acts and generosity in the *Mahābhārata.*

76 Known for his superhuman strength in the *Mahābhārata.*

77 *Rājavinoda,* II.26.

As is common in Sanskrit praise poems, the poet also dedicates several verses to descriptions of his protagonist's military prowess. But, as he did in his descriptions of Mahmud's predecessors, the poet steps away from the universal descriptions to remind us of the Sultan's position as the ruler of the *gurjara* lands: he is the one 'who serves *gurjarabhūmi* with care', yet, 'is eager to hold Dhara's (*dhārāpūrī'*) hand' reminding us of his conquest of the fort of his rivals in Malwa.[78] While no other specific places are mentioned in the rest of the genealogy, Mahmud Shah is also described as the destroyer of forts, and as creator of cities filled with lush fruit trees and virtuous people.[79]

As transcendent as it aims to be, Udayaraja's genealogy of the dynasty of the Gujarati sultan also shows awareness of the region's specific history and his contemporary political surroundings. Despite the exaggerated claims about the Muzaffarid sultans' moral and martial powers which draw from the stock metaphors of the genre, some of the military achievements Udayaraja describes locate the poem and its political commitments squarely within the time and space of sultanate rule. The genealogical portion of the poem traces Mahmud's dynasty to divine origins, claiming a Khastriya, or Rajput, lineage. As great kings of the warrior caste, repeatedly compared to the epic heroes and kings, the sultans are, implicitly – and explicitly in the case of Mahmud – depicted as upholders of moral order in the world. By deploying the notion of Puranic sacral kingship in a regionally grounded idiom, the *Rājavinoda* establishes homology with, and superiority over, the other Hindu rulers in and outside the region who would have been familiar with such literary devices. As a legitimate Indic warrior king, Sultan Mahmud's sphere of influence would not be restricted to the polities of Gujarat. We find this paramount king who has established his authority over the entire subcontinent – the poet refers to him as the 'protector of the world' – at the centre of a far more universal geography, involving rulers from all the directions of the subcontinent.

Gurjaradesha as the Centre of Bharatavarsha: The Sultan as Paramount King

In what is perhaps the most animated section of the *Rājavinoda*, in the fourth chapter, the poet imagines his protagonist as being surrounded by the society

[78] *Rājavinoda*, II.20.

[79] *Rājavinoda*, II.24.

of kings. The scene opens with the goddess Sarasvati entreating Indra to watch as the kings from different lands are led into the court.[80] Rulers from kingdoms in all the different quarters accept Mahmud's authority and participate in his court rituals in all their pomp and glory. The scene draws entirely from the conventions of classical Sanskrit poetry. The kings of these different countries stand in ceremony and appear, one after the other before the Sultan as he sits grandly on his eight-cornered throne; none of these kings are mentioned by name but only referred to by the place they rule. Each one wishes to outshine the other in the curiosities and presents that they bring forth in his honour. The court of the emperor of Gujarat is the foremost among them all, and the virtues of their own kingdoms are humbled by this great Sultan's domain.

The king of Vanga, the land where the Ganga becomes 'thousand faced',[81] offers the Gujarati sultan jewels from the western ocean.[82] Next,

> The Pandya king, who bows down before the great Lord [Mahmud Shah] in respect, offers strings of pearls, resembling a piece of the moon in the oyster shells from which they are gathered.[83]

The lord of Anga, who humbly offers a hundred women dressed in vivid outfits and ornaments, follows this king from the south;[84] the lord of Ratnapura brings forth diamonds, while the Kalinga lord brings the gift of strong elephants.[85] Sprightly soldiers from Trilinga's army then perform a war dance, and after this passionate display of arms, the Malwa king places everything he has at the Sultan's feet in order to protect his own life.[86] Thereafter the pageant continues apace:

> That even greater king Kumbhakarṇa[87] … he too serves King Mahmud, offering much gold in tribute.[88]

---

[80] *Rājavinoda,* IV.1.

[81] This could be a reference to the upper reaches of the Hoogli, known as Bhagirathi, which is considered the source of the Ganges.

[82] *Rājavinoda*, IV.2.

[83] *Rājavinoda*, IV.3.

[84] *Rājavinoda*, IV.4.

[85] *Rājavinoda,* IV. 5, 6.

[86] *Rājavinoda,* IV.11.

[87] This could be a reference to Rana Kumbha of Mewar.

[88] *Rājavinoda*, IV.12.

The invincible lord of Kāmarūpa bows down before his prowess.[89]

After experiencing this regal pleasure-grove, the king of Magadha, does not return to nor desires [his own] royal abode.

He does not praise [his own] arbour nor is he desirous of the joys of residing in Puṣpapurī [his capital]..[90]

From that country where the rivers Ganga and Yamuna meet, the lord of Prayaga brings water in numerous, shining, golden pots.[91] Dramatically, the king of Mathura permanently subordinates himself by acting as the sultan's doorkeeper and spreading the fame of Mahmud, the 'lord of the earth'.[92] The rulers of Kanyakumbja and Nepal are similarly humbled.[93] Others shower him with appreciation:

O brave one, you are Indra, Varuna, the wealth-granting Kubera,

Thus the Kashmir lord praises King Mahmud.[94]

And finally, the 'king of the mudgals, possibly the Delhi sultan, offers his crown to Mahmud, the *gurjara* emperor.[95]

In these verses, Mahmud's kingdom of Gujarat, located in India's western quarter, becomes the centre of the political geography, even though it is the kingdoms of the Gangetic basin that traditionally form the centre of the subcontinent. The rulers of all these lands come to pay their tribute to the great Sultan, all accepting his position as the universal king and ensuring the prosperity of his domain. The wealth they bring, be it women, jewels, or elephants, represents the Sultan's superiority above them all. Yet this display of inordinate wealth does not quite complete the scene, which continues, as do other parts of the narrative, with the spectacle of poetry, music, and dance. In court of this 'lord of the earth' there is an abundance of poets; the singers experiment with different tunes in his praise, the wrestlers display their art for the amusement of the audience; and beautiful maidens perform dances.[96] We are told:

89 *Rājavinoda*, IV.13. Kamarupa refers to the area in and around modern-day Assam.
90 *Rājavinoda*, IV.14.
91 *Rājavinoda*, IV.15.
92 *Rājavinoda*, IV.17.
93 *Rājavinoda*, IV.18,19.
94 *Rājavinoda*, IV.20.
95 *Rājavinoda*, IV.22.
96 *Rājavinoda*., IV.25–27; IV. 28–31.

> As this great king Mahmud is everyone's lord prosperity is ever-increasing,
> Who can equal the one who holds the lands from the *malaya* mountains to the Himalayas and from west to east?[97]

As has been established, the pursuit of pleasure was a crucial aspect of the ideal Indic king's sovereignty. In that sense, then, the king was 'pleasure-seeker-in-chief', as the sultan with his courtly entertainments also appears to be.

This scene at the court, in which powerful kings from numerous well-known regions offer various forms of wealth, is reminiscent of the one at Champaner's Chauhan Chieftan Gangadas's court in which the messengers from different directions report the political news from these to the king.[98] However, in Mahmud Shah's case, it is not merely visiting messengers but the rulers of these lands themselves that come to pay their tribute. This notion of the protagonist sultan as the controller of all the directions of the subcontinent reaches a culmination in the *Rājavinoda*'s final chapter in the epic poem, which is entitled 'achieving victory' (*vijayalaksmilabh*). Here, the rulers from all the different directions of the subcontinent, travel to Mahmud's court and accept their subordinate status. In conjunction with the previous chapter, 'the celebration of victory' (*vijayotsva*), in which the sultan appears be making elaborate preparations for battle, this final chapter acts as something of a conquest of directions or *digvijaya,* that was also typically part of the duties of a traditional Indic king. Mahmud Shah, the 'paramount king among kings', the *nripacakravarti*, has established mastery over the rulers of the entire subcontinent.[99] This subcontinental victory, however, enhances the beauty and prosperity of his regional kingdom, *gurjarabhumi*.[100]

In Udayaraja's imagination of his protagonist, we witness the interplay between the Sultan's position as a regional king and as a Kshatriya paramount whose influence extends across the subcontinent. However, the trope of the kings from the different regions submitting to his power by presenting him with a variety of gifts has the effect of reinforcing his position as a regional monarch. In the last chapter of the epic, in the final conquest of the directions, the poet reaffirms the Sultan's lordship of the Gurjara land, depicting him as an important regional king, and one who could extend his power into neighbouring areas, if he so desired. This also bolsters the genealogy's description of his

[97] *Rājavinoda*, IV.23.
[98] Chapter 3 in this monograph.
[99] *Rājavinoda,* VII.39.
[100] For instance, *Rājavinoda,* VII. 34, 35.

ancestors' achievements within and beyond the region, and further establishes Mahmud's claim as the unparalled ruler of Gujarat.

Moreover, the goddess of learning's arrival at the court has already shifted the heavens to his earthly domain to a region which, as we know, is seen as superior to all others in the subcontinent and through this description has become the subcontinent's centre. The sultan, in his panegyrist's representation of him, has thus succeeded in establishing his sovereignty over every sphere: divine, subcontinental, regional, and local.

Conclusion

The claims Udayaraja makes for Sultan Mahmud and his predecessors as the rulers of the *gurjaradesha* reveal that the poet sought to firmly locate his protagonist and both his protagonist's ancestors as the legitimate rulers of the region. The *Rājavinoda* joins *Gaṅgadāsapratāpavilāsanāṭaka* and the *Māṇḍalikanṛpacarita* in projecting its protagonist as an ideal Indic monarch. For Udayaraja, Mahmud Shah is a fierce warrior and a benevolent king, and the poet draws extensively on the stock imaginary of *kavya,* in order to enhance this depiction. Yet in Udayaraja's imagining, the Sultan is not merely a local king. He is the ruler of the entire region of Gujarat, and, at the same time, morally, militarily, and monetarily superior to other real or imaginary rulers of the subcontinent, including those of Delhi. Consequently, the *Rājavinoda* does engage with elements of Mahmud and his ancestors' local and regional achievements but also draws more prominently on the universally recognised ideals of an Indic king. What emerges is an image of an independent regional monarch with access to a variety of cultural resources, including Sanskrit, which retained currency as a language of power in the fifteenth century.

This interweaving of specific historical events with pan-Indian metaphors illuminates how power was being rearticulated and reconfigured at the regional level. The poet deploys the resources of highly aestheticised Sanskrit poetry to celebrate his patron and turn his regional kingdom in western India into the centre of not only the subcontinent, but the universe: after all, Sarasvati, the goddess of learning, has chosen to leave the heavens and move to Mahmud's court, by implication shifting the location of heaven itself. The trope of the kings from all over the subcontinent, including the rulers of Delhi, offering Mahmud tribute also shifts the earthly centre to Gujarat in western India, clearly indicating where power is now located.

While the Muzaffarid sultans themselves did not make their links to their Rajput past explicit, we find detailed mention of their origins in Sikandar, who enumerates several generations of their ancestors in his seventeenth-century account. The sultans would also have been aware of the older Sanskrit literary tradition – a tradition that was also deployed by their predecessors, the Delhi sultans, in their inscriptions – as one that was being claimed by their local adversaries as well. The sultans had consolidated their rule through the development of local consensus; the local Rajput chieftains in particular achieved concentrated power through conquest and negotiation, often through marriage alliances between them and the sultans. Seen in this light, it is evident that the *Rājavinoda*, although a rare example in terms of scale and the claims it makes, was part of the process of regionalisation wherein the sultan could be depicted in similar ways to the local Rajput chieftains but also in fact as their superior.

Less than five decades after Mahmud Begada's death in 1511, the Mughal emperor Akbar inaugurated one the most successful and diverse polities in Indian history. Establishing a local consensus through kinship ties with Rajput kingdoms was a critical aspect of this process; much could be accomplished through intermarriage, but strategically worded genealogies also proved to have great currency. The Mughals were great patrons of Persian, and in fact Persian remained the primary public language, but as recent scholarship has shown, Brajbhasha and Sanskrit also figured prominently in the Mughal political and cultural imagination.[101] As an inflection point in the complex history of multilingualism in fifteenth century promoted by the Gujarati sultans, *Rājavinoda's* portrayal of its protagonist as a great Indic king appears to foreshadow some of these developments, which saw much greater elaboration under the Mughals.

[101] Allison Busch has discussed the role of Brajbhahsha patronage at the Mughal court and the courts of various Mughal nobles in several works. See for instance, Busch, 'Hidden in Plain View,' and *Poetry of Kings*. For Sanskrit at the Mughal court see Truschke, *Culture of Encounters*.

5

Rās Mālā
Re-Discovering a Warrior Past

When, in the late sixteenth century, the Mughals in north India eventually overpowered the regional kingdom of Gujarat, the system of negotiated harmony that had developed between the Muzaffarid sultans and local chieftains was unseated. While the regional sultanate came to an end, the Rajput chieftaincies were subsumed into a new imperial administration. Decades before that, in 1511, Sultan Mahmud Begada had succumbed to ill health and had been buried at the imperial necropolis of Sarkhej, on the outskins of Ahmadabad, close to the remains of the revered Sufi, Sheikh Ahmad Khattu. During his fifty-two-year reign, Begada had overpowered the two great forts of Champaner–Pavagadh and Junagadh and integrated the numerous other local chieftains into the regional imperium, both through conquest and through the imposition of a tribute-paying system. By securing the support of spiritual leaders and other diverse communities, both professional and religious, the sultans, particularly Mahmud Begada, had managed to create a regional consensus. The prosperity of the region, ensured by its fertile lands, flourishing seaports, and the revenue system established by Sultan Ahmad and his successors, made these rulers reliable paymasters in the north Indian military marketplace. Over time, the sultans had emerged as important cultural patrons; cities like Ahmadabad and Chamapaner grew as significant centres of sultanate-style architecture and became home to a number of scholars and littérateurs.

Sultanate rule, and its network of relationships with local chieftains, persisted for sixty years after Begada's death. While the Mughal emperor Humayun had defeated the Gujarati sultan Bahadur Shah in *c.* 1535, it was his son Akbar's conquest of Gujarat in late sixteenth century that made the region an imperial province, or *subah*; it remained so until the late eighteenth century. And then, as the Marathas became well-ensconced in the region with Mughal decline, the different parts of Gujarat came to be controlled by the Gaekwad family, which had established itself in Baroda beginning in the early decades of the eighteenth century. The Gaekwads conducted repeated and violent revenue extraction incursions in different parts of the region, targeting the chieftaincies of the areas surrounding their kingdoms, such as Mahi Kantha and the Saurashtra/Kathiawad peninsula. These attacks were eventually put to an end when the British annexed Gujarat, along with Kathiawad to the Bombay Presidency in 1808.

Soon after they took over the region, the British embarked on the process of committing Gujarat to history, as they did in other parts of the subcontinent. In this period, during which the discipline of history itself was being formally institutionalised in Britain, the region of Gujarat, along with Kathiawad and Kachchh, came to be a part of the colonial historical imagination. Some of the earliest expressions of this imperial narrative imperative was based on the oral traditions of the Bhats, Charans, and other poet communities, who were the repositories of genealogies and histories of the warrior-kings of Gujarat and parts of western India.

One such influential work, *Rās Mālā: or the Hindoo Annals of the Province of Goozerat in Western India,* was first published in 1856. It was written by an officer of the East India Company who was stationed in Ahmadabad and other parts of Gujarat in the mid-nineteenth century. The officer, Alexander Kinloch Forbes (1821–1865), composed the monumental historical narrative within the context of the early colonial encounter in Gujarat, at a time when traditional notions of sovereignty, hierarchy, kingship, and the legitimate rights to rule over the numerous kingdoms of the region were being rapidly reconfigured. *Rās Mālā* is a reconstruction of the history of the region, focusing principally on the chieftains, whom Forbes often refers to as 'Râjpoots'. Forbes casts the Rajputs as the founders and the legitimate heirs of the region. He does so by emphasizing two other elements: one, the oral traditions that speak of these warrior clans, and two, the Rajputs' prominence in the fifteenth century in relation to the regional sultans. In this regard, *Rās Mālā* reclaims the fifteenth century as the most formative period of the region's past. While Forbes's voluminous history, and work as a promoter of the Gujarati language, had a deep impact on Gujarati writers, these particular aspects of its history did not end up finding much popularity among the regional intellectuals that followed him.

Rās Mālā was originally published in London and has seen several reprints since. It was also translated into Gujarati in 1869.[1] Divided into two volumes

[1] Forbes, *Rās Mālā*.

and four books or sections, Forbes's provincial history consists of over eight hundred pages, including the author's own coloured illustrations and architectural drawings of Hindu and Islamic monuments from different parts of Gujarat. The text itself is based on a variety of sources, among them Jain and Persian accounts, colonial writings, and, most significantly, the oral narratives of the Bhats, Charans, and other traditional genealogists and preservers of oral traditions that had been an integral part of the Rajput chieftaincies and princely houses of Gujarat. Forbes was assisted in his endeavours by a Shrimali Brahmin poet named Dalpatram Dahyabhai (1821–1898), who became the chief interlocutor between the traditional poets and the colonial officer.

Rās Mālā's value for our study lies in Forbes's understanding of the chieftains as forming the basis of Gujarat's political landscape. Rather than focusing on imperial rulers like the Mughals and Marathas, Forbes foregrounds the role of the political structures and relations defined by these numerous chieftains who held much smaller patrimonies and lands but were a significant influence on the politics of the region. Forbes is primarily concerned with these groups and their interactions with the regional Muzaffarid sultans. While the oral accounts he uses cannot be accurately dated, the memories they preserve of these fifteenth-century encounters provide an alternative picture to the one drawn in courtly accounts discussed in the previous chapters. For Forbes, these were the chieftains who went on to make up the Princely states of Gujarat, Kathiawad, and Kachchh; their political impact had longevity.

Forbes's *Rās Mālā* was also one of the first works to have extensively used the oral 'bardic' sources associated with the chieftains of Gujarat in an attempt to reconstruct their past. Earlier, seventeenth-century Marwari historian Munhata Nainsi wrote accounts based on oral traditions that included genealogies of some Rajputs associated with Gujarat.[2] Many of Gujarat's Rajput clans are also included in James Tod's monumental nineteenth-century work *Annals and Antiquities of Rajasthan.* While Nainsi viewed his narrative as a history of the Marwar kingdom, Tod was primarily concerned with the entire northwestern region of Rajputana or Rajasthan that had become more predominantly associated with the royal Rajput clans.

By contrast, *Rās Mālā* presents itself as a history of the region the author considered Gujarat. Forbes often uses the generic term 'bardic authority' to describe the oral narratives of the Bhats and the Charans. The works of these poets form an important parallel tradition to the Gujarati and Sanskrit texts

[2] Nainsi Munhata, *Muṅhatā Naiṇsīrī Khyāt.*

discussed in the preceding chapters. Forbes's detailed engagement with 'bardic authority' reflects the fact that it was these oral traditions and the stories of their warrior patrons that remained in circulation over several centuries and were the main sources of the region's history identified by him in the early years of colonial rule.

Based on oral sources, *Rās Mālā* was one of the few volumes covering a vast temporal expanse of Gujarat's history prior to the publication of the official colonial Gazetteers in the second half of the nineteenth century. In his introduction to the 1878 edition of the book, Major J. W. Watson, then the British Resident based in Rajkot, noted, 'There are but few other books of reference about Goozerat, and none of them so encyclopaedic in character.'[3] The *Rās Mālā* remains an important 'source' for Gujarati history and several Gujarati writers and historians have viewed it as a historical work or 'history book' as well as a source of historical raw materials for the study of the region's medieval past.[4] In the nineteenth century, as the only work of its kind, it shaped Gujarati writers' views of their own region and its history.[5]

Several historians have written about the production of knowledge in colonial India. Scholars like Bernard Cohn, Ronald Inden, Nicholas Dirks [6] and others have argued that the colonial rule introduced entirely new forms of knowledge in India that were imposed on colonial society and facilitated the colonial agenda of conquest. On the other hand, scholars C. A. Bayly, Eugene Irschick, Thomas Trautmann, Norbert Peabody, and Phillip Wagoner have suggested that the colonised were not merely passive recipients of these new forms of knowledge but often collaborated in their formation through their

---

[3] Watson, introduction to Forbes, *Râs Mâlâ*, ix.

[4] Sherry Chand and Kothari, 'Undisciplined History,' 72–73.

[5] Isaka, 'Gujarati Intellectuals and History Writing,' 4867–72. Isaka has discussed how *Rās Mālā* shaped the structure and understanding of Gujarati historical writing. She argues that these writers did not blindly emulate Forbes's work but in fact produced their own understanding of the region, recognising the importance of the regional sultanate. Isaka suggests that Forbes and other colonial writers were uniformly critical of the Muslim rule. However, while Forbes appears generally critical of 'Mohammedan sword', my reading suggests that his understanding of the regional sultans was complex and he in fact equates them to the Chaulukya rulers, whom he sees as a great Hindu dynasty.

[6] Cohn, *An Anthropologist Among the Historians;* Inden, 'Orientalist Constructions of India,' 401–46 and *Imagining India,* Dirks, 'Colonial Histories and Native Informants,' 279–313, and *Castes of Mind.*

own expertise in indigenous knowledge systems.[7] This symbiosis led to the continuation of a number of indigenous forms of knowledge in the colonial period and often played an important role in the way colonial knowledge was systematised and codified.[8] *Rās Mālā* makes this second line of argument particularly persuasive. A careful reading of *Rās Mālā* reveals a multilayered text that was based on a wide variety of sources and was a product of numerous contributors, especially for Forbes's chief assistant, Dalpatram, and the traditional genealogist-poets. This involvement, I suggest, shaped the manner in which *Rās Mālā* represented the chieftains of Gujarat and their precolonial political structures. However, I extend the arguments made by these scholars to suggest that in foregrounding the bardic and mostly non-classical and non-Sanskritic works of literature, Forbes's *Rās Mālā,* 'A Garland of Chronicles', portrayed a region shaped by the Rajput chieftains rather than in more contemporary narratives, a land of trade and commerce.

The project of collecting materials on the history and culture of Indian people by British officials was not a new one. Forbes was continuing a colonial tradition, and he appears to have been familiar with James Forbes's and Mountstuart Elphinstone's writing on western India, as well as with Grant Duff's work on the Marathas and John Malcolm's work on central India. At the time Forbes came to India, James Tod's momentous work on the Rajputs, *Annals and Antiquities of Rajasthan*, was already well known. With his training in the Company's Haileybury College in England, and the influence of the grand old men of the British administration in India weighing on him, Forbes set out on a crusade to understand, and thus arguably to control, indigenous society on its own terms. His journey was undoubtedly fuelled by personal curiosity, but it also served a colonial purpose, taking him into the realm of indigenous knowledge institutions and to the politics of the Indian Princely States.

Gujarat in Forbes's Time

The British took over the administration of Ahmadabad and other parts of Gujarat from the Marathas in 1808 and incorporated them into the wider area of

---

[7] Bayly, 'Knowing the Country: Empire and Information in India,' and *Empire and Information*; Irschick, *Dialogue and History*; Trautmann, 'Inventing the History of South India,' 36–54; Peabody, 'Cents, Sense, Census,' 819–50; Wagoner, 'Precolonial Intellectuals,' 783–814.

[8] For a more detailed exposition of the two strands of arguments, see Wagoner, 'Precolonial Intellectuals,' 783–86. See also Sreenivasan, *Many Lives of a Rajput Queen*, 119–20.

the Bombay Presidency. This led to the introduction of a new climate of peace for the promotion of trade, a development that was greatly appreciated by the merchant classes who were quick to adapt to the ways of the new government.[9] In Ahmadabad and other major cities of Gujarat, there generally emerged an attitude of cooperation between the British and the indigenous merchants, both of whom understood the value in increasing profits. In these big cities, the impact of the British government was primarily manifested in a new climate for enterprise and the gradual emergence of a new social class consisting of Western-educated government officials, lawyers, teachers, and small traders. Several men from the traditionally wealthy families also became involved in governmental affairs, and thus promoted and benefited from the social and economic processes that had been set in motion by the British.[10]

While the British annexed some parts of Gujarat, particularly trading centres like Ahmadabad, Surat, and Bharuch, the kingdoms of most of the indigenous chieftains were not brought under their direct control. Like the regional sultans, Mughals, and Marathas before them, the British brought the kingdoms of the plains under their control with ease but found it difficult to do the same with those that lay in areas of difficult topography, such as the salt flats of Kachchh or the jungle uplands of Rewa Kantha and Kathiawad.[11] Their remoteness from the heartland of imperial power made setting up administration hazardous and costly. The fragmented and fissiparous thrust of the politics in these regions posed further difficulties in establishing direct control.[12] The British organised and grouped these 'native' or Princely states into various agencies, which, according to their size and power, were supervised on behalf of the East India Company's government by Residents or Political Agents.

This pattern of political administration led to a two-tiered administrative system in the region: in one part of Gujarat, a fragmented political system was replaced by a uniform administration connected to the Bombay Presidency and the wider colonial imperial network; in other parts, the British engagement was active, but the integration of the Princely states into the wider all-India colonial network was only gradual.[13] In the first half of the nineteenth century, the British government struggled to control the Maratha incursions into these

[9] Mehta, *The Ahmedabad Cotton Textile Industry*; Joshi, 'Dalpatram and the Nature of Literary Shifts, 327–57.

[10] Mehta, *The Ahmedabad Cotton Textile Industry*, 7.

[11] Copland, *The British Raj*, 2.

[12] Copland, *The British Raj,* 15–16.

[13] Desai, *Social Change in Gujarat*, 96.

states, to curb the internal warfare between them, and as their predecessors in the region had done to establish lasting revenue relations. During this period in which the British were expanding their reach over different parts of Gujarat, and were competing with the Marathas and the chieftains for the region's political and economic resources, questions of sovereignty were of utmost importance.

It was against this backdrop that Alexander Forbes came to western India. Like many of the East India Company's administrators, Forbes was of Scottish descent. He had been an apprentice at a London-based firm of architects in the late 1830s, but he was soon nominated to the Civil Service of the East India Company in 1840. After training at the Company's Haileybury College, he travelled to India in the winter of 1843, where he was appointed Assistant Collector of Ahmednagar in the Bombay Presidency. This was the beginning of Forbes's long career in western India. Today, Forbes is remembered more for his literary and cultural engagement in the region than for his administrative acumen, for, from the outset, he encouraged the development of literary societies, newspapers, and schools.

Forbes's attitude to governance was deeply influenced by the European Romanticism of early British administrators in India such as Thomas Munro (1761–1827), John Malcolm (1769–1833), and Mountstuart Elphinstone (1779–1859). Their philosophical sensibilities led to a personalised, benevolent, and paternalistic style of rule.[14] Good governance was to be nurtured by developing sympathetic understandings of India and its people. Further, as administrators, they were sensitive to history as an organic expression of a society's character and thus were anxious to conserve India's enduring institutions as they saw them. Men like Malcolm endeavoured to rehabilitate and reclaim for the Company what they conceived of as an Indian tradition of personal government.[15] They believed in a style of governance that was committed to a sympathetic understanding of India and its people through the development of an intimate knowledge of the country. Elphinstone, for instance, wrote a two-volume work on Indian history with extensive borrowings from the work of the early philologist 'orientalists' but based the authority of his scholarship on his own extensive perusal of historical documents and personal experience of being in India. He was convinced that India could not be understood merely through its texts and grammars,[16] nor separated from its people. Such ideas are visible in Forbes's personal practices as well as in the

[14] Metcalf, *Ideologies of the Raj*, 24–26.
[15] Metcalf, *Ideologies of the Raj*, 25.
[16] Dirks, 'Colonial Histories,' 281.

institutions he established and nourished, and they are expressed explicitly, as we shall see, in the design and intention of *Rās Mālā.*

In his memoir of Forbes, Manasukhram Suryarama Tripathi's observations reflect an inclination towards this paternalistic style of governance. Tripathi, who was the honorary secretary of the Gujarati Sabha, a literary organisation that Forbes helped set up, at the time of the Forbes's death, notes that when the administrator travelled all over the region he preferred to go on foot.[17] On these journeys Forbes would always carry a map, a bag of money, a pistol, and a stick. On the way, as he met different people he would speak to them as though he was an ordinary man rather than an important officer of the East India Company. This way, writes Tripathi, Forbes would learn all the news of the land: local habits and practices; people's joys, sorrows, and superstitions; and help anyone who appeared to be in distress or difficulty.

In a later memoir, in the 1924 reprint of *Rās Mālā,* H. G. Rawlinson notes that Forbes was aware of the shortcomings of the 'native' princes' and chieftains' policies of governance. Yet he was critical of the Company government's attempts to impose control over the Indian kingdoms by interfering in matters of succession and other internal issues.[18] He instead believed that reform and improvement in these kingdoms would have to come from without, not 'in a policy of wholesale annexation, but in establishing a civil service with tact, sympathy, and knowledge of the people, to be able to guide the administration of the native states along proper lines'.[19] It was in these terms that Forbes perceived his project of collecting, collating, and writing the history of the region for the aid of his colleagues and successors.

Forbes's activities in creating and encouraging the nascent institutions of civil society, such as literary societies, newspapers, and schools, in the parts of Gujarat in which he served, illuminate his personal interest in the region, in addition to his philosophy of governance. For instance, in 1848, while serving as a judge and sessions judge in Ahmadabad, Forbes was instrumental,

---

[17] Tripathi, *Fārbas jīvan caritra*, 17. This memoir was written in order to accompany the Gujarati translation of the *Rās Mālā*, published in the same year.

[18] Rawlinson, 'Alexander Kinloch Forbes,' xi. Unless otherwise specified, I use this edition of the text throughout the chapter. It is noteworthy that after its publication in 1856, the *Rās Mālā* was reprinted with an introduction by J. W. Watson and a memoir of the author by A. K. Nairne in 1878. See A. K. Forbes, *Rās Mālā*. In 1924, it saw another reprint, this time with a memoir by Rawlinson. The 1997 edition that I have used is the reprint of the 1924 publication.

[19] Rawlinson, 'Alexander Kinloch Forbes,' xi..

along with other officials, in establishing the Gujarat Vernacular Society for the promotion of the Gujarati language. Forbes had first been introduced to Indian languages and literature, particularly through Sir William Jones's work on Sanskrit, while studying at Haileybury. In India, he passed examinations in Hindi and Marathi and later, when posted in Ahmadabad, he also began learning Gujarati, initially from a certain Rao Bahadur Bhogilal Pranvallabhdas and then from Dalpatram, whom he met in 1848.

In 1850, Forbes was appointed assistant judge and sessions judge in Surat. As in Ahmadabad, here, too, he initiated and became involved in a number of civic activities. He started a weekly newspaper called *Surat Samachar* and helped to set up a library. At the behest of the Bombay government, he also took on the post of the 'city improvement officer', during which he worked towards creating awareness about various civic matters among the people of Surat.[20] In 1851, Forbes returned to Ahmadabad as the first assistant collector, and in 1852 he was appointed Political Agent at Mahi Kantha. In the following year, he became the assistant judge and sessions judge at Ahmadabad. In 1854, Forbes returned to England, where he completed *Rās Mālā.*

Back in India in 1856, Forbes was sent to Surat as acting judge and later worked in the same capacity at Khandesh. In 1859, however, his expertise on the region was acknowledged by Lord Elphinstone, the then Governor of Bombay Presidency. Elphinstone appointed him Political Agent of Kathiawad, with the particular aim of subjugating some 'recalcitrant chieftains' and the piratical 'rebel' Vaghers of Okhamandal. After serving in Gujarat for a few more years, Forbes was appointed judge at the *Sadar Adalat* (High Court) at Bombay in 1862. In Bombay, Forbes continued to be involved in various activities related to the promotion and preservation of Gujarat's history and culture. In 1864, he was offered the presidency of the Bombay Branch of the Royal Asiatic Society but he declined the position, and chose to be its vice-president instead. In the same year, he was appointed vice-chancellor of the Bombay University. In Bombay, as in Ahmadabad, he received the support of the city's elites for his zeal for establishing societies and newspapers promoting the Gujarati language. Thus, a number of prominent citizens of Bombay interested in Gujarat approached him to help set up the Gujarati Sabha for the same cause. The Sabha, which was later renamed the Farbas (Forbes) Sabha, was established in March 1865 with Forbes as its president. Soon after this, Forbes, who had suffered from a long term illness, died in Pune in the August of the same year.

---

[20] Tripathi, *Fārbas jīvan caritra* 11–12.

The Gujarati Sabha's formation can be seen as a major step by the nationalist-minded elite of the region towards the invention of a common self-identity, a process that had taken hold in other parts of the subcontinent as well. Not long after the publication of Forbes's voluminous work did a number of these elites also begin the collection and composition of literary works they associated with Gujarat. Forbes's scholarly endeavours and involvement in these institutions provided legitimacy and facilitated this production of a new regional identity. In addition to his involvement with the urban elite, Forbes also appears to have been engaged in the production of a more specific idea of Gujarat as a region based on its literary past, particularly in less urban areas where vestiges of the Rajputs, their clans, and poets, were still visible. In the following sections, I explore these aspects of Forbes's collection project and its ultimate product, *Rās Mālā.*

Rās Mālā **and Gujarat's Bardic Tradition**

Alexander Forbes used a variety of sources in the writing of *Rās Mālā*, but the Bhats, Charans, and other communities of itinerant poets were his most important. Thus, not only were the Rajputs Forbes's protagonists, but their own poet-historians also animated the narrative. In the preface to *Rās Mālā*, Forbes notes that not long after he had moved to Gujarat, that he came across documents that bore the characteristic signatures of 'two bards', signs indicative of an economic structure that he had never encountered before.[21] These documents and their composers aroused his curiosity, and he sought more information about these men, their dialect, and their repertoire, which would, he believed, be the 'means of unlocking the casket in which the treasure was contained' – meaning the indigenous economic and social system of Gujarat.[22] To circumvent administrative difficulties, Forbes sought the aid of local elites and scholars; what he found were accounts and administrative documents written by bards, whose role in the political, social and religious world of the chieftains was on the decline. The bardic documents that Forbes was interested in were directly connected to the different ruling clans scattered all over the region and with whom the British were interacting at the time as part of their policy of territorial expansion. It may have been the richness of information about the chieftains contained in these sources that prompted Forbes to take

[21] Forbes, *Rās Mālā*, vol.1, xx.
[22] Forbes, *Rās Mālā*, vol.1, xx–xxi.

steps toward reviving the bardic institution for a new era, albeit without the poets' prior political and administrative functions.

Since at least the twelfth century, communities of Bhats and Charans had been an integral part of the numerous royal houses of Gujarat, Kathiawad, and Kachchh, for whom they kept genealogical records and maintained family histories. The Charan poets often travelled with their patrons during battles and performed praises of their deeds in order to inspire the warriors. Serving several other political and ritual functions for the Rajput clans, the poets' position *vis-á-vis* their patrons had been a complex one as these bards performed numerous secular and religious roles. As poets, they composed and chanted verses in their own unique styles and metres. Their compositions were generally in praise of a renowned warrior from the patron's putative ancestor, in commemoration of a victory, or in praise of a present chieftain. Historically, they were known for accompanying the armies of their patrons into battle and for inspiring the soldiers to fight by loudly chanting poems about the commanding chieftain and his lineage.[23] The two main castes of Bhats and Charans were further subdivided in smaller groups, some of whom kept written records of the genealogies and poems, while others committed them to memory.[24] As not only poets but genealogists, these bards helped affirm their patrons' links to prestigious mythological or historical ancestors and assert their social positions among other Rajput groups.

In addition, bards commanded great respect among their patrons because they themselves were considered directly linked to the goddess; hence, their presence was perceived as sacred, or even favourable, in mediations related to diplomatic or revenue transactions between kingdoms. Their ethical and moral power in these instances was further enhanced by their willingness to perform self-harm, or *traga*, which sometimes included suicide, self immolation, or the murder of a female relative, to enforce compliance with an agreement. Shedding the blood of a Charan or Bhat was seen to bring great misfortune to the person responsible, as it was believed that these groups were mother goddess worshippers and in fact the goddess's children. This symbolic but very real power allowed the bardic group to play key roles in the functioning of western Indian society until the early nineteenth century. Inevitably, the linguistic wares of these godly poets were fiercely protected, as they both

23 Singhji, *The Rajputs of Saurashtra*, 239.

24 See Shah and Shroff, 'The Vahīvancā Bāroṭs of Gujarat,' 40–70. This study by Shah and Shroff is a seminal work on these genealogists whose traditions still remain neglected in contemporary scholarship.

legitimised and perpetuated rule in many of the chieftaincies, and served important diplomatic and martial purposes. The bards' hold over the ruling houses of the region thus posed a significant challenge to the authority of the colonial administration's financial, territorial, and legal aims. In the early years of colonial rule, the British systematically delegitimised their duties, curtailing their administrative functions, and rendered them redundant to the new political order.[25] By the time that Forbes started working in Gujarat, the role of bards, an institution that was once crucial to the identity and authority of the Rajput chieftains, was on the decline.

Rās Mālā and its Making

Rās Mālā begins with a description of what Forbes considers to be Gujarat's natural boundaries, and in the first section, tells the story of the early medieval (eighth- to thirteenth-century) dynasties of Patan and Kathiawad. The second book is an account of the 'Mohumeddan' period in Gujarat, but true to Forbes's own agenda, it focuses mainly on the Rajput chieftains, their clans, and their political relations with the regional sultans during the fourteenth to the sixteenth centuries. In the third book, which covers the eighteenth and early nineteenth centuries, Forbes writes of the Maratha empire, and then the beginning of British rule in India. Even though the periodisation in the second and third books is determined by the dominant rulers of those periods, namely, the 'Mohumeddans' and the 'Mahrattas', respectively, Forbes is primarily concerned with the 'Rajpoots' or warrior chieftains who, he believed, formed the substratum of the political landscape of the region during this time. 'The story of these Hindoo chieftainships is our principal concern,' he notes.[26] In both these books, Forbes focuses on the chieftains' relations with the two categories of dominant rulers and eventually with their involvement with the British.

Finally, in the fourth book, entitled *Conclusions*, Forbes's focus shifts to a mixture of topics including the different Hindu castes of Gujarat; Rajput land tenures under the 'Mohumeddans', Marathas, and the British; as well as to festivals and other social rites and rituals that were current among the Hindus in the region at the time. The focus on the chieftains renders the rule of the Mughals, and the Marathas, marginal to Forbes's imagination of Gujarat's history. Forbes almost entirely ignores Mughal rule over Gujarat but expresses

[25] Neil Rabitoy discusses this process in detail. See Rabitoy, 'Administrative Organisation and the Bhats,' 46–73.

[26] Forbes, *Rās Mālā*, vol.1, 276

his admiration for the regional sultans. The Marathas, however, are treated with utmost disdain. He regards them as 'vulgar', 'wily', and 'mercenary' at various points in the book. This attitude is shaped perhaps by Forbes's own experience of the turbulent relations between the British and the Marathas; his genuine affection for the subjects of his study, the chieftains; and his view that the British were the most benevolent of the rulers to have controlled the region in the face of its current political condition.[27] Thus, *Rās Mālā* covers a vasr-temporal range but focuses most specifically on the chieftains and their clans, their kingdoms, and their political relations. Like other colonial writers, Forbes also views the arrival of the British as the panacea of the region. The historical account in the text ends in 1838, with the settlement of and control of the district of Mahi Kantha, where he would become Political Agent, when 'the British influence became paramount throughout Goozerat'.[28]

As noted, the sources of *Rās Mālā* are varied, though it is the contents and the tone of 'bardic' legends that dominate the narrative. The first book combines Jain texts such as Hemacandra's twelfth-century grammatical and historical work, *Dwayaśraya*, and Merutunga's fourteenth-century work *Prabandhacintāmaṇi,* 'wishing-stone of chronicles'.[29] Brahmin poet Krishnaji's poem dedicated to the Chaulukya rulers, entitled *Ratan Mālā* or 'garland of jewels', and the work of the bardic poet Chund Bardai, who wrote the biography of the legendary Chauhan king Prithviraja. In the second book, Forbes relies more on the accounts of the Persian histories like the *Tārīkh-i Firishtā* and the *Mir'āt-i-Aḥmadī* to discuss the specific details of the regional sultans but still bases the account more substantially on the bardic narratives. Similarly, in the third book, which is also the last of the historical sections of *Rās Mālā*, Forbes's account relies on these oral narratives about the chieftains but uses Alexander Grant Duff's *History of the Mahrattas* (1826) and James Forbes's *Oriental Memoirs* (1813–1815) to describe the history of the Marathas. While the Rajputs remain the focus of the narrative in this section, British involvement in Gujarat is clearly seen as beneficial both for the Indian chieftains as well as the Marathas.

Forbes, however, is cautious about the 'factual' value of the Indian sources he uses. He writes, 'The present work is wholly popular, and advances no claims to scientific value.'[30] For instance, he sees the Hindu traditions as

---

[27] Rawlinson, 'Alexander Kinloch Forbes,' xvi; see also Sherry Chand and Kothari, 'Undisciplined History,' 76.

[28] Forbes, *Rās Mālā*, vol. 2, 218.

[29] See Chapter 1 in this monograph for more on these texts.

[30] Forbes, *Rās Mālā,* vol. 1, xxii.

'destitute of historical foundation'[31] and warns against the exaggerations that are integral to bardic tales. The Jain accounts, he says, are more concerned with 'ecclesiastical transactions' than 'civil affairs' but, in both cases, 'they rather content themselves with anecdotes than attempt a connected relation'.[32] He is, however, somewhat more convinced of the Jain sources' validity as records of 'facts' than their Hindu counterparts.[33] He is also critical of the 'Mohumeddan historians', who for the most part describe the Hindu chieftains 'only under the title of infidels, insurgents or rebels' even though it is clear, he claims, that neither the sultans nor the Mughals were ever able to effect their complete subjugation.[34] Forbes's critique of the 'Musalaman' period is not different from the norm at the time, yet he is in constant admiration of the regional sultans, at least until Sultan Mahmud Begada's rule.

Even though the poetry may have exaggerated facts, which, Forbes notes, was also the case in the medieval kingdoms of Europe; 'there is often in the bardic sketches much of spirit, and of effective, however rude, colour and drawing.'[35] To justify the poems' accuracy, Forbes further cites the author of a book entitled *The Lives of the Queens of England* (1844). Overall, the bardic accounts that he collected were, he thought, similar to those found in England and in Europe. He writes, 'Where they are written, and *are intelligible without oral explanation* (author's emphasis), [they] may rank with the contemporaneous ballad poetry of other nations; where unwritten, they approximate to common oral tradition.'[36]

The *Rās Mālā* was clearly composed for an English readership and is generously interspersed with references to European mythology and folk legends, as well as parallels drawn from the Shakespeare's plays. Thus for instance, the birth of the founder of Anhilvada–Patan, Vanraja, is compared with the birth of king Edward's son in Shakespeare's *King Henry IV*.[37] Similarly,

---

[31] Forbes, *Rās Mālā,* vol. 1, 228–29.

[32] Forbes, *Rās Mālā,* vol. 1, 228–229.

[33] Forbes, *Rās Mālā,* vol. 1, 229.

[34] 'The Mohummedan historians, for the most part, refer to them only under the titles of infidels, insurgents, or rebels. From the accounts, however, which the Moslems themselves have left us…it is clear that Goozerat was very far from having been conquered even by the lieutenants of Allah-ood-deen. The task had to be attempted again and again by his successors, and was in fact…never fully accomplished.' Forbes, *Rās Mālā,* vol. 1, 276.

[35] Forbes, *Rās Mālā*, vol. 2, 265.

[36] Forbes, *Rās Mālā,* vol. 2, 265–66.

[37] Forbes, *Rās Mālā*, vol. 1, 33.

the legend of Siddharaja's use of spirits (*bhoots*) to construct a water tank is compared to the practice in France of attributing 'everything possessing any extraordinary character … by the credulity of the former generations, either to the fairies, the devil, Caesar.'[38] These parallels seem to give *Rās Mālā* a universal and familiar quality for the English or European reader.[39] In the preface to the book, Forbes specifies his perceptions of the uses to which his work may be put. He writes, '… it may … be of use to the local officer, and may interest some few even of my countrymen at home, in the fortunes of their fellow subjects – the Hindoos in Goozerat.'[40] Indeed, in the 1878 edition of *Rās Mālā*, J. W. Watson, then the Political Agent of Rajkot, reiterated Forbes's work's continuing use for the purposes of the administration.[41]

As legible as Forbes wanted his work to be to English audiences, the bulk of *Rās Mālā* is based not on European classics or even familiar literary forms but on Forbes's collection and interpretation of the bardic legends. As his assistant, Dalpatram was tasked with facilitating Forbes's understanding of these oral traditions of the Bhat and Charanas. He gave Forbes ready access to this otherwise closed and secretive world, providing skilled and erudite translation and exegesis of the poetic historical epics of the Bhats and Charans. He became so indispensable because, through his own personal acquaintance and reputation, he allowed Forbes access to this otherwise hidden world. The precise style and politics of the traditional poets of the region would probably not have been comprehensible to Forbes without Dalpatram's guidance. However, the poets of the region were not merely neutral containers of historical wisdom; their presentations, as I have noted, were eulogistic, but also dynastic, and directed by the needs of courtly politics of the time. It was the accounts of such men that became the basis of much of the *Rās Mālā*.

Prior to his meeting Forbes in 1848, Dalpatram had been closely associated with this category of court poets. Despite being born to a family of priests, Dalpatram had chosen to follow the Swaminarayan sect and a career in composing poetry in Brajbhasha, the language associated with Bhats. He travelled extensively over Kathiawad and Kachchh, attending poetic gatherings or *sabhas*. In these gatherings, many of which took place in temple precincts and sometimes at royal courts, Bhats and Charans would be encouraged, either by the patron or the audience, to prove their skills over one another.

[38] Forbes, *Rās Mālā*, vol. 1, 159.
[39] See Sherry Chand and Kothari, 'Undisciplined History', 75.
[40] Forbes, *Rās Mālā*, vol. 1, xxii.
[41] Watson, Introduction, ix.

Dalpatram often competed in these sessions and succeeded in proving his poetic abilities against the traditional poets. He gradually became well known in and outside Kathiawad and was honoured by the king of Idar and later by the *maharao* or ruler of Kachchh. He was also invited by poetry-loving *seths*, wealthy merchants, of Ahmadabad to perform at gatherings held in their homes.[42] Yet, despite his popularity among the wealthy elite, patronage remained intermittent, and he was not able to find a permanent patron to fulfil his ambition of becoming a 'court poet', or *rajakavi,* who could compose in Brajbhasha and in the Dimgal style, like some of the Bhats. Since Dalpatram was a Brahmin by caste, his desire to find a position equal to the Bhats, however, speaks of the significance of their literary works and social positions in Gujarat and western India.

Forbes heard about Dalpatram and his skills in poetry through Bholanath Sarabhai, a colleague at the court in Ahmadabad. In the winter of 1848, he summoned Dalpatram from his hometown, Wadhwan, to Ahmadabad, in order to assist him in his task of gathering Gujarat's history and poetry. Dalpatram subsequently wrote of his meeting and interaction with his English employer in very emotional terms.[43] Forbes's own account does not mention the encounters

---

[42] Dalpatram, *Kaviśvar Dalpatram*, vol.1, 174–76.

[43] Dalpatram describes the experience in the following words:

> After studying the different poetic ornamentations,
> My heart was bound to poetry;
> I was looking everywhere for a leader of men,
> I was calling out for him in the world of god,
> In the court of a generous and sincere patron,
> I had the desire to find a place,
> As these thoughts came to my mind, says Dalpat,
> Fārbas's summons arrived just at that opportune moment.
> At the gates of Khanpur [Ahmadabad] near the banks of the river,
> I met him at the sun-moon palace [name of Forbes's residence];
> It was the year 1848 of the Christian era,
> There was complete affection in the first meeting itself,
> It increased five times when he [Forbes] was close and ten times when he was afar,
> The love increased during the pleasant companionship…'

Dahyabhai, *Fārbasviraha,* vol. 1, 2–3. During the period in which they worked together, close bonds of friendship developed between Forbes and Dalpatram. These are reflected in this long poem in Gujarati, which can be translated as 'The Sadness of Separation from Forbes' that Dalpatram composed after Forbes's death. In this poem, Dalpatram expresses deep sadness for the loss of bygone days shared with Forbes and describes his mentor and friend in eulogistic and even somewhat romantic terms.

between the two men with the same degree of sentiment. However, Forbes acknowledges the debt he owes to his Indian collaborator by noting that since they first met his 'valuable co-adjutor' had been almost constantly by his side.[44] Forbes furnished his new assistant with the means to travel all over Gujarat so as to look for chronicles and to copy inscriptions. He himself travelled to many parts of the region during his official work and took every opportunity to gather information about its history from local poets and Jain repositories known as *bhandars*. In these travels, Dalpatram acted as his assistant, guide, and interpreter.

The efforts of the two men did not only result in the compilation of the *Rās Mālā* but also led to the formation of a number of societies and newspapers for the promotion of Gujarati language and of the ideas of reform.[45] Dalpatram became actively involved in the work of the Gujarat Vernacular Society, and from 1855 onwards served as its secretary and the editor of its journal. Prior to this he had also been involved in Forbes's reformist and philanthropic activities. Dalpatram continued to be involved in the Society's work after Forbes's death.[46] Of more specific significance to the making of the *Rās Mālā* is the fact that Forbes based the fourth book of the text almost entirely on two Gujarati essays by his assistant.[47]

---

[44] Forbes, *Rās Mālā*, vol. I, xxi.

[45] See also Mehta and Mehta, 'Dalpatrām ane Aleksāndar Forbes,' 14.

[46] Dalpatram went on to become one of the preeminent reformist poets writing in Gujarati in the nineteenth century. As has been noted, prior to meeting Forbes and becoming involved in his historical endeavours, Dalpatram had been well known for his poetry in Brajbhasha, rather than Gujarati. However, his engagement with the welfare of Gujarat and the promotion of the Gujarati language seems to have developed only after his interaction with Forbes and his involvement with the Gujarat Vernacular Society. This is also the time when he began composing poetry in Gujarati. In this regard, Dalpatram appears to have shifted away from his earlier ambition of becoming a court poet in favour of a newer, more urbanised role as an assistant to a colonial officer, preferring to be the latter's guide and interpreter. It is worth reiterating that his interaction with Forbes, the idea that this great colonial officer was leading Gujarat to the restoration of its past glory, and his own role as an agent of this restoration were crucial in Dalpatram's re-articulation of himself as an urban reformist poet serving the cultural and ideological needs of the Ahmadabadi elite, rather than a wandering poet seeking his fortunes in the princely houses whose influence and power were on the decline.

[47] This section differs from the rest of the book as it introduces its reader, who Forbes imagined to be a young British officer serving in the region, to different aspects of Hindu society in Gujarat. It deals, as has been noted, with the descriptions of the dominant castes, customs, religious and secular practices, and with land tenures. The bulk of this

About the title of his work, Forbes notes, 'In imitation of the titles of some the legends from which it is derived, I have called my compilation "Rās Mālā" or "A Garland of Chronicles".'[48] *Rās Mālā's* title itself draws from different aspects of the region's oral traditions. While the use of the term 'chronicle', a historical account that is chronological or arranged according to linear time, the Gujarati term *rasa* does not carry the same association of linearity or time.[49] The word *rasa*, or *rasau*, has at least three meanings, all derived from oral traditions of different kinds. One meaning of *rasa* has origins in the Jain tradition of composing biographical and historical works with moral teachings for the community. While many of the works were written down, they were also recited by Jain preceptors to convey the deeds of great men of the faith. *Rasa* is also the type of poem set to music that is associated with a folk dance form in Gujarat, and finally, *rasa* or *rasa lila* are the terms used for the Puranic deity Krishna's dancing dalliances with his female friends, the *gopis*.[50] The *Rās Mālā* does follow a broad chronological approach but, as we shall see, its use of literary works and oral traditions as sources gives it a far more fluid character compared to the more standard Western-style works of history that were being written in the nineteenth century.

Chieftains and Sultans in *Rās Mālā*

Rās Mālā does not follow a strict dynastic approach to the history of Gujarat but interweaves stories of individual kings and ambitious warriors, descriptions of places of interest, and the oral histories of different clans in a fluid manner. The sources set the texture of the narrative, which often oscillates between

section is based on essays entitled 'Demonology and Popular Superstitions in Gujarat' (*Bhoot Nibandh*), and an 'Essay on Caste' (*Jñāti Nibandh*), both by Dalpatram and translated by Forbes in 1850. Both these essays were based entirely on the author's own experiences and native knowledge of the region. Forbes's conclusions about the nature of contemporary Gujarati society were thus drawn from this Brahmin poet-scholar's observations and experiences. Soon after its establishment in 1848, the Gujarat Vernacular Society announced an essay competition on the topic of spirits and popular superstitions prevalent in Gujarat. Forbes encouraged Dalpatram to send an entry, not so much for the grand prize money of rupees one hundred and fifty but for the prestige it would bring him if he won. After its translation by Forbes in 1850, the *Bhoot Nibandh* was also translated in to Urdu and Marathi.

48 Forbes, *Rās Mālā*, vol. I, xxii.

49 Sherry Chand and Kothari, 'Undisciplined History,' 72.

50 Sherry Chand and Kothari, 'Undisciplined History,' 72.

the formal scholarly tones of the author's own writing and the more informal voice of the bard or a Jain narrative; it also contains occasional quotes from Persian histories. Legends about Rajput warriors are often interspersed with descriptions of towns and cities within Gujarat in which history, mythology, and Forbes's own observations about the place are vividly woven together. In this regard, the narrative reflects a differential temporality, where different time periods along with their varying mythologies, histories, and territories appear to have seamlessly merged with one another. Interestingly, however, the fluidities and multiplicities contained in *Rās Mālā* appear to jostle with the aims of colonial power as well as contribute to the colonial knowledge-building processes that were at work in this period.[51]

As a colonial officer who was concerned with revenue settlement and the control, pacification, and administration of areas that were not entirely under British influence, Forbes was certainly creating a compendium useful for the future generations of Englishmen who he imagined would serve in Gujarat. Like his predecessors, such as Tod or Mckenzie, he understood that his endeavour to gather and compile the information about the people of the region was directly linked to the needs of colonial government that was trying to establish its control in different parts of the subcontinent. Forbes's own views are also not devoid of the impulses of his time, which sought to present a picture of a homogenous region with social and political institutions that could be compared against those at home. However, a close reading of the text also reveals the tensions that exist between Forbes's precolonial sources and his own attempts to unite, classify, and familiarise.

Even though the kingdoms and territories he wrote about were subsumed in Bombay Presidency at the time, Forbes saw Gujarat as a distinct geographical region with a distinct identity. In his view Gujarat was composed of two portions: the continental segment, or Gujarat proper, and the peninsular projection into the Arabian Sea. The range of hills connecting the Vindhyas formed its eastern boundaries, while the Aravalli ranges to the north separated it from Malwa, Mewar, and Marwar. Kachchh and its salt desert, the Rann formed the northwestern and western boundaries, while the Gulf of Cambay constituted Gujarat's southern tip.[52] However, while Forbes set out the boundaries in such clear terms, his own account of the history of Rajputs gives a far more fluid picture of the political and cultural composition of the region. In *Rās Mālā*'s

[51] For the politics of the colonial involvement in collecting empirical data about India, see Ludden, 'Orientalist Empiricism,' 250–78.

[52] Forbes, *Rās Mālā*, vol. 1, 3.

bardic accounts, 'Rajpoot' warriors and kings originate, move, and settle in parts of Gujarat, Malwa, Sindh, and Rajasthan. This becomes particularly clear in the third book of the *Rās Mālā*, which focuses on British relations with the Rajputs and Marathas, Gujarat continues to appear as a cluster of small independent states rather than a homogenous region.

For instance, according to Forbes's bardic accounts, after the fall of Anhilvada–Patan at the hands of Sultan 'Ala' al-Din Khalji, various branches of the Vaghelas seem to have established themselves in different places, including Gondwana in central India.[53] Within Gujarat the Vaghelas also appear to have first settled to the west of the river Sabarmati and later in areas closer to the sultanate capitals of Ahamdabad and Champaner. Similarly, he records that a branch of the 'Purmâr race' and 'Shodhâ tribe', consisting of some two thousand people including their wives and children, entered Gujarat from Sindh on account of a famine in their original homeland of Parkar.[54] They established themselves at Muli in Kathiawad and were later joined by the Jutts, who were also from Sindh and migrated to Gujarat for the fear of the Padshah, who coveted their leader's daughter.[55] Throughout the *Rās Mālā*, particularly in the accounts of the reign of the regional sultans, we encounter the movement and settlements of numerous clans including Kolis and Kathis in different parts of the region. The Rathods of Idar, who feature prominently throughout *Rās Mālā*, on the other hand, were in fact able to retain their patrimonies and also expand and strengthen their hold in the surrounding areas, resulting in Idar emerging as the largest kingdom in the Mahi Kantha area during Forbes's own time. *Rās Mālā's* accounts thus attribute the acquisition, maintenance, and expansion of the patrimonies of the Rajput chieftains to the sultanate reign.

The fluid nature of the region is highlighted in several other accounts of the Rajputs during the rule of the regional sultans. For instance, in the story of Haloojee and Lugdheerjee, the Sodha Parmara chieftains from Kathiawad (as well as in the story of Jug Dev and the Vaghela brothers, explored in the sections to follow), we see the different levels of movement and migration that are reflected in the bardic accounts. Briefly, the tale is as follows. The beautiful daughter of the chief of the pastoralist Jutts who lived in Sindh was coveted by the 'Sindh padishah'. Consequently, the chieftain and his clansmen, 'about seventeen hundred in number', moved to Muli. At the time Muli was held by two brothers of the Sodha Paramara line, Haloojee and Lugdheerjee, who promised

[53] Forbes, *Rās Mālā*, vol. 1, 275 and 281.
[54] Forbes, *Rās Mālā*, vol. 1, 282–83.
[55] Forbes, *Rās Mālā*, vol. 1, 347.

to protect the Jutts. When the Sindhi monarch pursued the Jutts to Kathiawad, however, the Paramaras could not keep their promise because one of their own men betrayed them, and also because they lacked a proper protective fort.[56] The Jutt girl was forced to flee and eventually buried herself alive in a nearby village while Haloojee was imprisoned by the Sindhi army. Lugdheerjee at this point sought the aid of the 'King of Goozerat', who, at the time, was Sultan Mahmud Begada. The Sultan's armies arrived from Ahmadabad and the ruler of Sindh was successfully defeated in Bhuj. Haloojee converted to Islam and was offered lands by the Sultan within the sultanate territories. But Haloojee instead asked for the wasted lands of Ranpur, which had once belonged to his uncle, a Gohil, 'and had been ploughed and sown with salt by the padishah'.[57] Lugdheerjee, on the other hand, 'retained his religion and the Moolee estate acquired by his ancestors'.[58] The Jutts, we are told, treat the Muli Paramaras with a 'peculiar respect' in remembrance of the protection afforded to them.[59]

In this account, and in several others presented in *Rās Mālā* , the landscape is not a homogeneous unified region, but rather one of mobility, where different groups seeking service, protection or lands moved around freely. In the story of Haloojee and Lugdheerjee we also witness a freedom in the choices the brothers are able to make in embracing Islam or not in return for the Sultan's help. Forbes's idea of the region appears then to be led by his own colonial cartographic impulses to unite and categorise it in recognisable terms. In this regard as in other aspects, his sources reveal a somewhat different story.

The temporal contours of *Rās Mālā* are bound within the period between what Forbes calls 'ancient India' and the arrival of the British in Gujarat. This period, in Forbes's view, was 'more practically connected to present Hindoostan' than the previous one.[60] In the preface he defines the scope of the book with the following words:

> It is to the story of the city of Wun Raj [Anhilvad Patan], and of the Hindoo principalities and chieftainships which sprang up amidst its ruins, and which have many of them, continued in existence to the present day, that the reader's attention is in the present work invited.[61]

---

[56] Forbes, *Rās Mālā*, vol.1, 348
[57] Forbes, *Rās Mālā*, vol.1, 348
[58] Forbes, *Rās Mālā*, vol.1, 348
[59] Forbes, *Rās Mālā*, vol.1, 350
[60] Forbes, *Rās Mālā*, vol.1, ix–xx
[61] Forbes, *Rās Mālā*, vol.1, ix–xx.

Forbes finds further justification for this choice of subject in the fact that

> any stranger who is for any length of time resident in the land of the Hindoos, can hardly fail to notice many customs and usages of that people which are evidently relics of society not long gone ... The very remains of the Moslem power themselves are most strongly impressed by the character of the race whose rule was supplanted by that of the crescent ...[62]

In his study of this 'middle' period, Forbes finds a continuity of social and political traditions that are of utmost significance for his interpretation of the history of the region. Forbes does not have an explicit term for the period that lies between the 'ancient' and 'modern.' He does, however, draw extensively, though intermittently, on terminology from the feudal formations of medieval Europe to describe land and military relations in the region under scrutiny.

The 'story of the city of Wun Râj' is viewed by Forbes as the most glorious part of the region's pre-British history. While he is wary of falling prey to the exaggerations of its chroniclers, he himself sees the reign of the city's various dynasties, namely the Chavadas, Chaulukyas, and the Vaghelas, as a time of prosperity and grandeur, which were coveted by Muslim invaders like 'Mohumed Ghoree' and later 'Allh-ood-din Khyljy'. His understanding of the role of these dynasties in the history of the region is clearly reflected in his suggestion that at the time when the 'Chowrâ dynasty, under Wun Râj, first established itself at Unhilwârâ, the country of Goozerat was destitute of any other inhabitants than the wild aboriginal tribes.'[63] However, in the reign of the last of the Chaulukya or Solanki princes, he continues, 'we behold the same tract of country united under one strong government, studded with wealthy townships, adorned with populous cities, fenced with strong fortresses.'[64] Forbes clearly sees these rulers as the founders of all that is to be admired in the region's past.

Further, according to Forbes, the stability and prosperity that was brought by the rulers of Anhilvada was never to be found in the dynasties that followed. He writes:

> Never was she [Gujarat] for one hour not unwounded by domestic strife, from that day on which the sceptre was struck from the hand of Bheem Dev II, to

[62] Forbes, *Rās Mālā*, vol.1, ix.
[63] Forbes, *Rās Mālā*, vol.1, 248.
[64] Forbes, *Rās Mālā*, vol.1, 248–49.

> the long distant period when Rajpoot, Moslem, and Mahratta at length agreed to sheathe their swords, and repose for the just arbitrement of their quarrels on the power, the wisdom, and the faith of the sea-dwelling stranger.[65]

'Ala' al-Din's raids to Patan and Somanatha mark the final blow to the glory of Vanraj's great city. Forbes is certainly disapproving of the 'Moslem sword, then wielded by the furious hands of Allah-ood-deen, whose patronymic Khyljy is familiar to every peasant of Goozerat, under the substituted form "Khoonee," or "the murderer."'[66] Yet, even though he expresses his disapproval for this sultan and his lieutenants, his views about the period that follows betray a sense of ambiguity. The arrival of the Delhi sultans to the city of Anhilvada exhibits, according to him, a sense of anarchy. The chieftains that maintained their independence and form the subject of his study are also objects of his admiration. Forbes does repeatedly mention the fact that despite every attempt by 'Ala' al-Din and his successors, the regional sultans, the Mughals, and the hated Marathas, these chieftains managed to continue as independent rulers of their territories.

Despite his disapproval of the 'Moslem sword', Forbes is not critical of the dynasty of the regional sultans whose rule follows the period of disorganisation. He compares Ahmad Shah to Wan Raj, ancestor of the Chaulukya dynasty, calling him the 'founder of a new and brilliant dynasty'; Mahmud Begada to Siddharaja Jayasimha, considered one of the most prominent Chaulukya kings.[67] His account of many of their exploits is based directly on the *Mir'āt-i Aḥmadī*, but the dominating voice in these chapters is still that of the 'bardic authority' and their tales of the chieftains. As such, the influence of the sultans' rule is of course audible, but is somewhat muted by the colonial officer's reliance on the accounts of the Bhats and Charans. For Forbes, the period of sultanate rule is dominated by the movements of different 'clans' and chieftains trying to establish or maritime their control over agricultural lands, clusters of villages, or as is the case of the Gohils of Peerum, over parts of the maritime territory. It is this aspect of Gujarat's pre-British history that dominates *Rās Mālā*'s depiction of the region and which, according to Forbes, continues until the settlements of 'native' chiefs of these lands by the British.

---

[65] Forbes, *Rās Mālā*, vol.1, 249.

[66] Forbes, *Rās Mālā*, vol.1, 226.

[67] Forbes, *Rās Mālā*, vol. 1, 249. Of Begada he says, '…he inscribes upon the rolls of fame a title almost as glorious as the Lion of Unhilpoor'.

'Rajputs' in *Rās Mālā*

Forbes's account of the precolonial history of Gujarat, like the text itself, appears to be a patchwork of different ideas merged with the colonial writer's own observations and prejudices. As a colonial writer of the pre-1857 era, Forbes was perhaps not as explicitly concerned with the question of sovereignty as his successors would be and does not engage in an elaborate discussion of either this question or the nature of kingship.[68] Despite giving precedence to the 'Hindoo' chieftains in his account of Gujarat's history and society, he says little about the origins of the group as a whole in the *Rās Mālā*. Unlike James Tod, whose work he draws on extensively, Forbes does not explicitly mention a common origin theory or myth in relation to the chieftains. He often uses the categories 'Rajpoot' and 'Kshutrees' (Kshatriyas) interchangeably and does not make their meaning explicit. The two terms refer, throughout the book, to any non-Muslim chieftain or man of arms, and Forbes does not differentiate them by their origins or descent. The Chaulukya kings, whose chronicles and inscriptions make no mention of the term Rajput, are thus seamlessly equated with several lineages like the Gohils, Parmars, or Kathis of the later period, who were itinerant pastoralist groups that subsequently came to settle in the region.

On the basis of the collection of Jain chronicles, the *Ratan Mālā*, and some inscriptional records, Forbes evaluates, in his narrative, the position of the king or 'sovereign' in the days of Anhilvada's glory. The 'sovereign,' according to Forbes, is undoubtedly the most prominent figure in these records, 'supported by the white-robed priests of the Jain religion, or the Brahmanical wearers of the badge of regeneration.'[69] He imagines the 'sovereign' as the centre of a 'warlike circle', in which, after him and his priests, 'stand the warriors of Rajpoot race in ringed tunics' and the 'Wâneea [mercantile class], Muntreshwurs [ministers], already in professions puritans of peace, but not enough drained of their fiery Kshutree blood.'[70] These are followed by the 'half-warrior' minstrels and bards, and then the 'peaceful cultivators', and finally the 'wild aborigines of the ravine and of the hill'.[71] Forbes had little else to say about the nature of the sovereign and his kingdom and also does not engage in a discussion of the court and administrative hierarchies of the later 'Rajpoot' chieftains in the region.

[68] Inden, *Imagining India*, 176.
[69] Forbes, *Rās Mālā*, vol. 1, 230.
[70] Forbes, *Rās Mālā*, vol. 1, 230–31.
[71] Forbes, *Rās Māla*, vol. 1, 231.

The term 'Rajpoot' in fact appears to have multiple meanings in the text. The tale of 'Jug Dev Purmâr', who leaves his maternal home in order to seek his fortunes in a foreign land, represents a typical picture of 'Rajpoot life' for Forbes, and, offers an example of the multiple meanings the term Rajpoot holds in *Rās Mālā*. This story occupies comparatively long chapter in Book I and is based on a 'bardic' account rather than the written Jain texts or the *Ratan Mālā*, which Forbes otherwise frequently draws on in this section of his narrative. The tale, very briefly, is as follows: Jug Dev, the son of king Oodayaditya's unfavoured wife, is insulted on several occasions by the favorite queen. As such, he leaves his mother's home to find opportunity in a foreign land. 'I will get service somewhere,' he reassures his mother, a woman of the Solanki lineage.[72] After killing a couple of tigers who had become a menace to travellers and cows, and acquiring a retinue of loyal 'Rajpoots', horses, and elephants, Jug Dev eventually acquires lands and a wife in return for offering his loyal service to Siddharaja, the King of Patan.[73] Jug Dev is thus a fearless, chivalrous, and loyal warrior embodying all the qualities of a 'Rajpoot', and his story is often told by the bards to inspire their patrons. The Rajputs, defined in Forbes's narrative by such bardic accounts, are men of arms who moved around the region in search of land and patronage and were ever-ready to lay down their lives in battle.

The story of Jug Dev shows how Forbes, inspired by bardic accounts, represented the ideal Rajput. In this tale, the word 'Rajpoot' first refers to Jug Dev himself as a warrior. Second, it refers to his father, Oodayaditya, the Paramara king of Dhara. Third, it is also used for the men who go on to constitute his retinue, which he acquires en route to the Solanki kingdom. Finally, the category also seems to suggest that 'Rajpoots', like Jug Dev, were also itinerant men with access to weaponry, looking to settle or escape a contingent situation in return for military service. Money, elephants, horses, women, and men were the kind fortunes in store for these warriors. Instead of defining 'Rajpoots' in terms of lineage or courtly belonging, Forbes highlights personal prowess. In this respect, he differs sharply from James Tod, whose monumental work on the Rajputs of Rajasthan, published before the *Rās Mālā*, puts great emphasis on clan exclusivity and genealogy.

Forbes is similarly unconcerned with the delineation of the different clans and their individual characteristics in the *Rās Mālā*. The status of mixed groups

---

[72] The king's favourite wife belonged to the Vaghela lineage, which is also associated with Gujarat.

[73] Forbes, *Rās* Mālā, vol. 1, 117–49.

such as the 'Gohil Koolis', whose ancestry involved the intermarriage between a Gohil Rajput and Bheel woman, is also not explained.[74] Yet there is an implicit assumption in his writings that the Hindu chieftains of Gujarat were closely linked to the Chaulukyas, many branches of the former descending directly from the Chaulukyas or having loyally served them, 'never reverted to their *natural relations* to the paramount power which they bore during the sway of the dynasty of Unhilwârâ' (Anhilvada).[75] Like many other writers of his time, Forbes also does not clearly articulate the difference between how he is using terms like *clan*, *tribe*, or *race*,[76] each of which he uses to describe different groups or families of chieftains, thus leaving the actual nature of their social structure somewhat ambiguous to the reader. One reason for Forbes's unclear articulation of the origin and nature of the chieftains as a social group perhaps lies in their diverse histories and spheres of influence. Although he does not write about the origins of most of them, his account gives the reader a sense of the movements and migrations that so characterised their society.

An important and related feature of 'Rajpoot-hood' and political relations between the sultans and the chieftains during sultanate dominion, according to Forbes's narrative, was the institution of 'outlawry', or what he calls *Bâhirwutoo*.[77] The bardic accounts that Forbes uses in his descriptions of this period speak of outlawry as the mode of protest adopted by the chieftains who had lost their lands to the sultans to exert pressure and have them returned. Being well-acquainted with the countryside, these men would seek asylum outside the village settlements in forested tracts and engage in plunder and pillaging. The somewhat complex story of the brothers Wurhojee and Jetojee, who belonged to the Vaghela lineage that had ruled over Anhilvada–Patan prior to the entry of the Delhi sultans into the region is related in *Rās Mālā*. It offers one example of how the outlaws or *baharvatiyas* functioned according to Forbes's bards.[78] When the Gujarat sultan Ahmad Shah took over their lands, these two brothers moved their families to a pair of nearby villages and became outlaws plundering and ravaging the areas around Ahmadabad with their bands of horsemen. All of sultan Ahmad's attempts to apprehend them failed. However, with no reliable means of subsistence at hand, the two brothers

[74] Forbes, *Rās Mālā*, vol. 1, 346.

[75] Forbes, *Rās Mālā*, vol. 1, 275–76. Emphasis mine.

[76] Bayly, 'Caste and "Race" in the Colonial Ethnography of India,' 175.

[77] Modern Gujarati: *baharvatu*. The word is derived from the combination of the words *bahar* or outside and *vat* or path.

[78] For all the details of the tale see Forbes, *Rās Mālā*, vol. 1, 316–23.

gradually began to lose their followers. One night, while on an expedition, one of their men passed by a group of 'Rajpoots' near a water tank led by a certain Bhundaree Ukho. Catching site of the man, the peasant who drove this Ukho's cart said, 'Sir! I think the outlaws are come to the tank; we had better move on quickly.'[79] Ukho replied, 'Fear them not, there is no Rajpoot among them like me, or they would have recovered their *gras* within three days.'[80] On hearing this, the brothers decided to take this man up on the challenge and took him along on a raid of Ahmadabad.

In Ahmadabad, the capital of the sultans, it was a Friday, and the sultan's queen, or *begum*, and the other ladies of the palace were being escorted to a holy tomb near Sarkhej on the outskirts of Ahmadabad. At the tomb, the escorts remained at a short distance while the ladies proceeded alone to pay their respects to the saint. Seeing this as an opportunity, Ukho said to the brothers, 'Unless you seize these ladies, you will not recover your lands.'[81] The horsemen surrounded the women. Upon being asked by the queen who they were, the brothers said they were Wurho and Jeto, who, having lost their hereditary estates, were determined to die and therefore would attack the queen's retinue. Realising that such an act would result in losing her honour and hence her life, the queen promised the men that she would procure the recovery of their lands immediately. Then, forbidding her escorts from attacking them, she proceeded to Ahmadabad and sat 'moodily in the palace, forbidding the lights to be lit.'[82] Being apprised of the situation, the sultan came to her and asked her what had happened. She told him, saying, 'I have given my oath, therefore, you must send for the two brothers, and reinstate them in their lands. If they had driven off my carriage, where would have been the sultan's honour?"[83] The Sultan then invited the brothers, who had been waiting on the outskirts of the city, and promised them dresses of honour. They were given five hundred villages, which they equally divided between themselves. In turn, they gave the sultan their sister in marriage. The brothers were thus incorporated into sultanate polity, although according to another bardic story that follows in the text, they were despised by other Hindu chieftains.[84] While in the case of Haloojee we find one of two Rajput brothers establishing an affinity with the sultans by

[79] Forbes, *Rās Mālā,* vol. 1, 317.
[80] Forbes, *Rās Mālā,* vol. 1, 317.
[81] Forbes, *Rās Mālā,* vol. 1, 317.
[82] Forbes, *Rās Mālā*, vol. 1, 318.
[83] Forbes, *Rās Mālā*, vol. 1, 318.
[84] Forbes, *Rās Mālā*, vol. 1, 320.

embracing Islam, here we find a kinship bond created between them through marriage. Forbes's account of the sultanate of Gujarat mentions several other instances of outlawry resulting from the sultans' attempts to make claims over the chieftains' lands or honour and the negotiations and accommodations that may have followed.

Despite devoting pages of tales to courageous and enterprising bands of warriors in the first three books of the *Rās Mālā*, by the fourth book, Forbes has surprisingly little praise for the contemporary condition of his protagonists. This account projects the heroes of the earlier books as leading an 'indolent and monotonous life' in times of peace.[85] The Rajputs' primary activities seem to be sleeping, eating, entertainment, and drug-taking. After Forbes's afternoon siesta, 'which lasts until about three in the afternoon', the Rajput chieftain 'prepares for the great business of the day, the distribution of the red cup, kusoomba or opium.'[86]

In Forbes's account the meaning of the idea of the Rajput thus exhibits the amorphous picture that emerged from his sources. Here, the Rajputs, are akin to the open-ended social category that constituted the military labour market in which marriage alliances and military service propelled the rise in status of these upwardly mobile groups. Furthermore, in this view, the Rajputs and sultans are not always at odds but in fact part of the evolving system of patronage in the fifteenth century.

Conclusion

Today, Alexander Forbes's *Rās Mālā* has become the 'classic' text on Gujarat's history, a starting point for anyone wishing to study the region's past. However, what appears to be a definitive work was, as I have shown, formulated through a complex process of interaction between Forbes, Dalpatram and the Bhats and Charans. All these actors were representatives of important constituents of nineteenth-century Gujarati society, a society that was reconfiguring itself in response to the new order of politics and patronage introduced by the British, marking the end of the supremacy of the Rajput system and decades of turmoil under the Marathas.[87]

---

85 Forbes, *Rās Mālā*, vol. 2, 261.

86 Forbes, *Rās Mālā*, vol. 2, 50–65.

87 For Forbes's attempts to 'revive' the institution of the Bhats and Charans in the new context, see Kapadia, 'Alexander Forbes and the Making of a Regional History.'

In his narrative of the region's history, Forbes foregrounded the role of Rajput chieftains. While, on one hand, his approach follows from the British empire's bias against imperial Muslim rulers that preceded their own rule, Forbes's account displays a more nuanced view of the fifteenth-century and the regional Muzaffarid sultanate that had dominated the region. Furthermore, in Forbes's imagination, it was the rise of the Rajput chieftains and their warrior identities that ultimately shaped the region's history. Forbes's re-invention of the fifteenth century as a key moment in this history results from his understanding of the period as one produced through the interactions between sultans and chieftains and the poets who sang of them. Thus, while contemporary Bhats and Charans had been nearly silenced under the British administration, their ancestor's voices remained audible in the first colonial history of Gujarat.

Forbes's idea of the history of Gujarat as one shaped by these Rajput chieftains and their interactions with sultans, however, did not find popularity among the region's nationalist elite writers in the decades that followed. Instead, for this elite, who were a product to the new colonial education system, it was the Chaulukyas and the Vaghelas of Anhilvada–Patan who were deemed Gujarat's legitimate 'Rajputs' and the true upholders of Gujarat's past political 'glory'.

Conclusion

Two conventional ideas have coloured our view of Gujarat's pre-modern history: first, as in the rest of the subcontinent, that the fifteenth century, a century of transitions, was merely a twilight during which nothing noteworthy happened; and second, that the period in which the regional Muslim sultanate (and later the Mughals) ruled, brought any regional creative and political processes to an abrupt end. As the influential politician K. M. Munshi wrote, 'these developments had a negative influence on the literature of Gujarāt' and the literary productions in this era 'not only ignored political conditions, but provided easy ways to forget them'.[1] This narrative of the Chaulukya–Vaghelas being the last bastions of Gujarat's 'Hindu' culture, before it was destroyed by 'Muslim' domination, continues to shape the popular imagination of the region's history. Munshi's views, which portray the history of pre-modern Gujarat in terms of religious binaries rather than as a period of complex collaborations, have had a lasting impact on the region's popular imagination as well.[2]

In this book, I have tried to provide a corrective to this surprisingly persistent view that has shaped the understanding of Gujarat's and India's pre-modern history. I have shown that periods of change and flux, which do not necessarily coincide with large empires, may be productively examined by focusing on

[1] Munshi, *Gujarāta and Its Literature*, 112.

[2] For instance, in the popular and superbly produced TV commercials recently sponsored by the Gujarat Tourism Department, the historical sites related to the Muzaffarid sultans are hardly featured. The campaign has focused instead on Hindu temples such as Dwaraka, Somanatha, and Ambaji, or sites constructed during the Chaulukya or pre-Chualukya centuries, such as the sun temple Modhera, the Sidhpur temple complex, and a number of step-wells, obscuring the rich historical remains that sultanate cities like Ahmadabad and Champaner have to offer. This is despite the fact that the ruins of Champaner have now been designated as world heritage site by UNESCO.

the political and cultural processes that were at work within regional and local contexts. Literary narratives offer a particularly rich source for unpacking this history in a century of transitions in which such texts were often the only sources left behind by critical political actors like the local chieftains. While the regional sultans do have a legacy of historical documents and other material remains, literary works add of nuance to the ways in which their rule might be understood.

The regional kingdoms and sultanates that evolved in the subcontinent in the fifteenth century gave impetus to what has been called the 'vernacular millennium', but the regional languages were not the only ones that flourished in these new courts, or beyond them. Fifteenth-century polities, as is clear in case of Gujarat, were multilingual and multicultural, promoting classical and new regional styles of literature, architecture and other cultural effusions. I have focused on one sphere of this interconnected multilingual world by reconstructing ways in which a body of upwardly mobile regional political elites chose to represent their positions in the political landscape, their identities as warriors and kings, and their territorial domains during this century when the centralising authority from Delhi had declined.

This monograph has analysed narratives in both the Dimgal tradition and Sanskrit from the local kingdoms of the region, as well as an epic poem in Sanskrit addressed to one of the most influential rulers of the time, Sultan Mahmud Begada. This monograph has also explored the significance of the fifteenth century through the work of the colonial officer, Alexander Forbes, and in particular, his re-invention of Gujarat's history through the study of its warrior past. As I have shown, to compose the *Rās Mālā*, an account of the region's history and society during the medieval period, Forbes collected a vast number of legends about local chieftains that were circulating during his years of service. With the exception of the *Raṇmallachanda,* which finds mention in surveys of Gujarati literature, the other narratives I have focused on have never been read as products of their specific contexts. Together, these fifteenth-century and nineteenth-century representations have shown how the social structures and political predilections that made up this region and time period developed and continue to evolve over time.

Through a close reading of these literary representations, I have reconstructed ways in which political interactions between the Muzzafarid sultans and the local chieftains who occupied different parts of the Gujarat region between *c.* 1394 and 1511 were portrayed in these works. The local warrior chieftains and their clans, many of whom later styled themselves 'Rajputs', remained at the foundations of the regional polity as they held access to crucial material and military resources. The sultans and the local chieftains were thus embroiled in constant tensions and negotiations throughout sultanate rule. Establishing and consolidating their hold over the region was a complex process for the new sultans, who were erstwhile nobles of the Delhi sultanate. I have shown that, contrary to the dominant perception of simple confrontation between religious communities, the rise of both the local Rajput chieftains and the regional sultans during the fifteenth century was part of the same continuing processes of state building and identity formation. Their rise may be more productively understood as an output of the military labour market and the self-fashioning imperatives of groups who shared the common challenge of asserting their authority; in the process, they were able to draw on shared literary and social conventions as well. In the fifteenth century, these men were still establishing their physical presence through forts and courts in their patrimonies and giving their ideals and aspirations shape in the narratives discussed in the foregoing pages. To represent their kingly ideals, the chieftains and the sultans drew on multiple literary resources available at the regional and subcontinental levels.

The pattern of power-sharing created in the fifteenth century was to have a lasting effect on the region, as many of the local chieftains who managed to establish their strongholds in their patrimonies under sultanate rule continued to maintain them under the Mughals, Marathas, and the British. The fact that this was an exceptional outcome is clear from the fact that, of the five hundred and fifty or so princely states at the time of India's independence from British rule in 1947, over two hundred were located in mainland Gujarat and the peninsulas of Saurashtra/Kathiawad and Kachch.

In sum, I have argued that narratives from the courts of fifteenth-century Gujarat, far from being devoid of political content, as Munshi suggested, were in fact a product and reflection of their contemporary contexts. The multilingual environment of the fourteenth and fifteenth centuries produced a vast body of literary texts in different genres that have often been dismissed as lacking in historical value. I have tried to resurrect such a body of texts representative of those that were produced within a growing landscape of warrior ethos in Gujarat and all over western India. Through their use of eclectic tropes and varieties of languages, these biographical accounts of historically known figures reflect a continuous dialogue between the local, regional, and universal aspects of this ever-evolving ethos. For these men, once pastoralist warriors of obscure origins who emerged as chieftains and rulers, the patronage of such narratives was the way in which they could inscribe themselves into history, and lay claim to identities that would grant them status and prestige. However, unlike the sultans who emerged as the most successful of the warrior groups, many of the chieftains that occupied the interstices of the regional polity did not leave behind material remains that could tell their stories in posterity. In the absence of such evidence, the literary compositions of poets and panegyrists were a way to ensure their lasting legacy. These texts also become, as I have shown, important ways in which their histories can be discerned in the absence of large imperial documentation projects or extensive material remains.

In these narratives, the power and heroism of local chieftains, whether a warrior like Ranmal or the protagonists of Sanskrit compositions, such as Gangadas or Mandalik, were defined by their ability to challenge the imperial ruler's authority. This could be achieved, as Ranmal or Gangadas did, by directly challenging the sultans' claims over their territories or, as we saw in the narrative about Mandalik, by reinforcing his position in his own local domains. This notion of resistance is also found in Forbes's representation of the Rajput warrior-kings. As my reading of his work shows, the term 'Rajput' seems to have carried a number of meanings for the colonial officer. The Rajput in Forbes's narrative is a warrior in search of territories, a mercenary soldier, as well as a king with claims to a prestigious lineage and kingdom. The last of these, namely, the Rajput as a 'king', was only one part of Forbes's understanding of the appelation. In all three representations, however, the notion of 'resistance', be it to an Islamic imperial authority or to a tyrannical or unfair overlord (as in the case of Sunugjee, Ranmal's ancestor, or Jug Dev Parmar), formed a common feature of the Rajput character. Yet, as the constant use of eclectic tropes and the sultans' claims to an exalted Kshatriya status show, these assertions of heroic resistance were shaped less by religion than by immediate political contingencies.

When studied in their historical contexts, the Dimgal and Sanskrit narratives, as well Forbes's use of bardic materials, reflect their protagonists' anxieties and struggles over status and sovereignty during the social and political flux of the fifteenth century. With the decline of the Chaulukya–Vaghela dynasties, groups such as the Rathods of Idar, the Chauhans of Champaner, the Chudasamas of Junagadh, and several others, such as the Parmars, Gohils, Solankis, and Vaghelas, were gradually able to consolidate their hold over the territories they had acquired by grant or force. However, the appearance in the region of ambitious sultanate governors like Zafar Khan, and the subsequent establishment of the Gujarat sultanate, led to shifts in a political scenario that was already precariously balanced. These transitions are revealed in the narratives' representations of their protagonists and their political worlds.

In the story of the Idar chieftain Ranmal Rathod, his panegyrist Sridhara Vyasa's inclusion of multiple literary and cultural elements produced a narrative that gave an animated sense of the warrior ethos that was emerging among chieftains at the time. This narrative integrated both the classical elements of 'Kshatriya-hood' as well as the more open-ended identity of the 'Rajput' to which different categories of fighting men could now aspire. In the poet's imagination, Ranmal, the ruler of a small hill kingdom and an embodiment of this ethos, was able to challenge the powerful sultanate armies and retain his sovereignty over his territories. While sultanate sources constantly projected Ranmal and later his descendants as recalcitrant landlords, Sridhara Vyasa's narrative in oral-performative style may have served the purpose of creating a heroic personality and memory for the warrior chieftain and for others who heard or read about him.

While the Sanskrit narratives about Gangadas and Mandalik, who appear to have held larger territories than did Ranmal at the time, are composed in the courtly *kavya* style and therefore draw on the classical norms of Kshatriya-hood, they were also set firmly within the regional context of fifteenth-century Gujarat. The notions of kingship represented in these works speak of their protagonists in the universalised terms of *kavya*, and include elements from epic and Puranic mythology. Yet the Vijayanagara poet Gangadhara's engagement with the specificities of politics and geography make these narratives regional epics that would have reinforced their patrons' moral and martial positions within and around their own little local kingdoms. However, in the case of Ranmal, as well as the other two chieftains, the need to maintain a firm hold over their territories and social status through the promotion of martial values in politically uncertain times, is apparent.

In the Sanskrit biography of Mahmud Begada it is possible to see yet another aspect of the literary representation of regional kingship and the warrior ethos. Mahmud, as I have demonstrated, aspired to and achieved region-wide recognition of his authority. Apart from his successes at subduing the local chieftains and gaining control over their resources, he was also an important player in the wider politics of the subcontinent in which the regional rulers now competed with one another for supremacy. As any successful Kshatriya king of the past, Sultan Mahmud, too, wanted to benefit from the power and prestige of Sanskrit. Unlike the narratives about the local chieftains, Mahmud's biography does not focus on specific details of regional history and politics, but instead locates its protagonist as a *cakravarti,* a universal, paramount king and a Kshatriya, who has descended from the lineage of none other than the great epic warrior, Rama. The universal values of kingship available in the cosmopolitan Sanskrit language were harnessed to suit the Muslim sultan's political aspirations. Given Mahmud's wider interest in the patronage of religion, architecture, and other literary languages, this panegyric, along with the monumental praise-poem of the Dohad inscription and the persistence of Sanskrit and multilingual epigraphs, more generally, suggests that the sultans, much like the other big and small political players, were drawing on the multiple cultural resources that the region had to offer.

In the context of fifteenth-century Gujarat, it is possible to discern various perceptions of kingship, all projected through patronised authorship. The military resources of the Delhi sultans as well as their regional successors were far greater than those of the local chieftains. Although, as the Persian accounts of the period suggest, these men were able to negotiate terms with the imperial authorities due to the strategic locations of their territories, none of them could make claims over the entire region, or achieve the status of *gurjara* lord. Despite their lofty claims of their protagonists' prowess in battle against the *yavana* kings, the authors of these narratives do not assign correspondingly majestic titles to the local heros. Similarly, the protagonists' territorial claims also remain restricted to their own 'little kingdoms'. The sultan in Udayaraja's Rājvinoda, on the other hand, is adorned with the titles that were traditionally reserved for independent kings, with resonances whose power could be felt beyond his own kingdom. The sultan's pan-regional status is further reinforced by the trope of the rulers of different kingdoms subcontinent paying him their respects.

This book also illuminates Sanskrit's role in Gujarat's multilingual environment. The small but significant body of narratives in Sanskrit, along with the persistence of Sanskrit inscriptions in the region, makes clear that the language continued to hold a political import. In the second millennium, Sanskrit did not entirely lose its position as a language of power but rather was reconfigured to suit the needs of the emerging regional elite. The differences in the way it was used by the chieftains and the sultan are indicative of the literati's willingness and ability to modify classical literary devices to suit new patrons, regardless of their religious affiliations. In the geographically restricted regional polities, the transition to vernaculars was neither simple nor complete. The form of Gujarati that is spoken in the region today was only one of the many languages that were once used in this area. The use of the language in the modern state was, in fact, standardised by colonial officers like Forbes from the nineteenth century onwards. The sources presented and analysed here, however, show that the region had multiple linguistic traditions that interacted closely with one another.

One reason why the fifteenth century has been overshadowed in the historiography of pre-modern South Asia is that the Mughals are credited with inaugurating an era of unprecedented political and cultural innovations. However, as I have tried to show in this study of the vibrant regional context of Gujarat, a number of new social configurations and literary expressions were emerging under Muzaffarid rule. This study has opened up new avenues for understanding the role of patronage and political integration at work in this region on the eve of the trans-regional Mughal empire.

Read together, these narratives reveal a complex interaction between the two groups, the Rajput chieftains and the sultans, and challenge the conventionally held characterisation of the history of pre-modern Gujarat in terms of the clash between Hindu and Muslim polities. In the narratives addressed to the chieftains, their conflict with, and resistance to, the sultanate forces often forms the central axis around which the story revolves. Yet, the eclectic tropes used to describe the religious 'Other', and the shared conventions deployed by poets to fashion their protagonists' claims, complicate the picture. As inheritors of the Delhi empire's political legacy, the Muzaffarids promoted a rich Indo-Muslim polity. But as rulers of a diverse region, and themselves bearers of the legacy of a continuing Rajput warrior ethos, they were also keen to draw on the linguistic and cultural conventions of the Sanskrit cosmopolis. In this respect, their aspirations, and the way they expressed them poetically, mirrored those of their Rajput rivals.

In modern India, religious binaries are once again posing a threat to the pluralism that constituted India's pre-modern past. The need to remember the complex political interactions, multiple linguistic traditions, and fluidity that made up the fifteenth century has become even more crucial in this environment. This was, after all, the period in which a modest chieftain like Ranmal could claim to be following in the footsteps of the Turko-Mongol warrior, Timur, and a time in which a regional Muslim sultan's panegyrist could situate his earthly patron within the Puranic solar lineage, offering him shared ancestry with the great epic warrior Rama. My study of narratives from fifteenth-century Gujarat, I hope, is a step towards reclaiming the rich diversity and fluidity that shaped this century of transitions.

Bibliography

Abbot, Rev. J. E. 1896–97. 'Bai Harir's Inscription at Ahmadabad; AD 1499.' *Epigraphia Indica* IV: 297–300.

Acharya, G. V. 1933, 1935, 1942. *Historical Inscriptions of Gujarat*. 3 vols. Bombay: Sri Forbes Gujarati Sabha.

Ahmad, Aziz. 1963. 'Epic and Counter-Epic in Medieval India.' *Journal of the American Oriental Society* 83 (4): 470–76.

Alam, Muzaffar. 2004. *The Languages of Political Islam: India 1200–1800*. New Delhi: Permanent Black.

Alam, Muzaffar, Françoise 'Nalini' Delvoye and Marc Gaborieau, eds. 2000. *The Making of Indo-Persian Culture*. New Delhi: Manohar.

Alam, Muzaffar and Sanjay Subrahmanyam, eds. 2003[1998]. *The Mughal State*. New Delhi: Oxford University Press.

Ali, Daud. 2004. *Courtly Culture and Political Life in Early Medieval India*. Cambridge: Cambridge University Press.

———. 2013. 'Temporality, Narration and the Problem of History: A View from Western India c. 1100–1400.' *Indian Economic and Social History Review* 2 (50): 237–59.

Arai, Toshikazu. 1998. 'Jaina Kingship in the *Prabandhacintāmaṇi*.' In *Kingship and Authority in South Asia*, edited by John F. Richards, 92–132. New Delhi: Oxford University Press.

Asher, Catherine B. and Cynthia Talbot, eds. 2006. *India Before Europe*. Cambridge: Cambridge University Press.

Aufrecht, Theodore. 1962 [1902]. *Catalogus Catalogorum: An Alphabetical Register of Sanskrit Works and Authors by Theodore Aufrecht*, vol. 1. Wiesbaden: Franz Steiner Verlag GmbH.

Balachandran, Jyoti Gulati. 2012. 'Texts, Tombs and Memory: The Migration, Settlement and Formation of Learned Muslim Community in Fifteenth-Century Gujarat.' Unpublished Phd dissertation, University of California, Berkeley.

Bangha, Imre. 2014. 'Early Hindi Epic Poetry in Gwalior: Beginnings and Continuities in the *Rāmāyaṇa* of Vishnudas.' In *After Timur Left: Culture and Circulation in Fifteenth Century North India*, edited by Samira Sheikh and Francesca Orsini, 365–402. New Delhi: Oxford University Press.

Bühler, George. 1892. 'The Cintra Praśasti of Sarangadeva.' *Epigraphia Indica*, I: 271–87.

———, ed. 1892. *The Jagadūcharita of Sarvānanda: A Historical Romance from Gujarat*, Indian Studies, 26 (no. 1). Wien: Sitzungberichte der Kais. Akademie der Wissenschaften in Wien.

———. 1897. 'A Jaina Account of the End of the Vaghlelas of Gujarat.' *Indian Antiquary* (July): 194–95.

Bayley, Clive Edward. 1970 [1886]. *Local Muḥammadan Dynasties of Gujarāt*. New Delhi: S. Chand and Co.

———. 1993. 'Knowing the Country: Empire and Information in India,' *Modern Asian Studies*, 27 (1): 3–43.

———. 1996. *Empire and Information: Intelligence Gathering and Social Communication in India, 1780–1870*. Cambridge: Cambridge University Press.

Bayly, Susan. 2006. 'Caste and "Race" in the Colonial Ethnography of India.' In *The Concept of Race in South Asia*, edited by Peter Robb, 165–218. New Delhi: Oxford University Press.

Bednar, Michael B. 2007. *Conquest and Resistance in Context: A Historiographical Reading of Sanskrit and Persian Battle Narratives*. Austin: The University of Texas at Austin.

Bhati, Narayan Singh. 1989. *Prācīn Ḍiṇgaḷ Gīt Sāhitya*. Jodhpur: Rajasthan Granthaghar.

Blochmann. H. 1875. 'Eight Arabic and Persian Inscriptions from Ahmedabad.' *Indian Antiquary* (4): 367–68.

Bronner, Yigal and David Shulman. 2006. '"A Cloud Turned Goose": Sanskrit in the Vernacular Millennium.' *Indian Economic and Social History Review*, 43 (1): 1–30.

Busch, Allison. 2010. 'Hidden in Plain View: Brajbhasha Poets at the Mughal Court.' *Modern Asian Studies* 44 (2): 267–309.

———. 2011. *Poetry of Kings: The Classical Hindi Literature of Mughal India* New York: Oxford University Press.

Campbell, James Macnabb. 1896. *Gazetteer of the Bombay Presidency*, vol. I, part 1. Bombay: Government Central Press.

Chaghatai, M. A. 1941. *Muslim Monuments in Ahmedabad Through their Inscriptions*. Poona: Deccan College Research Institute.

Chattopadhyaya, B. D. 1998. *Representing the Other? Sanskrit Sources and the Muslims (8th to 14th Centuries)*. New Delhi: Manohar.

———. 1999. 'Origin of Rajputs: The Political, Economic and Social Processes in Early Medieval Rajasthan.' In The Making of Early Medieval India, 57-88. New Delhi: Oxford University Press.

———. 1999a [1994]. *The Making of Early Medieval India*. New Delhi: Oxford University Press.

———. 1999b. 'Urban Centres in Early Medieval India: An Overview.' In *The Making of Early Medieval India*, 155–82. New Delhi: Oxford University Press.

———. 1999c. 'Political Processes and the Structure of Polity in Early Medieval India.' In *The Making of Early Medieval India*, 183–222. New Delhi: Oxford University Press.

Cohn, Bernard S. 1987. *An Anthropologist among the Historians and Other Essays*. New Delhi: Oxford University Press.

Commissariat, M. S. 1938 and 1957. *A History of Gujarat; Including a Survey of its Chief Architectural Monuments and Inscriptions*, 2 vols. Bombay: Longman, Green and Co. Ltd.

Copland, Ian. 1982. *The British Raj and the Indian Princes: Paramountcy in Western India, 1857–1930*. New Delhi: Orient Longman.

Cort, John E. 1996. 'Genres of Jain history.' *Journal of Indian Philosophy*, 23 (4): 469–506.

———. 1998. 'Who is King? Jain Narratives of Kingship in Medieval Western India.' In *Open Boundaries: Jain Communities and Cultures in History*, edited by John E. Cort, 85–110. New York: SUNY.

Dahyabhai, Dalpatram. 1867. *Kavitvilās*. Ahmedabad: Gujarat Vernacular Society.

———. 1898 [1869]. *Fārbas Viraha*. Ahmedabad: Gujarat Vernacular Society.

Dalal, C. D. 1920. *Hammiramadamardana of Jayasimha Suri*, Gaekwad's Oriental Series, No. X. Baroda: M.S. University.

Dalal, C. D., ed. 1978 [1920]. *Prācīn gurjara kāvya-saṅgraha: A Collection of Old Gujarati Poems from the 12th to the 15th centuries*. Vol. 1. Baroda.

Dalpatram, Nanalal. 1933. *Kavīśvar Dalpatrām*. Vol. 1. Ahmedabad.

Dar, M. I. 1953. 'Gujarat's Contribution to Gujari and Urdu.' *Islamic Culture* 27:18–36.

Datta, Amaresh. 1987. *Encyclopaedia of Indian Literature*. New Delhi: Sahitya Akademi.

Davis, Richard H. 1999. *The Lives of Indian Images*. New Delhi: Motilal Banarasidass.

De Clercq, Eva. 2014. 'Apabhramsha as Literary Medium in Fifteenth-Century North India.' In *After Timur Left: Culture and Circulation in Fifteen-century North India*, edited by Francesca Orsini and Samira Sheikh, 339–64. New Delhi: Oxford University Press.

Delvoye, Françoise 'Nalini'. 1994. 'Indo-Persian Texts on Music Patronage in the Sultanate of Gujarat.' In *Confluence of Cultures: French Contributions to Indo-Persian Studies*, edited by Françoise 'Nalini' Delvoye and M. Gaborieu, 253–80. New Delhi: Oxford University Press.

———. 1998. 'Music Patronage in the Sultanate of Gujarat: A Survey of Sources.' In *New Developments in Asian Studies: An Introduction*, edited by P. van der Velde and A. McKay, 342–60. New York: Columbia University Press.

Desai, Neera. 1978. *Social Change in Gujarat: A Study of the Nineteenth Century Gujarati Society*. Bombay: Vora and Co.

Desai, Z. A. 1960–61. 'Mir'at-i-Sikandarī as a Source for the Study of Cultural and Social Conditions of Gujarat under the Sultanate (1403–1572).' *Journal of the Oriental Institute* 10: 235–78.

———. 1962. 'Arabic Inscriptions of the Rajput Period from Gujarat.' *Epigraphia Indica Arabic and Persian Supplement*: 1–24.

———. 1971. 'Some Fourteenth Century Epitaphs from Cambay in Gujarat.' *Epigraphia Indica Arabic and Persian Supplement*: 2–58.

———. 1975. 'A Persian–Sanskrit Inscription of Raja Karna Dev Vaghela of Gujarat.' *Epigraphia Indica Arabic and Persian Supplement*: 13–20.

———. 1987. 'Khaljī and Tughluq inscriptions from Gujarat.' *Epigraphia Indica Arabic and Persian Supplement*: 1–40.

Dhaky, M. A. 1961. 'The Chronology of Solanki Temples of Gujarat.' *Journal of the Madhya Pradesh Itihas Parishad* 3: 1–81.

Dhruva, H. H. 1881. 'The Dohad Inscription of the Chaulukya King Jayasimha.' *Indian Antiquary* 10 (June):158–62.

Digby, Simon. 2004. 'Before Timur Came: Provincialization of the Delhi Sultanate through the Fourteenth Century.' *Journal of the Economic and Social History of the Orient*, 47 (3): 298–356.

———. 2014. 'After Timur Left: North India in the Fifteenth Century.' In *After Timur Left: Culture and Circulation in Fifteenth Century North India*, edited by Francesca Orsini and Samira Sheikh, 47–59. New Delhi: Oxford University Press.

Dirks, Nicholas B. 1993. 'Colonial Histories and Native Informants: Biography of an Archive.' In *Orientalism and the Postcolonial Predicament: Perspectives on South Asia*, edited by Carol Breckenridge and Peter van der Veer, 279–313. Philadelphia: University of Pennsylvania Press.

———. 2003. *Castes of Mind: Colonialism and the Making of Modern India*. New Delhi: Permanent Black.

Eaton, Richard M. 2000. *Essays on Islam and Indian History*. New Delhi: Oxford University Press.

———. 1993. *The Rise of Islam and the Bengal Frontier, 1204–1760*. Berkeley, Los Angeles, London: University of California Press.

Eaton, Richard M. and Philip Wagoner. 2014. *Power, Memory, Architecture: contested sites on India's Deccan Plateau, 1300–1600*. New Delhi: Oxford University Press.

Firishta, Abdu'l-Qasim. 1981 [1829]. Ta'rīkh-i Firishta, translated by John Briggs as *History of the Mahomedan Power in India till the Year AD 1612*, 4 vols. London: Longman, Rees, Orme, Brown and Green (repr. New Delhi: Oriental Books Reprint Corporation).

Forbes, Alexander Kinloch. 1856. *Rās Mālā or Hindoo Annals of the Province of Goozerat, in Western India*. London: Richardson Brothers.

———. 1869. *Rās Mālā, Athvā Gujarāt Prāntano Itihās*. Translated by Ranchodbhai Udayrama Dave. Mumbai: Shree Forbes Gujarati Sabha.

———. 1878. *Rās Mālā: Hindoo Annals of the Province of Goozerat in Western India, New Edition with an Introduction by Major J.W. Watson and a Memoir of the author by A.K. Nairne*. London: Richardson Brothers.

———. 1997 [1924]. *Rās Mālā: Hindoo Annals of Western India. Edited with Historical Notes and Appendices by H.G. Rawlinson*. New Delhi: Low Priced Publications.

Gadre, A. S. 1943. 'The Nānaka Praśastis of Vīsaladeva of Gujarat (1271 AD).' In *Important Inscriptions from the Baroda State*, vol. 1, 74–79. Baroda: M. S. University.

Gangadhara. *Gaṅgadāsapratāpavilāsanāṭakam*. MS in the British Library MSS 2388.

Gangadhara. 1954a. 'Mandalika Mahākāvya of Gangādhara Kavi.' *Bharatiya Vidya* 15 (1): 35–57. (Also see Velankar).

Gangadhara. 1954b. 'Śrī-Gaṅgādharakavi-kṛt śrī Māṇḍalīka-mahākāvyam.' *Bharatiya Vidya* 15 (2): 13–40.

Gangadhara. 1973. *Gaṅgadāsa-pratāpavilāsa-nāṭakam: A Historical Play by Gaṅgādhara*. Edited by Bhogilal J. Sandesara. Baroda: Oriental Institute.

Gode, P. K. 1940. 'Dates of Udayarāja and Jagaddhara.' *Journal of the University of Bombay*, 10 (2): 101–15.

Guha, Sumit. 1999. *Environment and Ethnicity in India 1200–1991*. Cambridge: Cambridge University Press.

———. 2004a. 'Transitions and Translations: Regional Power and Vernacular Identity in the Dakhan, 1500–1800.' *Comparative Studies of South Asia, Africa and the Middle East* 24 (2): 23–31.

———. 2004b. 'Speaking Historically: The Changing Voices of Historical Narration in Western India, 1400–1900.' *The American Historical Review* 109 (4): 1084–103.

Hertel, Johannes. 1922. *On the Literature of the Shvetambaras of Gujarat*. Leipzig: Sächsische Forschungsinstitute.

Inden, Ronald. 1986. 'Orientalist Constructions of India.' *Modern Asian Studies*, 20 (3): 401–46.

———. 2000 [1990] *Imagining India*. London: Hurst and Company.

———. 2006a. 'Hierarchies of Kings in Early Medieval India.' In *Text and Practice: Essays on South Asian history*, 129–59. New Delhi: Oxford University Press.

———. 2006b. *Text and Practice: Essays on South Asian History*. New Delhi: Oxford University Press.

Inden, Ronald, Jonathan Walters and Daud Ali. 2000. *Querying the Medieval: Texts and the History of Practices in South Asia*. New York: Oxford University Press.

Irschick, Eugene. 1994. *Dialogue and History: Constructing South India, 1795–1895*. Delhi: Oxford University Press.

Isaka, Riho. 2002. 'Gujarati Intellectuals and History Writing in the Colonial Period.' *Economic and Political Weekly* 37 (48): 4867–72.

Jackson, Peter. 1999. *The Delhi Sultanate: A Political and Military History*. Cambridge: Cambridge University Press.

Jain, V. K. 1990. *Trade and Traders in Western India, 1000–1300*. New Delhi: Munshiram Manoharlal.

Jha, Pankaj Kumar. 2014. 'Beyond the Local and the Universal: Exclusionary Strategies of Expansive Literary Cultures in Fifteenth-Century Mithila.' *Indian Economic and Social History Review* 51 (1): 1–40.

———. 2016. 'Literary Conduits for "Consent": Cultural Groundwork of the Mughal State in the Fifteenth Century.' *The Medieval History Journal* 19 (2): 322–50.

Jhaveri, Krishnalal M. 1993 [1914]. *Milestones in Gujarati Literature*. New Delhi, Madras: Asian Educational Services.

Joshi, Jogidas A. 1924. *Īḍar Rājyano Itihās* (History of the Idar State), vol. 1. Himmatnagar.

Joshi, Svati. 2004. 'Dalpatram and the Nature of Literary Shifts in Nineteenth Century Ahmedabad.' In *India's Literary History: Essays on the Nineteenth Century*, edited by Stuart Blackburn and Vasudha Dalmia, 327–57. Delhi: Permanent Black.

Joshi, Umashankar, Ananatarai Raval, and Yashvant Shukla, eds. 2001. *Gujaratī Sāhityano Itihās* (History of Gujarati Literature), vol. 1 and vol. 2, part 1. Ahmedabad: Gujarat Sahitya Parishad.

Jamindar, Rasesh. 2000. 'Contribution of the Sanskrit Epigraphs of Gujarat in the Making of National Heritage.' *Journal of the Oriental Institute* 50 (1–4): 195–204.

Kamphorst, Janet. 2006. 'Rajasthani Battle Language.' In *Voices from South Asia: Language in South Asian Literature and Film*, edited by Theo Damsteegt, 33–78. Zagreb: Department of Oriental Croatian Philological Society.

Kapadia, Aparna. 2005. `What Makes the Head Turn: Three Narratives of Love and War from Medieval Westen India.' Unpublished MPhil Dissertation, Jawaharlal Nehru University, Delhi.

———. 2010. 'Alexander Forbes and the Making of a Regional History.' In *The Idea of Gujarat: History, Ethnography, and Text*, edited by Edward Simpson and Aparna Kapadia, eds. 50–65. New Delhi: Orient Blackwsan.

Kapadia, Aparna and Edward Simpson, 'Gujarat in Maps'. In Edward Simpson and Aparna Kapadia. eds. 20–31. New Delhi, Orient Blackswan.

Karashima, Noboru, ed. 1999. *Kingship in Early Indian History*. New Delhi: Manohar.

Keay, John. 2000. *India: A History*. London: Harper Collins.

Keith, A. B. 1929. *The History of Sanskrit Literature*. Oxford: Clarendon Press.

Khan, Ali Muhammad. 1965. *Mir'āt-i-Aḥmadī: A Persian History of Gujarat*. Translated by M. F. Lokhandwala. Baroda: Oriental Institute.

Kokil, Muhammad Umar. 1938. 'Gujarātnā Sultānonā Samaymā Saṁgīt' (Music in the Time of the Sultans of Gujarat), *Fārbas Gujaratī Sabhā Traimāsik*, 3 (3): 394–400.

Kolff, Dirk H. 1990. *Naukar, Rajput and Sepoy: The Ethnohistory of the Military Labour Market in Hindustan, 1450–1850*. New Delhi: Cambridge University Press.

Konow, Sten. 1909–10. 'Balera plates of Mularāja.' *Epigraphia Indica* X: 76–79.

Kotani, Hiroyuki. 1999. 'Kingship, State and Locality in the Seventeenth-to-Nineteenth Century Deccan with Special Reference to Ritual Function.' In *Kingship in Early Indian History*, edited by Noboru Karashima, 237–71. New Delhi: Manohar.

Krshnaji. 1868. *The Ratan Málá*. Translated by Alexander Kinloch Forbes. Bombay: Reprinted from the Bombay Branch Royal Asiatic Society's Journal.

Lal, K. S. 1980. *Twilight of the Sultanate: A Political, Social and Cultural History of the Sultanate of Delhi from the Invasion of Timur to the Conquest of Babur, 1398–1526*. New Delhi: Munshiram Manoharlal.

Lambah, Abha and Alka Patel, eds. 2006. *The Architecture of the Indian Sultanates*. Mumbai: Marg Publications.

Losensky Paul E. and Sunil Sharma, eds. 2011. *In the Bazaar of Love: The Selected Poetry of Amīr Khusrau*. New Delhi: Penguin Books.

Ludden, David. 1993. 'Orientalist Empiricism: Transformations of Colonial Knowledge,' in *Orientalism and the Postcolonial Predicament: Perspectives on South Asia*, edited by Carol Breckenridge and Peter van der Veer, 250–78. Philadelphia: University of Pennsylvania Press.

Mahamahopadhyaya Kaviraja Shyamaladas. 1986 [1886], *Vir Vinod: Mewad ka itihas*, vol. 2 New Delhi: Motilal Banarsidas.

Mahamud, Hasan. 1988. Introduction to *Tārīkh-i Maḥmūd Shāhī*, edited by S. C. Misra. Baroda: M. S. University.

Majumdar, A. K. 1956. *Chaulukyas of Gujarat*. Bharatiya Vidya Series IV. Bombay: Bharatiya Vidya Bhavan.

Majmudar, M. R. 1965. *Cultural History of Gujarat (From Early Times to Pre-British Period)*. Bombay: Popular Prakashan.

Macdonell, Arthur A. 1900. *The History of Sanskrit Literature*. New York: D. Appleton.

Mehta, Makrand J. 1982. *The Ahmedabad Cotton Textile Industry: Genesis and Growth*. Ahmedabad: New Order Book Co.

Mehta, R. N. 1978. *Champaner: A Medieval Capital*. Vadodara: Heritage Trust.

———. 1979. *Chāṁpāner: Ek Adhyayan*. Vadodara: Mahārājā Sayājīrāo Viśvavidyālaya.

Mehta, Shirin M. and Makrand J. Mehta. Oct–Dec 1968. 'Dalpatrām ane Aleksandar Forbes: Gats̄ takani Ek Maitri Upar Dṛṣṭīpāt,' *Śrī Fārbas Gujarātī Sabhā Traimāsik*, 8–22.

Merutungacharya. 1901. *The Prabandhacintāmaṇi or Wishing-Stone of Narratives*. Translated by C. H. Tawney. Calcutta: The Asiatic Society.

Merutungacharya. 1932. *Prabandhacintāmaṇi*. Edited by Durgāshanker Kevalram Shāstri. Bombay: Forbes Gujarati Sabha.

Metcalf, Barbara, D. 1995. Presidential Address: 'Too Little Too Much: Reflections on the Muslims in the History of India.' *The Journal of Asian Studies*, 54 (4): 951–67.

Metcalf, Thomas R. 1994. *Ideologies of the Raj*. Cambridge: Cambridge University Press, 24–26.

Misra, S. C. 1982. *The Rise of Muslim Power in Gujarat: A History of Gujarat from 1298 to 1442*. Bombay: Munshiram Manoharlal.

Mita, Masahiko. 1999. 'Polity and Kingship of Early Medieval Rajasthan: An Analysis of the Naḍol Cāhmāna Inscriptions.' In *Kingship in Early Indian History*, edited by Noboru Karashima, 89–117. New Delhi: Manohar.

Munhata, Nainsi. 1962. *Muṅhatā Naiṇsīrī Khyāt*. Edited by Badariprasad Sakaria. 3 vols. Jaipur: Rajasthan Puratan Granthamala.

Munshi, K. M. 1944. *The Glory that was Gūrjaradeśa*, vol. 3. Bombay: Bharatiya Vidya Bhavan.

———. 1954. *Gujarāta and its Literature from Early Times to 1852*. Bombay: Bharatiya Vidya Bhavan.

Nayak, C. R. 1966. 'Gujarī Bhāshā.' *Svadhayaya* 4 (3): 268–85.

Obrock, Luther. 'History at the end of history: Śrīvara's Jainataraṅgiṇī.' *The Indian Economic and Social History Review* 50 (2): 221–36.

Orsini, Francesca, and Samira Sheikh, eds. 2014. *After Timur Left: Culture and Circulation in Fifteenth Century North India*. New Delhi: Oxford University Press.

Padmanabha. 1953. *Kānhaḍade Prabandha*. Edited by K. B. Vyas. Jaipur: Rājasthān Purātattva Mandir.

Panchal, Govardhan. 1998. 'A Glimpse into the Sanskrit and Other Forms of Drama in Medieval Gujarat.' In *Contribution of Gujarat to Sanskrit Literature*, edited by M. K. Prajapati, Hansa Hindocha, and H. R. Patel, 293–310. Patan: Dr. M. I. Prajapati Ṣaṣṭipūrti Sanmāna Samiti.

Paniker, K. Ayyappa, ed. 1999. *Medieval Indian Literature: An Anthology*, vol. 2. New Delhi: Sahitya Akademi.

Patel, Alka. 2004. *Building Communities in Gujarāt; Architecture and Society During the Twelfth through Fourteenth Centuries*. Leiden, Boston: E. J. Brill.

———. 2006. 'From Province to Sultanate: The Architecture of Gujarat during the 12th through 16th Centuries.' In *The Architecture of the Indian Sultanates*, edited by Abha Narain Lambah and Alka Patel, 68–79. Mumbai: Marg Publications.

Pathak, R. D. 1985. 'Gujari: The God-given Great Gift to the World.' In *The Growth of Indo-Persian Literature in Gujarat*, edited by M. H. Siddiqi, 98–104. Baroda: Dept. of Persian, Arabic and Urdu, M. S. University of Baroda.

Pathak, V. S. 1963. *Ancient Historians of India: A Study in Historical Biographies*. Bombay: Asia Publishing House.

Peabody, Norbert. 2001. 'Cents, Sense, Census: Human Inventories in Late Precolonial and Early Colonial India.' *Comparative Studies in Society and History*, 43 (4): 819–50.

Pearson, M. N. 1976. *Merchants and Rulers of Gujarat: The Response to the Portuguese in the Sixteenth Century*. New Delhi: Munshiram Manoharlal.

Pollock, Sheldon. 1996. 'The Sanskrit Cosmopolis, 300–1300: Transculturaltion, Verncularisation, and the Question of Ideology.' In *Ideology and Status of Sanskrit: Contributions to the History of the Sanskrit Language*, edited by E. M. Houben. 209–217. Leiden: Brill.

———. 1998a. 'India in the Vernacular Millennium: Literary Culture and Polity, 1000–1500.' *Daedalus* 127 (3): 41–74.

———. 1998b. 'The Cosmopolitan Vernacular.' *The Journal of Asian Studies* 57 (1): 6–37.

———. 2006. *The Language of the Gods in the World of Men: Sanskrit, Literature, and Power in Premodern India*. Berkeley, Los Angeles, and London: University of California Press.

Prajapati, M. K., Hansa Hindocha and H. R. Patel, eds. 1998. *Contribution of Gujarat to Sanskrit Literature*. Patan: Dr. M. I. Prajapati Ṣaṣṭipūrti Sanmāna Samiti.

Prasad, Pushpa. 1990. *Sanskrit Inscriptions of the Delhi Sultanate, 1192–1526*. New Delhi: Oxford University Press.

Rabitoy, Neil. 1974. 'Admininstrative Organisation and the Bhats of British Gujarat.' *Indian Economic and Social History Review* 11 (1): 46–73.

Rao, V. N. and David Shulman. 2012. *Śrīnātha: The Poet Who Made Gods and Kings*. New York: Oxford University Press.

Rao, Velcheru Narayana and David Shulman. 2002. *Classical Telugu Poetry: An Anthology*. Berkeley: University of California Press.

Richards, John F., ed. 1998. *Kingship and Authority in South Asia*. New Delhi: Oxford University Press.

Sandesara, B. J. 1953. *Literary Circle of Mahāmātya Vastupāla and its Contribution to Sanskrit Literature*, Shri Bhahadur Singh Singhi Memoirs, vol. 3. Bombay: Bharatiya Vidya Bhavan.

———. 1964. 'Śrīpāla: The Blind Poet-laureate at the Court of Siddharājā Jayasiṃha (1094–1143 AD) and Kumārapāla (1143–1174 AD) of Gujarat.' *Journal of the Oriental Institute*, 13: 252–59.

———. 1968. 'Detailed Description of the Fort of Chāmpāner in the Gaṅgadāsapratāpavilāsa, an Unpublished Sanskrit Play by Gaġādhara.' *Journal of the Oriental Institute*, 18: 45–50.

Sandesara, B. J. and A. M. Bhojak, eds. 1953. 'Gaṅgadāsapratāpavilāsa by Gaṇgādhara. A Historical Sanskrit Play Depicting the Conflict between Sultān Muhammad II of

Ahmedabad and the King Gaṅgadāsa of Chāmpāner.' *Journal of the Oriental Institute*, 4: 193–204.

Sankalia, H. D. 1937–38. 'Dohad Stone Inscription of Mahamuda (Begarah): V.S. 1545, Saka 1410.' *Epigraphia Indica*, 24: 212–25.

Sarvananda, 1892. 'The Jagadūcharita of Sarvānanda, A Historical Romance from Gujarat.' In *Indian Studies 1*, edited by George Bühler. Wein: Sitzungberichte der Kais. Akademie der Wissenschaften in Wien.

Shah, A. M. and R. G. Shroff. 1975. 'The Vahīvancā Bāroṭs of Gujarat: A Caste of Genealogists and Mythographers.' In *Traditional India: Structure and Change*, edited by Milton Singer, 40–70. New Delhi: Rawat Publications.

Sharma, Dashratha. 1966. *Rajasthan Through the Ages: From the Earliest Times to 1316 A.D.* Vol. 1. Bikaner: Rajasthan State Archives.

Shastri, Durgashankar Kevalaram. 1953 [1937–39], *Gujarātno Madhyakālīna Rājpūt Itihās*, 2 vols. Ahmedabad: Gujarat Vidyasabha.

Shastri, H. G. 1979. *Gujaratnā Aitihāsika Lekha (Historical Inscriptions of Gujarat)*. vols. 2 and 4. Bombay: Shree Forbes Gujarati Sabha.

Shastri, Keshavaram K. 2001. 'Rās ane Phāgu Sāhitya.' In *Gujaratī Sāhityano Itihās (History of Gujarati Literature)*, edited by Umashankar Joshi, Ananatarai Raval and Yashvant Shukla. Ahmedabad: Gujarat Sahitya Parishad.

Sheikh, Samira. 2008. 'Alliance, Genealogy and Political Power: The Cuḍāsamās of Junāgaḍh and the Sultans of Gujarat.' *Medieval History Journal* 11 (1): 29–61.

———. 2010. *Forging a Region: Sultans, Traders and Pilgrims in Gujarat, 1200–1500*. New Delhi: Oxford University Press.

———. 2014. 'Languages of Public Piety: Bilingual Inscriptions from the Sultanate of Gujarat, c. 1390–1538.' In *After Timur Left: Culture and Circulation in Fifteenth Century North India*, edited by Samira Sheikh Francesca Orsini, 186–209. New Delhi: Oxford University Press.

Shelat, Bharati and Zuber Qureshi, ed. 2012. *Kavi Udayarāja viracitaṃ: Rājavinodamahākāvyam*. Ahmedabad: Shah Wajihuddin Academy.

Sherry Chand, Sarvar V., and Rita Kothari. 2003. 'Undisciplined History. The Case of *Ras Mala*.' *Rethinking History* 7 (1): 69–87.

Sikandar b. Muhammad, Manjhu Gujarati. 1990. *Mir'āt-i Sikandarī*. Translated by Fazlullah Lutfullah Faridi. Dharampur: Education Society's Press, n.d. Reprint, Vintage Books.

———. 2002. *Mir'āt-i Sikandarī*. Hindi translation. Jaipur: Shabda Mahima Prakashan.

Simpson, E. and Aparna Kapadia, eds. 2010. *The Idea of Gujarat: History, Ethnography and Text*. New Delhi: Orient Blackswan.

Singhji, Virabhadra. 1994. *The Rajputs of Saurashtra*. Bombay: Popular Prakashan.

Sonawane, V. H. 1972. 'Māṇḍavī Step-well Inscription at Cāmpānera, Samvat – 1554, śaka – 1419.' *Journal of the Oriental Institute*, 20 (3): 223–27.

Sreenivasan, Ramya. 2002. 'Alauddin Khalji Remembered: Conquest, Gender and Community in Medieval Rajput Narratives.' *Studies in History*, new series. 18 (2): 275–96.

———. 2004. 'The "Marriage" of "Hindu" and *"Turak"*: Medieval Rajput Histories of Jalor.' *Medieval History Journal* 7 (1): 87–108.

———. 2006. 'Drudges, Dancing Girls, Concubines: Female Slaves in Rajput Polity, 1500–1850.' In *Slavery in South Asian History*, edited by Indrani Chatterjee and Richard M. Eaton, 136–61. Bloomington: Indiana University Press.

———. 2007. *Many Lives of a Rajput Queen. Heroic Pasts in India C. 1500–1900*. Ranikhet: Permanent Black.

———. 2014. 'Warrior-Tales at Hinterland Courts in North India, c.1370–1550.' In *After Timur Left: Culture and Circulation in Fifteenth Century North India*, edited by Samira Sheikh and Francesca Orsini, 241–72. New Delhi: Oxford University Press.

Sridhara Vyasa. *Raṇamallachanda,* MS no. 1541 of 1891–95. Pune: Bhandarkar Oriental Research Institute.

———. 1973. *Raṇmallachanda. Raṇmall Chanda of Śrīdhar Vyāsa: A Rare Historical Saga in Old Gujarati*. Edited and translated by K. B. Vyas. Vol. 59, Pune: Annals of the Bhandarkar Oriental Research Institute.

Subrahmanyam, Sanjay and David Shulman. 1999. 'The Men Who would be King? The Politics of Expansion in Early Seventeenth-Century Northern Tamilnadu.' *Modern Asian Studies* 24 (2): 225–48.

Swayam, S. 2004. 'Sites of Ritual Construction of Identities: A Fresh Look at Memorial Stones of Gujarat.' *Man in India*, 84 (3 & 4): 303–39.

Talbot, Cynthia. 2016. *The Last Hindu Emperor: Prithviraj Chauhan and the Indian Past, 1200–2000*. Cambridge: Cambridge University Press.

Talbot, Cynthia. 1995. 'Inscribing the Other, Inscribing the Self: Hindu–Muslim Identities in Pre-Colonial India.' *Comparative Studies in Society and History*, 37 (4): 692–722.

———. 2008. 'Becoming Turk the Rajput Way: Conversion and Identity in an Indian Warrior Narrative.' *Modern Asian Studies* 43 (1): 211–43.

Tambs-Lyche, Harald. 1997. *Power, Profit and Poetry: Traditional Society in Kathiawar, Western India*. New Delhi: Manohar.

Tessitori, L. P. 1914–16. 'Notes on the Grammar of Old Western Rajasthani with Special Reference to Apabhraca and to Gujarati and Marwari.' *Indian Antiquary,* 43, 44, 45.

Tirmizi, A. A. 1963. 'Tarikh-i-Salatin-i-Gujarat.' *Medieval India Quarterly*, 5: 33–72.

Tirmizi, S. A. I. 1968. *Some Aspects of Medieval Gujarat*. New Delhi: Munshiram Manoharlal.

Thapar, Romila. 2002. 'The Tyranny of Labels,' in *Cultural Pasts: Essays in Early Indian History*, 990-1014. New Delhi: Oxford University Press.

———. 2004. *Somanatha*: *The Many Voices of History*. New Delhi: Penguin–Viking.

———. 2013. *The Past Before Us: Historical Traditions of Early North India*. 1st ed. Cambridge, Massachusettes, and London: Harvard University Press.

Tod, James. 2005 [1829–1832]. *Annals and Antiquities of Rajast'han or the Central and Western States of Rajpoot India*, 2 vols. New Delhi: Rupa and Co.

Trautmann, Thomas. 1999. 'Inventing the History of South India.' in *Invoking the Past: The Uses of History in South Asia*, edited by Daud Ali, 36–54. New Delhi: Oxford University Press.

Tripathi, Manassukhram Suryaram. 1869. *Fārabas Jivan Caritra* (Life of Forbes). Ahmedabad: Gujarat Vernacular Society.

Truschke, Audrey. 2016. *Culture of Encounters: Sanskrit at the Mughal Court*. New Delhi: Allen Lane.

Udayaraja. 1956. *Rājavinodamahākāvyam or Mahamūda-suratrāṇa-caritra*, Rajasthan Puratan Grantha-Mālā, Granthak 8. Jaipur: Rajasthan Oriental Research Institute.

———. *Rājavinodamahakāvya*. BORI MS 18/1874–75.

Velankar, H. D. 1953. '"Māṇḍalīka": The Last Great King of Independent Saurāṣtra.' *Bharatiya Vidya* 14: 36–61.

———. 1954a. 'Mandalika Mahākāvya of Gangādhara Kavi.' *Bharatiya Vidya* 15 (1): 35–57.

Vose, Steven M. 2013. 'The Making of a Medieval Jain Monk: Language, Power, and Authority in the Works of Jinaprabhasūri (c. 1261–1333).' PhD dissertation, South Asia Regional Studies, University of Pennsylvania.

Warder, A. K. 1972. *Indian Kāvya Literature*, vol. 1. New Delhi: Motilal Banarasidass.

Watson, J. W. 1877. 'Historical Sketch of the Hill Fortress of Pāwāgadh, in Gujarāt.' *Indian Antiquary* VI: 1–9.

Wagoner, Phillip B. 1996. '"Sultan among the Hindu Kings": Dress, Titles, and the Islamization of Hindu Culture at Vijayanagara.' *Journal of Asian Studies*, 55 (4): 851–80.

———. 2003. 'Precolonial Intellectuals and the Production of Colonial Knowledge.' *Comparative Studies in Society and History*, 45 (4): 783–814.

Wink, André, 2002. *Al-Hind: The Making of the Indo–Islamic World*. 3 vols. Leiden: E. J. Brill.

Yashaschandra, Sitamshu. 2003. 'From Hemacandra to Hind Svarāj: Region and Power in Gujarati Literary Culture.' In *Literary Culture in History: Reconstructions from South Asia*, edited by Sheldon Pollock, 567–611. Berkeley: California University Press.

Ziegler, Norman P. 1976. 'Marwari Historical Chronicles: Sources for the Social and Cultural History of Rajasthan.' *Indian Economic and Social History Review* 13 (2): 219–55.

———. 2003 [1998]. 'Some Notes on Rājput Loyalties during the Mughal Period.' In *The Mughal State 1526–1750*, edited by Muzaffar Alam and Sanjay Subrahmanyam, 168–210. New Delhi: Oxford University Press.

Zutshi, Chitralekha. 2014. *Kashmir's Contested Pasts: Narratives, Sacred Geographies, and the Historical Imagination*. New Delhi: Oxford University Press.

Index